OUR COMPLETE DESTINATION GUIDE
n-depth reviews, detailed listings
nd insider tips

Northern
Atolls p93

North & South
Male Atol... ..50

Ari
Atoll
p81

Male p44

WITHDRAW

Southern
Atolls
p106

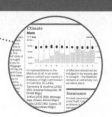

D1020607

THIS EDITION WRITTEN AND RESEARCHED BY

Tom Masters

Welcome to the Maldives

Unbelievable Beaches

The Maldives is home to perhaps the best beaches in the world; they're on almost every one of the country's nearly 1200 islands and are so consistently perfect that it's hard not to become blasé about them. While some beaches may boast softer granules than others, the basic fact remains: you'll find this whiter-than-white powder sand and luminous cyan-blue water almost nowhere else on earth. This fact alone is enough to bring nearly a million people a year to this tiny and otherwise little-known Indian Ocean paradise.

Resorts for Everyone

Every resort in the Maldives is its own private island, and with over 100 to choose from the only problem is selecting where to stay. At the top end, the world's most exclusive hotel brands compete with each other to attain ever-greater heights of luxury, from personal butlers and private lap pools to in-room massages and pillow menus. It's not surprising that honeymooners and those seeking a glamorous tropical getaway have long had the country at the top of their wish lists. But there's choice beyond the five- and six-star resorts. Other islands cater for families, for divers, for those on a (relative) budget, and anyone wanting a tranquil back-to-nature experience.

Unrivalled luxury, stunning white-sand beaches and an amazing underwater world make the Maldives an obvious choice for a true holiday of a lifetime.

(left) The Maldives is synonymous with tropical luxury (p14)
(below) Remarkable creatures like this crown jellyfish abound in the Maldives

Underwater World

With some of the best diving and snorkelling in the world, the clear waters of the Maldives are a magnet for anyone with an interest in marine life. The richness and variety is astonishing – baby sharks can be spotted in any lagoon in the country, while dazzling spectacles such as huge coral walls, magnificent caves and schools of brightly coloured tropical fish await you when you get down to the reef. Manta rays, turtles, friendly sharks and even the world's largest fish, the whale shark, can be seen all over the country and – amazingly – none of the life on the reef is dangerous. The best bit? The water is so warm many people don't even wear a wetsuit.

Independent Travel

What's more, these incredible islands are finally open to independent travellers, meaning you no longer have to stay in resorts and be kept separate from the local population, something that kept backpackers away for decades. Intrepid individuals can now choose their own itineraries and travel from island to island, living among the devout but extremely friendly local population. With a national ferry network now in place and a growing number of privately run guesthouses on inhabited islands, the Maldives and its people are now more accessible than ever.

› Maldives

Top Experiences ›

DEPTHS & ELEVATION

0m+
80m
200m
600m
1000m
2000m
3000m
4000m+
approximate values

INDIAN OCEAN

0 — 70 km
0 — 40 miles

Utheemu
Visit a 16th-century Maldivian mansion (p93)

Rasdhoo Atoll
Meet hammerhead sharks at dawn (p83)

Ari Atoll
Swim with a whale shark (p84)

Male
Explore the fascinating Maldivian capital (p44)

IHAVANDHIPPOLHU ATOLL

HAA ALIFU – NORTH THILADHUNMATHEE ATOLL

HAA DHAALU – SOUTH THILADHUNMATHEE ATOLL

Dhidhdhoo
Kulhuduffushi

MAAMAKUNUDHOO ATOLL

NORTH MILADHUNMADULU ATOLL

SHAVIYANI – Funadhoo

SOUTH MILADHUNMADULU ATOLL

NOONU – Manadhoo

RAA – Ugoofaaru

NORTH MAALHOSMADULU ATOLL

SOUTH MAALHOSMADULU ATOLL

Naifaru
LHAVIYANI

FAADHIPPOLHU ATOLL

BAA – Eydhafushi

GOIDHOO ATOLL

RASDHOO ATOLL

ALIFU

ARI ATOLL

NORTH MALE ATOLL

Thulusdhoo

Male Ibrahim Nasir International Airport

KAAFU

MALE ✪

SOUTH MALE ATOLL

Mahibadhoo

VAAVU

FELIDHOO ATOLL

Felidhoo

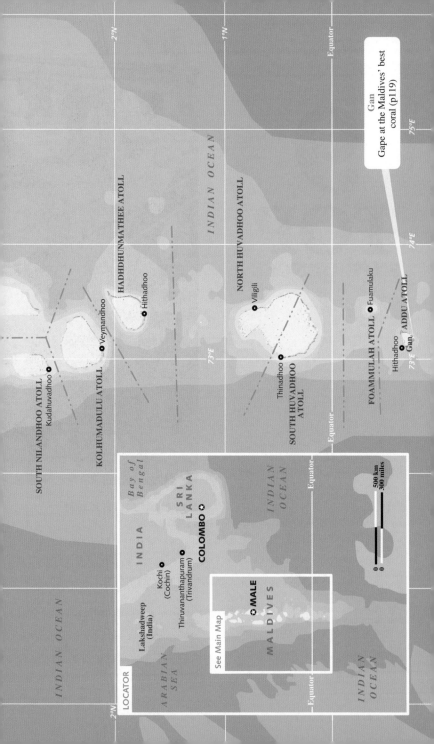

9
TOP
EXPERIENCES

Male

1 The Maldivian capital (p44) is definitely the best place to get to know locals and see what makes them tick. The brightly painted houses, crowded markets and convivial teashops where you can chat to locals and share plates of delicious 'short eats' are just some of the highlights of this fascinating capital city – and perfectly complement the resort experience. Male fishermen unloading at the docks

Breakfast with the Hammers

2 Hammerhead sharks, definitely one of the weirdest-looking creatures in the sea (and that's saying something), can be seen in abundance in Maldivian waters – if you know where to look for them. There are few more thrilling experiences than a dawn dive, descending free fall into the deep blue to 30m, before suddenly coming upon a huge school of hungry hammerhead sharks waiting to be fed. The best place to do this is at the world-famous Hammerhead Point (aka Rasdhoo Madivaru; p83) in Rasdhoo Atoll.

JOHN BORTHWICK/LONELY PLANET IMAGES ©

Watch a Bodu Beru Performance

3 Whether you're in a resort or staying on an inhabited island, the cultural highlight of almost any trip to the Maldives is seeing an incredible dance and drum performance known as *bodu beru* (p159), which means 'big drum' in Dhivehi. These traditional all-male performances are a thrilling experience, even if they can feel rather contrived in your resort's restaurant. The drum ceremony starts off slowly and builds gradually to an incredible climax, during which some dancers even enter a trance-like state.

Take a Seaplane

4 Few destinations can claim that the mode of transport in which travellers arrive is one of the highlights of their trip, but that's because there are few places in the world where you need seaplanes to reach your hotel. These zippy Twin Otters function like taxis in a country with no roads, and taking off from the water is an unforgettable experience, as is observing the spectacular coral atolls, blue lagoons and tiny desert islands from above.

Snorkel in Addu

5 When El Niño devastated the marine life of the Maldives and bleached the corals in 1998, the only area of the country to escape was the most southern atoll, Addu (p118). While the coral all over the country is recovering impressively, here the corals are absolutely spectacular, including huge staghorn corals that didn't survive elsewhere in the Maldives. Anyone who snorkels or dives here will be in awe of the strength and variety of colour, particularly off the island of Gan.

MICHELE WESTMORLAND/GETTY IMAGES ©

Learn to Dive

6 You simply *have* to get beneath the water's surface in the Maldives; the corals, tropical fish, sharks, turtles and rays all make up an unforgettably alien world, which is best experienced by diving (p29). All resorts have a dive school, and you will not regret deciding to learn here. The Maldives boasts excellent safety standards, modern equipment, passionate and experienced dive schools and – best of all – the water is so warm many people don't even bother diving in a wetsuit.

MEDIACOLOR'S/ALAMY ©

Visit an Inhabited Island

7 If you want to see the 'real' Maldives, try spending a few nights on an inhabited island in one of the new guesthouses (p166), a million miles from the spa and infinity pool of your resort. Here you can see colourful local life, try islander food and take in a traditional part of the world few people get to see. All resorts offer trips to nearby inhabited islands, so you don't even have to give up the comforts of your resort to enjoy a cultural experience. Cooking in the northern Maldives

Swim with a Whale Shark

8 The largest fish in the world, the whale shark (p144) is prevalent in Maldivian waters, especially in the south of Ari Atoll and during a full moon when the currents between the atolls are at their strongest. Swimming with one of these gentle giants is an incredible experience – they average almost 10m in length – and it's also totally safe, as despite their immense size, whale sharks feed only on plankton.

Be a (Luxurious) Castaway

9 Nearly every resort (p14) offers some variation on this theme: you and your partner or family are given a picnic basket (in the most luxurious resorts it may be a full meal set up for you by staff) and dropped off on an uninhabited, pristine island by dhoni. The crew then jump back on the boat and leave you to your own devices on a white-powder beach surrounded by a turquoise lagoon. Explore the island, dine on great food, sunbathe and swim – this is the modern castaway experience.

need to know

Currency
» Maldivian Rufiyaa (Rf), though US dollars (US$) are generally used in resorts.

Language
» Dhivehi, though English is spoken in resorts and widely elsewhere.

When to Go

▬ Tropical climate, wet/dry seasons

Hanimaadhoo
GO Dec–Apr

Male
GO Dec–Apr

Mahibadhoo
GO Dec–Apr

Kadhoo
GO Dec–Apr

Hithadhoo
GO Dec–Apr

High Season
(Dec–Feb)

» The Maldives enjoys its best weather.

» Expect little rain, low humidity and blue skies.

» Christmas and New Year involve huge price hikes and often minimum stays of 10-days or more.

Shoulder
(Mar–Apr)

» Great weather continues until the end of April, when the weather is at its hottest.

» Surf season begins in March and continues until October.

» Prices jump during Easter.

Low Season
(May–Nov)

» Storms and rain more likely, but weather warm and resorts at their cheapest.

» Prices rise in August for European summer holidays.

» Marine life more varied on the western side of atolls.

Your Daily Budget

Budget less than
$300

» Budget resorts cost US$150–300 per night.

» Guesthouses are cheaper at around US$100 per night.

» Reach guesthouses cheaply by taking public ferries.

Midrange
US$300-750

» Midrange resorts start from US$300 per night.

» Full board or all-inclusive options can save money.

» Speedboats to resorts cost around US$200

Top End
more than
US$750

» Top-end rooms start at US$750.

» Male's best hotel costs around US$350.

» Dine at the best restaurants in Male for around US$20.

Money

» Credit cards can be used in resorts and most guesthouses. ATMs are only reliably found in Male.

Visas

» Nobody coming to the Maldives requires a visa for a stay of 30 days or less.

Mobile Phones

» Local SIM cards can be bought in Male or other inhabited islands, but not at resorts. Most phones will automatically roam in the Maldives.

Transport

» Travel is by boat, plane or seaplane. Resorts will arrange for a transfer to/from the airport. There's a new ferry network.

Websites

» **Lonely Planet** (www. lonelyplanet.com/ Maldives) Info, bookings, traveller forums.

» **Official Tourism Site** (www. visitmaldives.com)

» **TripAdvisor** (www. tripadvisor.com) Resort reviews.

» **Minivan News** (www.minivannews. com) Reliable English newspaper.

» **Guesthouses in Maldives** (www. guesthouses-in-maldives.com) A great resource.

» **Island Life Maldives** (www. islandlifemaldives. com) Guesthouse and budget-travel website.

Exchange Rates

Australia	A$1	Rf15.75
Euro zone	€1	Rf20.08
Japan	¥100	Rf18.83
New Zealand	NZ$1	Rf12.42
Switzerland	CHF1	Rf16.67
UK	UK£1	Rf24.28
US	US$1	Rf15.34

For current exchange rates, see www.xe.com.

Important Numbers

Country code	☎960
International access code	☎00
Ambulance	☎102
Fire	☎118
Police	☎119

Arriving in Maldives

» **Male Ibrahim Nasir International Airport**

Speedboat – resorts in South and North Male Atoll transfer guests by speedboat (10 to 70 minutes).

Seaplanes – chartered transfers operate daily until around 5pm (seaplanes cannot fly after dark) to resorts outside South and North Male Atoll. Late arrivals need to overnight in Male and take a seaplane the next day.

Male ferry – the ferry leaves 24 hours a day to the capital (Rf10, five minutes, every 10 minutes).

What to Bring

As nearly all visitors head directly from the airport to their resorts or guesthouses on small, remote islands, it's important to bring everything you'll need for the duration of your stay. Going to the nearest supermarket to pick up something you've forgotten is simply not an option, and while all resorts have small shops selling essentials, they're generally overpriced and the selection tends to be tiny.

Some obvious things to pack include sunscreen and after-sun products (which will set you back a fortune in resorts), a sun hat, flippers, mask and snorkel, three-pin UK-style adaptors if you're coming from outside the UK, any birth control or medication you'll need, plenty of reading material and a good pair of UV-blocking sunglasses.

Choosing a Resort

Best Rooms

One & Only Reethi Rah For the most glamorous rooms imaginable, there's no beating the enormous villas and Asian furnishings.
Soneva Gili If you're looking for something more rustic, the vast timber water villas here are a triumph of simple luxury.

Best Pool

Coco Palm Bodu Hithi The super stylish glass-sided infinity pool is one of our favourites.

Best Beach

Kanahura The endless white-sand beach is unbeatable, and the resort also owns a private desert island for you to boat over to for a picnic lunch.

Best Restaurant

Fresh in the Garden For superb food in an incredible setting, we love the treetop restaurant at Soneva Fushi.

Best Spa

Huvafen Fushi Get ready for the ultimate massage in the incredible underwater spa.

Don't worry about being swayed by the judicious use of Photoshop in brochures – almost every resort in the Maldives will get you a superb beach, amazing weather and turquoise waters overlooked by majestic palms. Indeed, so uniform is the perfection, it's often hard to take memorable photographs here – they all just look like they've been lifted from a holiday brochure.

It's what nestles among the trees beyond the beach that should most concern you, and we're not talking about creepy crawlies. The standard of facilities and accommodation in Maldivian resorts varies enormously – from budget and extremely average accommodation to the best of everything if you can afford to pay through the nose for it. Therefore your choice of resort or guesthouse is absolutely key to getting the holiday you want. Take plenty of time and weigh up as many options as possible before settling for the place or places you'll book into. This chapter will help you identify the factors you need to take into consideration when selecting a resort, as well as listing some of our favourites in the country.

Atmosphere

What is surprising is that every resort has a fairly distinct atmosphere. It's unexpectedly simple, for example, to tell if you're visiting a honeymooners' paradise, a diving mecca or a family resort. This is impossible to judge from a website or brochure, so before choosing a resort decide on the type of holiday you want and the atmosphere most conducive to providing it. Honeymooners who find themselves surrounded by package-tour groups and screaming children may quickly come to regret booking into the first resort whose website they looked at. Similarly, divers and surfers may find the almost total social-life vacuum in a resort popular with honeymooners and couples a little claustrophobic after a week.

Back to Nature

The Maldives has built much of its tourism industry on the desert-island ideal: the fantasy of simplicity, tranquillity, beach and sea. Of course, the fact that many places also provide a butler, a gourmet restaurant and a fleet of staff who cater to your every whim makes the whole experience somewhat more fun than being a real castaway. These resorts tend to be well designed, use imported woods and natural fibres, have little or no air-conditioning and often open-air rooms with no window panes. The simplicity of such places (even at top-end resorts, which admittedly add supreme style and comfort to the mix), not to mention their peacefulness and relaxed feel, is what attracts people. These 'no shoes, no news' resorts are great for a romantic break, a honeymoon or total escape.

High Style

Few countries in the world have such a wealth of choice in the luxury market as the Maldives. All major luxury-hotel brands have or hope to have a presence here, and at times things can look like a never-ending glossy travel magazine. As well as our personal favourites, at the time of writing there was a host of new properties in the pipeline by such brand names as Raffles and Louis Vuitton, and these are likely to be bringing ever higher levels of comfort and pampering.

The pampering on offer here is almost legendary. You'll have your own *thakuru* (personal butler), who will look after you during your stay. And you'll nearly always have a sumptuous architect-designed villa stuffed full of beautifully designed furniture and fabrics, a vast, decadent bathroom (often open air) and a private open-air area (in a water villa this is usually a sun deck with a direct staircase into the sea). Some of our very favourite resorts in this category also include private pools – some big enough to do lengths in, but all a wonderful way to cool off or wash off the salt after a dip in the sea.

Food in these resorts is almost universally top notch. There will be a huge choice of cuisine, with European and Asian specialist chefs employed to come up with an amazing array of dishes day and night. Social life will be quiet, and will usually revolve around one of the bars. Most of the market here are honeymooners, couples and families, but kids will certainly not run riot (most resorts impose a limit on the number of children), and even if they do, there will be enough space to get away from them. Despite the general feel being romantic and stylish, activities will not be ignored – everything from diving to water sports and excursions will be well catered for. Essentially, if you can afford this level of accommodation, you are guaranteed an amazing time, whatever your interests.

RESORT TIPS

It's always worth checking a resort website yourself and even contacting the resort for specific, up-to-date information, as things change regularly. Is there construction work happening on the island? Is the spa finished yet? Does it still offer kiteboarding? Also, be aware that many resort websites haven't been updated since they were created. While there are exceptions, it's never a good idea to take the information there as fact – check when the page was last updated and also read up on the resort at www.tripadvisor.com.

Check the dive-centre website. It might provide a discount if you block book your dives before your arrival. Email it for specific dive information and to check that it will definitely be visiting any site you want to dive at during your stay.

If the trip is a honeymoon, or second honeymoon, or if you will be celebrating an anniversary or birthday, let your travel agent or resort know – there's usually something laid on in such circumstances. Some resorts normally require a wedding certificate before they do anything – couples claiming to be on their honeymoon just to get freebies are notorious!

Romance

Romance is big business in the Maldives, where more than a few visitors are on their honeymoon, renewing their vows or just having an indulgent break with their significant other. Almost anywhere is romantic. That said, the more budget the resort, the more families and big charter groups you'll get, and the intimacy of the romantic experience can be diminished if it's peace, quiet and candlelit dinners you're after. Romance does not necessarily mean huge cost. It's hard to think of anywhere more lovely than little Makunudu Island, for example, where there's no TV or loud music, just gorgeously simple and traditional houses dotted along the beach, and vegetation thick with trees planted by past honeymooners. However, the maxim of getting what you pay for is still true here – the loveliest, most romantic resorts are usually not the cheap ones.

Be aware that you cannot at present get married in the Maldives, although this may change in the near future. However, if you really want to, you can organise non-legally-binding services and effectively have your wedding here even if the legal formalities are completed elsewhere. Nearly all midrange and top-end resorts can organise such ceremonies, so check websites for details and special packages.

Diving

All resorts have their own diving school, and all are run to extremely professional standards as required by Maldivian law. Every resort has access to good diving, although nearly all diving is from boats – even if the house reef is excellent, any diver will tell you that variety is king. It's very hard to say that one resort has better diving than another, when in fact all the sites are shared. There are a few resorts that have obvious advantages, such as the Equator Village, where coral was not affected by the bleaching in 1998; Helengeli, from where some 40 dive sites can be reached, giving a huge choice; or a number of resorts in and around Ari Atoll, where the dive sites are excellent, including the Kuramathi resorts for hammerhead sightings, Chaaya Reef Ellaidhoo and Adaaran Club Bathala.

Ecotourism

Ecotourism can so often be a gimmick that it's important to know who's serious and who's just trying to attract a larger number of visitors. Despite the lip service paid by many resorts, relatively few have genuine ecotourism credentials. These credentials might include educational programs, sustainable development, environmentally friendly building practices, minimal use of air-conditioning and electricity in general, and a resort ethos that fosters environmental awareness and care (ie offering you not only Evian when you ask for water, but also water that has been desalinated on-site). The resorts we recommend in this category are leading the way in the use of materials, their interaction with the local ecosystem and the activities they offer guests. Those that are serious about their commitment to ecotourism include Soneva Gili, Soneva Fushi, Rihiveli Beach Resort, both Banyan Tree and Angsana properties, Coco Palm Bodu Hithi and Six Senses Laamu.

Guesthouses

A complete gear change comes in the form of the all-new guesthouses, which are hotels on inhabited islands, a new initiative in a country where tourism and the local population were always kept scrupulously apart. There are now dozens of these small hotels dotted around the country, and the experience offered here is one totally different to that offered in resorts. Forget the infinity pool and cocktails – you're on a dry local island here and swimming costumes aren't culturally acceptable – but you can still enjoy the beach on nearby uninhabited islands, do lots of diving, snorkelling, surfing, fishing, island hopping and cultural tourism. This is the best option for anyone who finds being separate from the local population in a self-contained resort an unappealing idea. For more on these options, see p166.

Activities

Few people will want to spend an entire holiday sunbathing and swimming, so resorts are careful to provide a program of excursions and activities for guests. Bear in mind that this is the only way you'll be able to leave the island during your stay, public transport from resort islands being nonexistent and opportunities for sightseeing almost as scarce. It's therefore important to give some thought to what you'd like to do other than sunworship, and check that the resort you're interested in can cater to your needs.

» (above) Perfect turquoise waters for sailing at Kandooma resort (p78), South Male Atoll

» (left) Perhaps more than anything the Maldives is known for its pristine diving

While all resorts have a diving centre, the uniformity ends there; you'll have to check to see if the resort you're planning to visit has a water-sports centre or its own spa, organises guided snorkelling, lays on marine biology lectures and morning yoga sessions or has a resident tennis pro. For example, the only resort to offer a golf course is Kuredu Island Resort in Lhaviyani, although there are plans to build a second course on one of the islands in the new wave of resort development. Other unique features are Soneva Fushi's observatory, Island Hideaway's marina and Huvafen Fushi's underwater spa.

Day Trips

Day trips from your resort are one of the very few ways you'll be able to see something of the Maldives. Even if you are an independent traveller, this is still a good way to see otherwise inaccessible islands. Most commonly offered are day trips to the charming capital of Male from resorts in North and South Male Atolls. There's enough to see and enough shopping to make this trip worthwhile, and it's a great way to get a feel for Maldivian people – you'll find the terrifyingly polite resort staff replaced by a friendly and funny city populace.

Another popular excursion is a trip to an inhabited island, which allows you to see a small island community, traditional housing, craftwork and lifestyle. The trip inevitably feels rather contrived, but can still be immensely enjoyable depending on how friendly the locals are and how many people are around (with children often in school or studying in Male, and menfolk away for work, some islands feel more like ghost towns than centres of population). While it's often more enjoyable to explore an island on your own, the resort guides will at least know all the locals and can be helpful in making contacts and telling you in detail about local life.

RESORT BASICS

You'll be met at the airport by your resort representative, who will usually take your ticket and/or passport from you for the duration of your stay, something that is quite normal here despite feeling rather odd to the seasoned traveller.

Unless you're arriving after dark you'll soon be transferred to your resort – either by a waiting dhoni, speedboat, airplane or seaplane from the nearby lagoon airport. You may have to wait for other passengers to get through customs, but it shouldn't be too long if your resort is on the ball. You can use US dollars or euros at the airport cafe, and change some cash into rufiyaa at the bank.

Travellers arriving after dark will have to spend a night at the airport hotel or at a hotel in Male; seaplane transfers are not carried out after sunset for obvious reasons. Speedboat transfers are also not normally undertaken after dark, but this is not always the case.

On arrival at the resort you'll be given a drink, asked to fill out a registration form and taken to your room. Resort staff will bring your luggage separately.

Room Types

Some resorts have just one type of room, which confusingly may be called 'Superior', 'Deluxe' or 'Super Deluxe'. Most bigger, newer resorts have several types of room, ranging from the cheapest 'Superior Garden Villas' to the 'Deluxe Over-Water Suites'. A 'Garden Villa' will not have a beach frontage, and a 'Water Villa' will be on stilts over the lagoon at a big cost hike.

More expensive rooms tend to be bigger, newer and better finished, and can have a bathtub as well as a shower, a minibar instead of an empty fridge, tea- and coffee-making facilities (even an espresso machine), a CD sound system and maybe even a Jacuzzi. Smaller over-water accommodation is called a 'water bungalow', although the terms 'water bungalow' and 'water villa' are fluid and largely interchangeable. More and more often in top-end resorts a private plunge pool (or even a lap pool) is part of the set up.

Single Supplements & Extra Beds

This book gives high-season (December to March) room rates for single/double occupancy when they differ, but most package-deal prices are quoted on a per-person basis, assuming double occupancy. Due to water villa (wv) popularity, this book also gives the

Fishing

Just about any resort will do sunset, sunrise or night-fishing trips, but they are a more authentically Maldivian experience at small, locally run resorts like Asdu Sun Island and Thulhagiri. Most resorts near Male can arrange a big-game fishing trip, including Bandos, Baros, Club Faru, Sheraton Maldives Full Moon Resort & Spa, Kurumba Maldives and Cocoa Island. These work out more economically if there are several participants, as costs are high: from $450 for a half-day trip for up to four people. Large boats, fully equipped with radar technology, are used to catch dorado, tuna, marlin, barracuda and jackfish among others.

Snorkelling & Diving

All resorts cater for divers and snorkellers, and most organise twice-daily diving excursions and usually at least one snorkelling trip a day. If you're keen on either,

it'll always be cheaper to bring your own equipment, including snorkel, mask and fins, plus buoyancy control device (BCD) and dive computer, if you're a diver. Dive schools vary enormously in quality and helpfulness, but all are of an exceptionally high safety standard, as regulated by strict Maldivian laws. Resorts themselves are not so important for divers – it's their location and the ease of access to dive sights nearby. Most resorts have at least 10 sites nearby and visit them in rotation. If there's a particular dive site you want to visit, you should contact the dive school at the resort and check it'll be running a trip there during your stay. See p29 for more about snorkelling and diving.

Spa Treatments

As a destination for relaxation, the Maldives has also become well known for offering a huge array of treatments in purpose-built

lowest high-season water villa price based on two people sharing. Solo travellers have to pay a 'single-person supplement' for the privilege of having a room all to themselves.

Extra people can usually share a room, but there's a charge for the extra bed, which varies enormously from resort to resort, as well as additional costs for meals and the obligatory US$8 per person per night 'bed tax', which is collected by the government for each tourist. In a package-tour price list, this appears as a supplement for children sharing the same room as parents, or for extra adults sharing a room.

For children two years and younger, usually just the US$8 bed tax is payable. From two to 12 years, the child supplement with full board will be from US$15 to US$30 in most budget to midrange resorts, but much more in expensive resorts. A more expensive option is to get two adjacent rooms, ideally with a connecting door. You might get a discount on the second room. Transfers to and from the airport for children are normally charged at half the adult rate.

Be aware that most resorts in the Maldives quote their prices exclusive of taxes, which are significant. In general all resorts add on a 10% service charge as a tip for staff, a 6% standard general sales tax (GST), introduced in 2012, and the US$8 bed tax per person per night. Therefore bear these extras in mind when you're totalling up a trip's cost.

Pricing Periods

Pricing patterns vary with the resort and the demands of its main market – some are incredibly detailed and complex with a different rate every week. The basic pattern is that Christmas-New Year is the peak season, with very high prices, minimum-stay requirements and surcharges for Christmas and New Year's Eve dinners. Early January to late March is high season, when many Europeans take a winter holiday. The weeks around Easter may attract even higher rates (but not as high as Christmas). From Easter to about mid-July is low season (and the wettest part of the year). July and August is another high season, for the European summer holidays. Mid-September to early December is low season again.

Specific markets can have their own times of high demand, such as the August holiday week for Italians, Chinese New Year in the Asian market or the end of Ramadan for some Middle Eastern guests.

SAFARI CRUISES

Safaris are a superb option for anyone wanting the best possible combination of diving sites, the chance to travel beyond the restrictions of a resort, and a sociable arena where both couples and noncouples will feel totally comfortable.

The massive expansion in the market for safari cruises has meant an increasingly sleek approach from the tour companies that run them. A typical, modern boat is air-conditioned and spacious, and serves varied and appetising meals. It should have hot water, a sun deck, fishing and diving gear, mobile phone, full bar, DVD player and cosy, comfortable cabins.

Costs start at around US$100 per person per day, including the US$8 per day per bed tax and all meals, plus roughly US$60 per day for diving trips. There's usually a minimum daily (or weekly) charge for the whole boat, and the cost per person is lower if there are enough passengers to fill the boat. You'll be charged extra for soft drinks and alcohol, which are priced comparably to most resorts. You might splurge for the occasional meal at a resort, but generally there are few extras to spend money on.

The most basic boats are large dhonis with a small galley and communal dining area, two or three cramped cabins with two berths each, and a shared shower and toilet. Passengers often drag their mattresses out on deck for fresh air, and sleep under the stars. Food is prepared on board and varies from very ordinary to very good – it usually features lots of freshly caught fish. The bigger, better boats have air-conditioning, more spacious accommodation, and a toilet and shower for each cabin. The best boats, like the best resorts, spare no effort in making their guests comfortable.

Most safari trips are for diving (see p30) or so-called 'surfaris' for surfing (see p36). A minority of safari trips are primarily for sightseeing, and usually offer a fair amount of fishing and snorkelling, stops at fishing villages and resorts, and picnics or a camp-out on an uninhabited island. Obviously it's important to make sure you're joining a trip that will cover what you want to do.

On a scheduled trip, a single passenger may have to share a cabin with another, or pay a premium rate. If you arrange your own group of six or so people, you can charter a whole boat and tailor a trip to suit your interests.

Choosing a Safari Boat

More than 80 safari boats are operating in the Maldives. Some specific suggestions are given here, but you'll need to do some research yourself. When you're considering a safari-boat trip, ask the operator about the following.

» Boat size – Generally speaking, bigger boats will be more comfortable, and therefore more expensive, than smaller boats. Most boats have about 12 berths or less. Few boats have more than 20 berths, and those that do may not be conducive to the camaraderie you get with a small group.

» Cabin arrangements – Can you get a two-berth cabin (if that's what you want)? How many cabins/people are sharing a bathroom?

spas. These include all types of massage, beauty treatments, Ayurvedic (Indian herbal) medicine, acupuncture and even traditional Maldivian treatments. All midrange and top-end resorts have a spa, and even some of the budget resorts now have them. The best are sometimes booked up weeks in advance, so plan ahead if you're interested in certain treatments. With staff often from Bali, Thailand, India and Sri Lanka, you're in safe (if expensive) hands. You can check most resort websites for a full treatment list, but resorts particularly well known for their spas include Soneva Fushi, Cocoa Island, Sheraton Maldives Full Moon Resort & Spa, Banyan Tree, One & Only Reethi Rah and W Retreat & Spa. The underwater spa at Huvafen Fushi is the first of its kind in the world and is truly unique; you can be massaged while watching the fish swimming around the glass walls of the room. Resorts well known for Ayurvedic therapy include Adaaran Select Meedhupparu, Taj Exotica, Vivanta by Taj Coral Reef, Four Seasons Landaa Giraavaru and Olhuveli Beach & Spa.

» Comforts – Does the boat have air-con, hot water and desalinated water available 24 hours?

» Companions – Who else will be on the trip, what language do they speak, have they done a safari trip before? What are their interests: diving, sightseeing, fishing, surfing?

» Food and drink – Can you be catered for as a vegetarian or vegan? Is there a bar serving alcohol, and if so, how much is a beer and a bottle of wine etc?

» Recreation – Does the boat have DVD player, iPod dock, fishing tackle, sun deck? Does the boat have sails or is it propelled by motor only?

Safari Boat Operators

Safari boats often change ownership, or get refitted or acquire a new name. The skipper, cook and divemaster can change too, so it's hard to make firm recommendations. The following boats have a good reputation, but there are many others offering decent facilities and services. The boats listed here all have a bar on board, oxygen for emergencies, and some diving equipment for rent. Universal's *Atoll Explorer* is like a mini cruise ship with a swimming pool on deck, while the *Four Seasons Explorer* is the most luxurious and expensive. The websites are those of the boat operators. Many of these operators have other boats as well, which may also be very good. If the website does not give booking information (or it's not in your language), most of these boats can be booked through the bigger tour operators in Male (see p57), or by overseas travel agents. The official **tourism website** (www.visitmaldives.com) has reasonably up-to-date details on almost every safari and cruise boat (click on 'Where to Stay' then 'Safari').

Adventurer 2 (www.maldivesdiving.com; ✸) Boat 31m, eight cabins, 20 berths, hot water.

Atoll Explorer (www.atollexplorer.com; ✸) Boat 50m, 20 cabins, 40 berths, hot water.

Dive Masters (www.guraabu.com.mv; ✸) Boat 30m, eight cabins, 19 berths, hot water.

Eagle Ray (www.maldivesboatclub.com) Boat 26m, seven cabins, 14 berths, hot water.

Four Seasons Explorer (www.fourseasons.com/maldivesfse; ✸) Boat 39m, 11 cabins, 22 berths, hot water and ultimate luxury.

Gulfaam (www.voyagesmaldives.com; ✸) Boat 20m, five cabins, 12 berths.

Manta Cruise (www.tripconcept.com) Boat 31m, nine cabins, 20 berths, hot water.

MV Carina (www.seamaldives.com.mv; ✸) Boat 33m, 11 cabins, 33 berths, hot water.

Sting Ray (www.maldivesboatclub.com.mv; ✸) Boat 31m, nine cabins, 22 berths, hot water.

Sultan of Maldives (www.sultansoftheseas.com; ✸) Boat 30m, eight cabins, 16 berths, hot water.

Surfing

The best resorts for surfing are Chaaya Island Dhonveli and Adaaran Select Hudhuran Fushi, which are both blessed with their own surf breaks and are very popular with surfers during the season. The popularity of surfing is increasing in the Maldives, with surfer arrivals going up massively in the past few years. However, it's really only these two resorts that are perfectly located near good breaks, although nearby resorts, such as Four Seasons Kuda Huraa, Paradise Island and Club Med Kani, can organise boat trips. Meemu Atoll is also great for surfing, and is largely unvisited by travellers, despite there being two nearby resorts making access fairly easy. Another fantastic option to avoid the crowds and explore a pristine region of the country is to join a 'surfari'. See p36 for details on surfing in the Maldives.

Water Sports

In addition to diving schools, most resorts have a water-sports centre (check before booking). These vary enormously. Some offer the most basic array of canoes and windsurfing,

MALDIVES RESORT RATINGS

To give you a simple idea of which resorts are best for which things, we've scored each resort out of three for each category, three being the very highest standard in its field. A zero means that the resort has nothing worth mentioning on a subject; for example, if it doesn't accept kids, it gets a zero for children's activities.

RESORT	PAGE	BEACH	ROMANCE	SOCIAL LIFE	PAMPERING	CHILDREN'S ACTIVITIES	FOOD	DESIGN	DIVING	SNORKELLING	WATER SPORTS
Adaaran Select Meedhupparu	p100	3	2	2	2	2	2	1	3	2	3
Anantara Dhigu & Veli	p78	3	2	2	2	3	1	2	3	3	3
Anantara Kihavah Villas	p102	3	3	1	3	3	3	3	3	3	3
Angaga	p88	3	2	2	1	2	2	2	3	3	2
Angsana Ihuru	p66	3	3	1	2	0	3	3	3	3	2
Angsana Velavaru	p113	3	3	1	3	1	3	3	3	3	3
Asdu Sun Island	p70	2	1	2	1	1	1	1	3	3	2
Ayada Maldives	p117	3	3	1	3	1	3	3	2	3	3
Bandos Island Resort	p72	2	1	3	1	3	2	1	2	3	3
Banyan Tree Madivaru	p86	3	3	0	3	1	3	3	3	3	2
Banyan Tree Vabbinfaru	p65	3	3	1	3	1	3	3	3	3	2
Baros	p66	3	3	1	3	1	3	3	3	2	3
Biyadhoo	p79	2	1	2	1	1	2	1	3	3	3
Centara Grand Island Resort & Spa Maldives	p87	3	2	2	3	3	2	2	3	2	3
Chaaya Island Dhonveli	p71	3	2	2	1	2	2	2	3	3	3
Chaaya Lagoon Hakuraa Huraa	p108	3	2	2	1	2	2	2	3	1	3
Chaaya Reef Ellaidhoo	p88	3	1	2	1	2	2	2	3	3	3
Coco Palm Bodu Hithi	p67	2	3	2	3	2	3	3	3	3	3
Coco Palm Dhuni Kolhu	p103	3	2	2	2	2	2	2	3	3	3
Cocoa Island	p76	3	3	1	3	1	3	3	3	3	3
Conrad Maldives Rangali Island	p87	3	3	1	3	3	3	3	3	3	3
Diamonds Athuruga Beach & Water Villas	p90	3	2	3	1	2	2	2	3	3	2
Dusit Thani Maldives	p102	3	3	1	3	3	3	3	2	2	3
Embudu Village	p79	3	1	2	1	2	2	1	3	3	2
Equator Village	p122	1	1	3	1	2	1	1	3	3	2
Eriyadu	p71	3	2	2	1	1	2	1	3	3	2
Filitheyo	p109	2	1	2	1	2	2	2	3	1	1
Four Seasons Kuda Huraa	p65	2	2	1	3	3	3	2	3	3	3
Four Seasons Landaa Giraavaru	p101	2	3	2	3	3	3	3	3	3	3
Gangehi Island Resort	p90	2	2	2	3	1	2	2	3	3	2
Helengeli Island Resort	p68	3	2	2	1	1	1	2	3	3	0
Hilton Maldives Iru Fushi Resort & Spa	p99	3	2	2	2	3	2	2	3	2	3
Holiday Island	p91	3	1	2	1	2	1	1	3	1	2
Huvafen Fushi	p64	3	3	1	3	1	3	3	3	3	3
Island Hideaway	p95	3	3	1	3	2	3	2	3	3	2
Jumeirah Dhevanafushi	p115	3	3	2	3	2	3	3	2	2	3
Jumeirah Vittaveli	p76	3	3	1	3	2	2	3	2	2	2

RESORT	PAGE	BEACH	ROMANCE	SOCIAL LIFE	PAMPERING	CHILDREN'S ACTIVITIES	FOOD	DESIGN	DIVING	SNORKELLING	WATER SPORTS
Kandooma	p78	1	2	3	2	3	2	3	3	2	3
Kanuhura	p104	3	3	2	3	3	3	3	3	3	3
Komandoo Island Resort	p104	2	3	1	2	0	2	3	3	3	3
Kuramathi	p83	3	1	3	1	1	2	1	3	3	3
Kuredu Island Resort & Spa	p105	3	2	3	2	2	2	1	3	3	3
Kurumba Maldives	p69	3	2	2	3	3	3	2	3	3	3
Lily Beach Resort	p90	3	2	3	2	2	2	2	2	3	2
LUX* Maldives	p88	3	3	1	3	2	2	3	3	1	3
Maayafushi	p91	2	1	1	1	1	2	1	3	3	1
Madoogali	p88	3	3	1	2	1	2	2	3	3	2
Makunudu Island	p67	3	3	1	2	1	2	2	3	3	1
Medhufushi	p109	3	2	2	2	1	2	3	3	3	3
Meeru Island Resort	p69	3	2	2	2	2	2	2	3	3	3
Mirihi	p86	3	2	1	3	2	2	2	3	2	2
Naladhu	p77	2	3	1	3	1	3	2	3	3	2
Nika Island	p89	3	3	1	3	1	3	2	3	3	3
Olhuveli Beach & Spa	p78	3	2	1	3	1	2	2	3	3	3
One & Only Reethi Rah	p63	3	3	2	3	3	3	3	3	1	3
Palm Beach Resort	p105	3	3	2	2	2	2	2	3	1	2
Paradise Island	p72	3	2	3	2	2	1	1	3	3	3
Park Hyatt Maldives Hadahaa	p117	3	2	2	2	3	3	2	3	2	2
Rania Experience	p111	3	3	0	3	1	3	3	3	3	2
Reethi Beach Resort	p103	3	2	2	1	1	2	2	3	3	3
Rihiveli Beach Resort	p76	2	2	3	2	2	2	1	3	1	3
Shangri-La Villingili Resort & Spa	p122	3	3	1	3	3	3	3	3	3	3
Sheraton Maldives Full Moon Resort & Spa	p67	3	3	1	3	2	3	3	2	2	2
Six Senses Laamu	p114	3	3	1	3	2	3	3	3	3	2
Soneva Fushi	p102	3	3	2	3	3	3	3	3	3	3
Soneva Gili	p64	3	3	1	3	1	3	3	3	3	3
Summer Island Village	p70	3	1	2	1	2	1	1	3	3	3
Sun Island	p91	2	1	3	1	3	3	1	3	3	3
Taj Exotica	p77	3	3	1	3	1	3	3	3	3	2
Thulhagiri	p70	3	2	2	1	1	2	1	3	3	2
Velidhu Island Resort	p89	3	2	2	1	1	1	1	3	3	3
Veligandu	p84	3	2	2	2	1	2	1	3	3	2
Vilamendhoo	p89	2	2	2	1	2	2	2	3	3	2
Vilu Reef	p112	3	3	2	3	1	2	2	3	3	3
Vivanta by Taj Coral Reef	p68	2	2	2	2	2	2	2	3	3	3
W Retreat & Spa	p86	3	3	3	3	1	3	3	3	3	3
Waldorf Astoria Maldives	p95	3	3	1	3	2	3	2	3	3	3
Zitahli Kuda-Funafaru Maldives	p99	3	3	1	3	1	2	3	2	3	3

JOHN BORTHWICK/LONELY PLANET IMAGES ©

» (above) Relaxing on one of the Maldives' thousands of perfect w sand beaches
» (left) Water villa living at Six Senses Laamu Resort (p114) on Hadhdhunmathee Atoll

EATING LOCAL IN RESORTS

It used to be rare to find Maldivian food in tourist resorts – the opinion was that Western stomachs couldn't cope with the spices. Now many resorts do a Maldivian barbecue once a week, which is very enjoyable if not totally authentic. These barbecues can be on the beach, by the pool or in the restaurant. The main dishes are fresh reef fish, baked tuna, fish curries, rice and *roshi* (unleavened bread). The regular dinner buffet might also feature Maldivian fish curry. Less common is the Maldivian breakfast favourite *mas huni*, a healthy mixture of tuna, onion, coconut and chilli, eaten with *roshi*. If there's nothing Maldivian on the menu, you could ask the kitchen staff to make a fish curry or a tray of 'short eats' – they may be making some for the staff anyway. Small resorts are usually amenable to special requests. Otherwise, do a trip to Male or an island-hopping excursion to a fishing village and try out a local teashop. They're always a fascinating and surprisingly tasty experience.

while others run the gamut from water skiing to kite-boarding and wakeboarding. The best resorts for sailing and windsurfing have a wide lagoon that's not too shallow, and lots of equipment to choose from.

Resorts with particularly strong watersports facilities include Kuredu Island Resort, Adaaran Select Hudhuran Fushi, Chaaya Island Dhonveli, Bandos, Kuramathi, Kanuhura, Meeru, Summer Island Village, Club Faru, Club Med Kani, Vilu Reef, Olhuveli and Reethi Beach.

You'll find jet skis and other not-so-cheap thrills at Kuredu Island Resort, Kanuhura, Chaaya Island Dhonveli, Chaaya Reef Ellaidhoo, Conrad Maldives Rangali Island, Reethi Beach, Fun Island, Holiday Island, Vilu Reef, Paradise Island, W Retreat & Spa, both Four Seasons resorts and Royal Island, among many others.

Food & Drink

A miniature revolution in fine cuisine has occurred in the past few years in the Maldives, with luxury hotels offering a huge choice from an ever-growing number of restaurants, allowing guests to eat somewhere different every day for several days.

However, the buffet – the standard lunch and dinner option – is still in evidence, and extremely variable it can be too. The usual truism that you get what you pay for is especially relevant here.

Alcohol is also becoming more of a feature at resorts – many have spent years building up wine cellars to rival any French restaurant, and as you'd expect these are not cheap. Reethi Rah claims to have over 8000 bottles of wine in its cellar, while Huvafen

Fushi's wine cellar is a work of art itself, buried deep below the island and hired out for private dinners at great expense.

However, in all cases alcohol is expensive and, with a few luxury exceptions, limited in range. In lesser resorts the available beers will not thrill connoisseurs – although Kirin and Tiger are commonly seen amid the Heineken and Carling. All-inclusive packages cover designated drinks, usually the cheapest non-brand-name beer going, a house red and white wine and non-brand-name spirits. People on these deals can usually be found drinking, perhaps to justify the price of the package.

Meals

The way you eat is entirely dependent on what kind of resort you stay in. Meal times can be a highlight or a low point according to how demanding you are and what meal plan you're on.

Typically, breakfast is a buffet wherever you stay in the Maldives. At the bottom end, there will be a fairly limited selection of cereals, fruit, pastries and yoghurts. At the midrange and top end you'll have an enormous spread, usually including omelette stations, fresh fruit, good coffee, brand-name cereals, freshly baked pastries, curries, rice dishes, full English-style breakfast, meat platters and oodles of sweet cakes. You get what you pay for, remember.

In budget resorts, lunch and dinner will usually be a buffet as well. This can quickly become repetitive, and while you'll never go hungry, you may find yourself craving some variety. Some budget resorts have à la carte restaurants where you can dine to have a change of cuisine and scenery – if you're on

RESORT TOP FIVES

Back-to-Nature Resorts

Soneva Gili (p64)

Makunudu Island (p67)

Soneva Fushi (p102)

Rihiveli Beach Resort (p76)

Banyan Tree Madivaru (p86)

Water Villas

Soneva Gili (p64)

One & Only Reethi Rah (p63)

Huvafen Fushi (p64)

W Retreat & Spa (p86)

Coco Palm Bodu Hithi (p67)

Romantic Resorts

Makunudu Island (p67)

Mirihi (p86)

Six Senses Laamu (p114)

Baros (p66)

Cocoa Island (p76)

High-Style Resorts

One & Only Reethi Rah (p63)

Four Seasons Landaa Giraavaru (p101)

Jumeirah Vittaveli (p76)

Waldorf Astoria Maldives (p95)

Dusit Thani Maldives (p102)

Diving Resorts

Helengeli Island Resort (p68)

Asdu Sun Island (p70)

Equator Village (p122)

Chaaya Reef Ellaidhoo (p88)

Kuramathi (p83)

Stylish Midrange Resorts

Great style and attractiveness at relatively affordable prices.

Veligandu (p84)

Diamonds Athuruga Beach & Water Villas (p90)

Olhuveli Beach & Spa (p78)

Kandooma (p78)

Kurumba Maldives (p69)

an all-inclusive deal, meals like this will be charged as extras. However, for the most part there's little or no choice at the budget end. Dinner will usually have the biggest selection, and may be a 'theme night' specialising in regional cuisines such as Italian, Asian, Indian or Maldivian.

If you're in a midrange or top-end resort, you'll have a totally different experience. Almost all resorts in these categories have at least two restaurants, with a few exceptions for small islands where the restaurants are à la carte and have sufficiently long or changing menus to keep you satisfied for a couple of weeks or more. The larger resorts will have multiple choices (Kurumba has eight!), usually including at least one of the following: Japanese, Thai, Chinese, Indian, Italian, French, seafood or fusion.

Another alternative to the usual buffet is a 'speciality meal'. This might be a barbecue or a curry night, served on the beach and open to anyone who pays an extra charge (unlike a theme night in the main restaurant, which is not charged as an extra). Or it can be a much pricier private dinner for two in romantic surroundings – on an uninhabited island, on the beach, or on a sandbar a short ride from the resort island. Most resorts will do special meals on request, and nearly all top-end places offer in-room dining for those enjoying themselves too much to leave their villas.

Meal Plans

Many guests are on full-board packages that include accommodation and all meals. Others take a half-board package, which includes breakfast and dinner, and pay extra for lunch. Some resorts offer a bed-and-breakfast plan, and guests pay separately for lunch and dinner. The advantage of not paying for all your meals in advance is that you permit yourself the freedom to vary where you eat (assuming your resort has more than one restaurant). However, at good resorts your full-board plan is usually transferable, meaning you can eat a certain amount at other restaurants, or at least get a big discount on the à la carte prices.

Room-only deals are also sometimes available, but they're rarely a great idea. Never underestimate the sheer expense of eating à la carte in the Maldives at any level, although at the top end it's positively outrageous – think US$75 per head without alcohol for a decent lunch. Self-catering is of course not possible, and there's nothing worse than being unable to eat properly due to financial constraints. Unless you're very comfortable financially and want to eat in a variety of different places, it's definitely a good idea to book full-board or at least half-board meal plans.

All-inclusive plans are some of the best value of all, although in general they're associated with the core package-tourist market and tend to be available only in budget resorts. These typically include all drinks (non-brand-name alcohol, soft drinks and water) and some activities and water sports/diving thrown in for good measure. Always investigate carefully exactly what's on offer meal-wise before you make a decision – the meal plan can make an expensive package worthwhile or a cheap one a rip-off. One upmarket all-inclusive resort is Lily Beach in Ari Atoll, where you'll get good wines and brand-name spirits for your (not inconsiderable) daily rate.

Entertainment

The Maldives is not a premium destination for entertainment. What little of it there is can be naff and uninspiring, and the resorts that insist on a nightly disco often find them empty. Simply put, honeymooners, divers and families, the core demographic of Maldivian tourism, don't really come here for any kind of entertainment, preferring quiet romance and daytime activities to night-time ones.

That said, don't miss a performance of traditional Maldivian *bodu beru* (big drum) players, who perform regularly at resorts. (If you're staying on an inhabited island, you might see the real thing performed by local youths after nightfall.) This is definitely a cultural and entertainment highlight – the passion and excitement of the performance alone is remarkable – and shouldn't be missed.

The biggest party and entertainment resort is Club Med Kani, with its all-inclusive bar and nightly disco, and to a lesser extent Bandos, where visiting air crews can often be the life and soul of the party. One classy exception is the ice-cool stylings of the subterranean nightclub at W Retreat & Spa, with its visiting international DJs and hardly an ABBA record in sight.

Luxuries

You've come to the right place if this is your main interest. The Maldives' top-end resorts (and even some of its midrange options) offer an eye-watering range of treatments, pampering and general luxury.

Currently indispensible in the luxury industry is the personal *thakuru*, or butler, otherwise known as a 'man Friday' or 'villa host'. The *thakuru* is assigned to you throughout your stay. He's your point of contact for all small things (restocking the minibar, reserving a table for dinner), but given that one *thakuru* will often be looking after up to 10 rooms at a time, the term 'personal' is pushing it a bit, especially when even in the best hotels in the country there are often language problems and some service issues.

The home of pampering at most resorts is the spa. Until recently they were considered optional for resorts, whereas now they are usually at the very centre of the luxury experience. Expect to pay from about US$50 for a simple massage at a budget or midrange place to US$350 for a long session of pampering at a top-end resort.

Spas generally offer a vast range of treatments from the sublime to the truly ridiculous. Some of our favourite names include Fit For Life Aromatic Moor Mud Wrap, Tamarind Fancy Wipe, Potato Purifier and Happy Man Relaxer (no jokes, please).

Beaches

There's almost no resort in the Maldives that does not have an amazing beach. Throughout the course of researching this book, the only really mediocre beach we saw was at the Equator Village. It's still swimmable, but it's narrow and strewn with seaweed, making swimming unpleasant. Beaches suffer a great deal from erosion but resorts work very hard to redress this with sandbags and seawalls in certain places. These can of course be unsightly, but they are necessary to hold the islands' beaches in place. Obviously, the more expensive the resort, the more effort is made to ensure that sandbags are never visible

For the record, here are a list of our favourite beaches in the country: Hilton Maldives Iru Fushi Resort & Spa, Kanuhura, One & Only Reethi Rah, Kuredu Island Resort & Spa, Palm Beach, Soneva Fushi, Reethi Beach, Waldorf Astoria Maldives, Coco Palm Dhuni Kolhu, Eriyadu, Angsana Ihuru, Bandos, Baros, Banyan Tree Vabbinfaru, Soneva Gili, Club Med Kani, Rihiveli, Paradise Island, Island Hideaway, W Retreat & Spa, Coco Palm Bodu Hithi, Sun Island,

Veligandu, Vilu Reef, Huvafen Fushi, Filitheyo, Fun Island and Conrad Maldives Rangali Island. This does not mean that resorts not on this list don't make the grade – these are just our top choices.

Children

If you're bringing children to the Maldives, it's very important to get your choice of resort right, as only some resorts have kids clubs or babysitters available, and activities for older children can be limited at resorts more used to welcoming honeymooning couples. If you aren't looking for kids clubs and your offspring are happy to spend the day on the beach, then almost every resort will be suitable. Note that Komandoo Island Resort does not accept children aged under six and W Retreat & Spa doesn't accept children under 12.

In general kids will love the Maldives, although more than a week might be pushing it unless you're staying in a big family resort where there are plenty of other children for them to play with and lots of activities. Nowadays nearly all top-end resorts have kids clubs, and these can be impressive places, with their own pools and a host of activities, which mean parents can drop off kids (usually under 12) at any time, for free during the day.

Some highly recommended resorts for children include Kuredu, One & Only Reethi Rah, Hilton Iru Fushi, Kanuhura, Bandos, Kurumba Maldives, Filitheyo, Club Med Kani, Paradise Island, the three Kuramathi resorts, Meeru, both Four Seasons resorts, Lily Beach and Sun Island.

Diving, Snorkelling & Surfing

Top Diving Sites

Some of the better-known dive sites are described in the chapters covering each atoll and marked on the maps. For examples of the different types of dive sites, look up the following:

British Loyalty Addu Atoll, p121
Dhidhdhoo Beyru Ari Atoll, p86
Embudhoo Express South Male Atoll, p75
Fish Head Ari Atoll, p85
Guraidhoo Kandu South Male Atoll, p75
Halaveli Wreck Ari Atoll, p85
Helengeli Thila North Male Atoll, p61
HP Reef North Male Atoll, p61
Kakani Thila Baa Atoll, p101
Maa Kandu & Kuda Kandu Addu Atoll, p121 & p121
Maaya Thila Ari Atoll, p85
Bodu Hithi Thila North Male Atoll, p61
Shark Point Addu Atoll, p61

Unless you take some time to explore the magical world underneath the water in the Maldives, you're seeing just one part of this incredibly diverse country. Yes, the flora and fauna on the tiny scraps of land poking their heads above the water are not the most spectacular or varied, but glance into the deep blue all around and you'll see marine life so incredible that you'll quickly understand why the Maldives is a favourite destination for divers from around the world.

The visibility is incredible, the water so warm that many divers don't even wear a wetsuit and the sheer variety of life underwater is fantastic. Because of the thoroughly professional and safety-conscious approach from all resorts, it's common to learn to dive in the Maldives as well. Even if you don't do a full PADI or equivalent course, a brief scuba introduction is very cheap and lots of fun, while snorkelling can be done by anyone who can swim.

A further advantage of the Maldives' submarine life is that it's not only plentiful, beautiful and accessible, but also extremely unaggressive. Despite Maldivian waters being rich in sharks, there's not one likely to attack humans, and the only plausible situation in which it would attack would be when it feels threatened.

If you plan to dive, decide what you want to see and how much diving you want to do before choosing a resort. Snorkelling is similar – some resorts don't have a good house reef and thus you have to go on a boat trip to see anything worthwhile. Surfing is the most seasonal activity of all, but it's increasingly popular in the east of the country, where some great breaks come in off the Indian Ocean.

Diving

Taking the plunge into the deep blue is one of the most exciting things imaginable and the rewards are massive, especially in the Maldives, which is rightly known as a world-class scuba-diving destination. The enormous variety of fish life is amazing, and there's a good chance you'll see some of the biggest marine creatures – a close encounter with a giant manta or a 2m Napoleon wrasse is unforgettable, and the sharks of the Maldives are legendary.

Diving Safaris

On a diving safari, a dozen or so divers cruise the atolls in a live-aboard boat fitted out for the purpose. You can stop at your pick of the dive sites, visit uninhabited islands and local villages, find secluded anchorages and sleep in a compact cabin. If you've had enough diving, you can fish, snorkel or swim off the boat.

Generally, bigger boats are more comfortable, more fully equipped and more expensive. For keen divers, a safari trip is a great way to get in a lot of dives at a variety of sites, and it will probably work out cheaper than a resort-based dive trip. See p20 for general information about safaris and choosing a safari boat.

Everyone on a diving safari should be a qualified diver. If you need to do a diving course, contact the boat operator in advance (you may need a minimum of two to four people for a course). Dive clubs can often get together enough members to fill a safari boat and design a program and itinerary that suits their needs. Ideally, everyone on board should be of a similar diving standard.

A diving safari should have a separate dhoni that has the compressor and most of the equipment on board. This means that compressor noise doesn't disturb passengers at night, and the smaller boat can be used for excursions near shallow reefs. All dive safari boats will have tanks and weights, and they'll be included in the cost of dives. Regulators, buoyancy control devices (BCDs), depth gauges, tank pressure gauges and dive computers are available on

most boats for an additional charge. It's best to bring your own mask, snorkel, fins and wetsuit. Ask about the availability of specialised equipment such as cameras, lights and nitrox. Check www.visitmaldives.com for reasonably up-to-date details on what each boat provides (click on 'Where to Stay' then 'Safari').

For safety, every dive-safari boat should have oxygen equipment, a first-aid kit, and good radio and telephone communications with Male. The divemasters should give thorough predive briefings and emergency plans, have a checklist of every diver and do a roll-call after each dive. It's good to have descent lines and drift lines available for use in strong currents, and to be able to hang a safety tank at 5m for deeper dives. Night diving requires powerful lights, including a strobe light.

Where to Dive

There are hundreds of recognised and named dive sites, and dozens accessible from nearly every resort. In general there are four types of dive sites in the Maldives.

Reef Dives

The edges of a reef, where it slopes into deep water, are the most interesting part of a reef to dive. Inner-reef slopes, in the sheltered waters inside an atoll, are generally easier dives and feature numerous smaller reef fish. The reef around a resort island is known as its 'house reef', and in general only the guests of that resort are allowed to dive or snorkel on it.

At some resorts qualified divers can do unguided dives on the house reef. This is cheaper and more convenient than a boat dive, and gives divers a chance to get really well acquainted with the reef. House reefs can be terrific for night dives too.

Outer-reef slopes, where the atoll meets the open sea, often have interesting terraces, overhangs and caves, and are visited by pelagics. Visibility is usually good, but surf and currents can make for a demanding dive.

Kandus

These are channels between islands, reefs or atolls. Obviously, kandus are subject to currents and this provides an environment in which attractive soft corals thrive. Water inside an atoll is a breeding ground for plankton, and where this water flows out through a kandu into the open sea, the rich supply of

REEF IN BRIEF

REEF	ATOLL	REEF TYPE	PAGE
Banana Reef	North Male	reef & kandu	p63
Devana Kandu	Vaavu	kandu & thila	p107
Embudhoo Express	South Male	kandu	p75
Fotteyo	Vaavu	kandu	p107
Fushifaru Thila	Lhaviyani	kandu & thila	p104
Kuda Giri	South Male	giri & wreck	p75
Kuda Kandu	Addu	kandu	p121
Kuredhoo Express	Lhaviyani	kandu	p104
Maa Kandu	Addu	reef & kandu	p121
Macro Spot	Dhaalu	giri	p112
Manta Reef	Ari	reef & kandu	p85
Milaidhoo Reef	Baa	kandu	p101
Orimas Thila	Ari	thila	p85
Panetone	Ari	kandu	p85
Rakeedhoo Kandu	Vaavu	kandu	p107
Rasdhoo Madivaru	Ari	outer-reef slope	p83
Two Brothers	Faafu	giri	p109
Vaadhoo Caves	South Male	kandu	p75

plankton attracts large animals such as manta rays and whale sharks. During the southwest monsoon (May to November), currents will generally flow out of an atoll through kandus on the eastern side, while in the northeast monsoon (December to March), the outward flow is on the western side.

Thilas & Giris

A thila is a coral formation that rises steeply from the atoll floor and reaches to between 5m and 15m of the water surface – often it's a spectacular underwater mountain that divers fly around like birds. The top of a thila can be rich in reef fish and coral, while the steep sides have crannies, caves and overhangs, which provide shelter for many small fish, and larger fish come, in turn, to feed on the smaller fish.

A giri is a coral formation that rises to just below the water surface. It has many of the same features as a thila, but the top surface may be too shallow to dive.

Thilas and giris are found inside kandus, where the nutrient-rich currents promote soft-coral growth. They also stand in the sheltered waters inside an atoll, where the sea is warmer and slower moving. Hard-coral structures on sheltered thilas and giris suffered most from the 1998 coral bleaching, and have been the slowest to recover.

Wrecks

While many ships have foundered on Maldivian reefs over the centuries, there are few accessible wrecks with any historical interest. Most were on outer-reef slopes and broke up in the surf long ago, leaving remnants to be dispersed and covered in coral. Any wreck sites of historical significance will require special permission to dive. The wrecks you can dive at are mostly inside the atolls and not very old. They are interesting for the coral and other marine life that colonises the hulk within just a few years. Quite a few of the wrecks have been sunk deliberately, to provide an attraction for divers.

Diving Seasons

January to April are generally considered the best months for diving, and should have fine weather and good visibility. May and June can have unstable weather – storms and cloudy days are common until September. October and November tend to have calmer, clearer weather, but visibility can be slightly reduced because of abundant plankton in the water. Some divers like this period because many large fish, such as whale sharks and mantas, come into the channels to feed on the plankton. December can have rough, windy weather and rain.

Learning to Dive

Diving is not difficult, but it requires knowledge and care, and a lot of experience before you can safely dive independently. It doesn't require great strength or fitness, although if you can do things with minimum expenditure of energy, your tank of air will last longer.

There's a range of courses, from an introductory dive in a pool or lagoon to an open-water course that gives an internationally recognised qualification (usually PADI). Beyond that, there are advanced and speciality courses, and courses that lead to divemaster and instructor qualifications. Courses in the Maldives are not a bargain, but they're no more expensive than learning at home and this way you are assured of high standards, good equipment and extremely pleasant conditions. On the other hand, if you do a course at home, you'll have more time for diving when you get to the Maldives.

The best option for learners is to do an open-water referral course in their home country (ie all the theory and basics in the pool), allowing you to complete the course in the Maldives in just two days rather than the four or five needed for the full course. After all, you didn't fly halfway around the world to sit in a room watching a PADI DVD, did you? If you do this, ensure you have all your certification from the referral course with you; otherwise you'll have to start from scratch.

If you're at all serious about diving, you should do an open-water course. This requires nine dives, usually five in sheltered water and four in open water, as well as classroom training and completion of a multiple-choice test. The cost in the Maldives is from US$400 to US$750. Sometimes the price is all-inclusive, but there are often a few extra charges. You can do the course in as little as five days, or take your time and spread it over a week or two. Don't try it on a one-week package – transfers and jet lag will take a day or so, and you shouldn't dive less than 24 hours before a flight. Besides, you'll want to do some recreational dives to try out your new skills.

The next stage is an advanced open-water course, which will involve five dives (including one night dive), and will cost from US$280 to US$400, depending on the dive school. Then there are the speciality courses in night diving, rescue diving, wreck diving, nitrox diving and so on.

Dive Schools & Operators

Every resort has a professional diving operation and can run courses for beginners, as well as dive trips and courses that will challenge even the most experienced diver. The government requires that all dive operations maintain high standards, and all of them are affiliated with one or more of the international diving accreditation organisations – most are with PADI.

Certificates

When you complete an open-water course, you receive a certificate that is recognised by diving operators all over the world. Certificates in the Maldives are generally issued by the Professional Association of Diving Instructors (PADI), the largest and the best-known organisation, but certificates from Confédération Mondiale des Activités Sub-aquatiques (CMAS; World Underwater Federation), Scuba Schools International (SSI) and a number of other organisations are also acceptable.

Equipment

Dive schools in the Maldives can rent out all diving gear, but most divers prefer to have at least some of their own equipment. It's best to have your own mask, snorkel and fins, which you can also use for snorkelling. The tank and weight belt are always included in the cost of a dive, so you don't need to bring them – sealed tanks are prohibited on aircraft anyway, and you'd be crazy to carry lead weights. The main pieces of diving equipment to bring with you are described in the following sections.

Wetsuit

The water may be warm (27°C to 30°C) but a wetsuit is often preferable for comfortable diving. A 3mm suit should be adequate, but 5mm is preferable if you want to go deep or dive more than once per day. Alternatively, it's possible to dive in a T-shirt if you don't feel the cold too much.

Regulator & BCDs

Many divers have their own regulator (the mouth piece you breathe through), with which they are familiar and therefore confident about using. BCDs (Buoyancy Control Devices) are the vests that can be controlled to inflate and deflate and thus increase or decrease your buoyancy, a vital tool for safe diving. Both pieces of equipment are usually included in full equipment packages, though serious divers will usually bring their own.

Dive Computer

These are now compulsory in the Maldives. They're available for rent, for US$5 to US$10 per dive, or as part of a complete equipment package.

Logbook

You'll need this to indicate to divemasters your level of experience, and to record your latest dives, which are then authenticated by the divemaster and stamped by the school.

Other items you might need are an underwater torch (especially for cave and night dives), waterproof camera, compass, and safety buoy or balloon, most of which are available for rental. Some things you won't need are a spear gun, which is prohibited, and diving gloves, which are discouraged since you're not supposed to touch anything anyway.

Diving Costs

The cost of diving varies between resorts, and depends on whether you need to rent equipment. A single dive, with only tank and weights supplied, runs from US$40 to US$100, but is generally around US$45 or US$50 (night dives cost more). If you need to rent a regulator and a BCD as well, a dive will cost from US$50 to US$110. Sometimes the full equipment price includes mask, snorkel, fins, dive computer and pressure gauge, but they can cost extra. A package of 10 dives will cost roughly from US$300 to US$500, or US$400 to US$700 with equipment rental. Other possibilities are five-, 12- and 15-dive packages, and packages that allow you as many dives as you want within a certain number of consecutive days. The very best diving operators will bill you at the end of your stay, having worked out which tariff is most economical for you based on the diving you've done. In addition to the dive cost, there is a charge for using a boat, which can be as much as US$20 per dive. There may also be a service charge of 10% if diving is billed to your room, so the prices really do add up. Ideally book your dives ahead of time, confirming the price, and shop around between resorts to find the best deals.

Marine Environment Protection

The waters of the Maldives may seem pristine but, like everywhere, development and commercial activities can have adverse effects on the marine environment. The Maldivian government recognises that the underwater world is a major attraction, and has imposed many restrictions and controls on fishing, coral mining and tourism operations. Twenty-five Protected Marine Areas have been established, and these are subject to special controls, while the country's first ever National Marine Park was being created in Noonu Atoll at the time of writing.

Visitors must do their best to ensure that their activities don't spoil the experience of those who will come in the future. The following rules are generally accepted as necessary for conservation, and most of them apply equally to snorkellers and divers.

» Do not use anchors on the reef, and take care not to ground boats on coral. Encourage dive operators and regulatory bodies to establish permanent moorings at popular dive sites.

» Avoid touching living marine organisms with your body or dragging equipment across the reef. Polyps can be damaged by even the gentlest contact.

» Never stand on corals, even if they look solid and robust. If you must hold on to prevent being swept away in a current, hold on to dead coral.

» Be conscious of your fins. Even without contact the surge from heavy fin strokes near the reef can damage delicate organisms. When treading water in shallow reef areas, take care not to kick up clouds of sand. Settling sand can easily smother the delicate organisms of the reef.

» Collecting lobster or shellfish is prohibited, as is spearfishing. Removing any coral or shells, living or dead, is against the law. All shipwreck sites are protected by law.

» Take home all your rubbish and any litter you may find as well. Plastics in particular are a serious threat to marine life. Turtles can mistake plastic for jellyfish and eat it. Don't throw cigarette butts overboard.

» Resist the temptation to feed fish. You may disturb their normal eating habits, encourage aggressive behaviour or feed them food that is detrimental to their health.

» Practise and maintain proper buoyancy control. Major damage can be done by divers descending too fast and colliding with the reef.

» Take great care in underwater caves. Spend as little time within them as possible as your air bubbles may be caught within the roof and thereby leave previously submerged organisms high and dry. Taking turns to inspect the interior of a small cave will lessen the chances of damaging contact.

Back from the Bleaching

It's true that coral bleaching killed nearly all of the hard coral in the Maldives, but that's not the end of the story. In a few places old coral has unaccountably survived, and you can occasionally be surprised by a big-table coral or a long-branching staghorn. The most southern atoll of the Maldives, Addu, was unaffected by coral bleaching and so still boasts extraordinarily colourful and varied hard corals, and is by far the best place in the country to dive and snorkel. Soft corals and sea fans were less affected by coral bleaching and have regrown more quickly. Magnificent soft-coral gardens thrive at many dive sites, especially around channels that are rich with water-borne nutrients, and a few fine specimens can be seen at snorkelling depths on many house reefs.

RISE & RISE OF THE ATOLLS

A coral reef or garden is not, as many people believe, formed of multicoloured marine plants. It is a living colony of coral polyps – tiny, tentacled creatures that feed on plankton. Coral polyps are invertebrates with sac-like bodies and calcareous or horny skeletons. After extracting calcium deposits from the water around them, the polyps excrete tiny, cup-shaped, limestone skeletons. These little guys can make mountains.

A coral reef is the rock-like aggregation of millions of these polyp skeletons. Only the outer layer of coral is alive. As polyps reproduce and die, the new polyps attach themselves in successive layers to the skeletons already in place. Coral grows best in clear, shallow water, and especially where waves and currents from the open sea bring extra oxygen and nutrients.

Charles Darwin put forward the first scientific theory of atoll formation based on observations of atolls and islands in the Pacific. He envisaged a process where coral builds up around the shores of a volcanic island to produce a fringing reef. Then the island sinks slowly into the sea while the coral grows upwards at about the same rate. This forms a barrier reef, separated from the shore of the sinking island by a ring-shaped lagoon. By the time the island is completely submerged, the coral growth has become the base for an atoll, circling the place where the volcanic peak used to be.

This theory doesn't quite fit the Maldives, though. Unlike the isolated Pacific atolls, Maldivian atolls all sit on top of the same long, underwater plateau, around 300m to 500m under the surface of the sea. This plateau is a layer of accumulated coral stone over 2000m thick. Under this is the 'volcanic basement', a 2000km-long ridge of basalt that was formed over 50 million years ago.

The build-up of coral over this ridge is as much to do with sea-level changes as it is with the plateau subsiding. When sea levels rise the coral grows upwards to stay near the sea surface, as in the Darwin model, but there were at least two periods when the sea level actually dropped significantly – by as much as 120m. At these times much of the accumulated coral plateau would have been exposed, subjected to weathering, and 'karstified' – eroded into steep-sided, flat-topped columns. When sea levels rose again, new coral grew on the tops of the karst mountains and formed the bases of the individual Maldivian atolls.

Coral grows best on the edges of an atoll, where it is well supplied with nutrients from the open sea. A fringing reef forms around an enclosed lagoon, growing higher as the sea level rises. Rubble from broken coral accumulates in the lagoon, so the level of the lagoon floor also rises, and smaller reefs can rise within it. Sand and debris accumulate on the higher parts of the reef, creating sandbars on which vegetation can eventually take root. The classic atoll shape is oval, with the widest reefs and most of the islands around the outer edges.

Geological research has revealed the complex layers of coral growth that underlie the Maldives, and has shown that coral growth can match the fastest sea-level rises on record, some 125m in only 10,000 years – about 1.25cm per year. In geological terms, that's fast.

The underlying hard-coral structure is still there of course – new coral grows on the skeletons of its predecessors. The healthiest living coral has many metres, perhaps kilometres, of dead coral underneath. New coral is growing on reefs all over the Maldives, though the large and elaborately shaped formations will take many years to build. It's fascinating to observe the new coral growth – the distinctly coloured patches with the finely textured surface of a living, growing organism. The first regrowth often occurs in crevices on old coral blocks, where it's protected from munching parrotfish. The massive Porites-type corals seem to come first, but they grow slowly – look for blobs of yellow, blue or purple that will eventually cover the whole block in a crust or a cushion or a brainlike dome. The branching corals (Acropora) appear as little purplish trees on a coral block, like a pale piece of broccoli. Growing a few centimetres per year (15cm in ideal conditions), they will eventually become big, extended staghorn corals or wide, flat-topped tables.

The recovery for coral is not uniform. Some parts of a reef can be doing very well, with 80% or 90% of the old surfaces covered with new and growing coral, while 100m along the same reef, new coral growth cover is less than 20%. Reef formation is a very complex natural process, but surprisingly the marine ecosystem as a whole seems to be undamaged by the coral bleaching. Fish life is as abundant and diverse as ever.

Snorkelling

Snorkelling is the first step into seeing a different world. Anyone who can swim can do it, it's cheap to rent the equipment (and often free at smarter resorts), and the rewards are immediately evident. The colours of the fish and coral are far better at shallow depths, because water absorbs light. Below 5m, colours start to become less sharp (many divers carry torches to compensate). This means a visual feast awaits any snorkeller on any decent reef.

Where to Snorkel

Usually an island is surrounded firstly by a sand-bottomed lagoon, and then by the reef flat (*faru*), a belt of dead and living coral covered by shallow water. At the edge of the reef flat is a steep, coral-covered slope that drops away into deeper water. These reef slopes are the best areas for snorkelling – around a resort island this is called the 'house reef'. The slope itself can have interesting features such as cliffs, terraces and caves, and there are clearly visible changes in the coral and marine flora as the water gets deeper. You can see both the smaller fish, which frequent the reef flats, and sometimes much larger animals that live in the deep water between the islands but come close to the reefs to feed.

You can also take a boat from your resort to other snorkelling sites around the atoll. A giri (coral pinnacle) that rises to within 5m of the surface is ideal for snorkelling, which is not difficult if it's in sheltered waters inside an atoll. A kandu (sea channel) will usually have excellent soft corals, schools of reef fish and large pelagic species (fish that inhabit the upper layers of the open sea).

The best resorts for snorkelling have an accessible house reef around at least part of the island, where deep water is not far offshore. There are usually channels you can swim through to the outer-reef slope. To avoid grazing yourself or damaging the coral, always use these channels rather than trying to find your own way across the reef flat. Another option is to walk out on a jetty to the reef edge – all resorts have at least one jetty, though sometimes they don't extend right to the edge of the reef.

Resorts that don't have an accessible house reef will usually provide a couple of boat trips per day to a good snorkelling site nearby, but this is a lot less convenient, as you're limited in time and seldom alone. Many resorts offer island-hopping trips or snorkelling excursions that stop at really superb snorkelling sites, and these are a far better option. Sometimes snorkellers can go out with a dive boat, if the dive site is suitable and there's space on the boat.

Preparation

Every resort will have snorkelling equipment that you can rent, though it's often free at smarter resorts. It's definitely better to have your own equipment, though, as it's cheaper in the long run and sure to fit properly. You can buy good equipment at reasonable prices in Male, though you're better off buying your gear at home before you leave.

Mask

Human eyes won't focus in water, but a mask keeps an air space in front of them allowing them to do so. Any mask, no matter how cheap, should have a shatterproof lens. Ensure that it fits you comfortably – press it gently onto your face, breathe in through your nose a little, and the suction alone should hold the mask on your face.

If you're short-sighted, you can get the mask lens ground to your optical prescription, but this is expensive. Alternatively, get a stick-on optical lens to attach to the inside of the mask lens, or simply fold up an old pair of spectacles and wedge them inside the mask. There's no problem with contact lenses under the mask.

Snorkel

The snorkel tube has to be long enough to reach above the surface of the water, but should not be either too long or too wide. If it is too big, you will have more water to expel when you come to the surface. Also, each breath out leaves a snorkel full of used air, and if the snorkel is too big, you will rebreathe a larger proportion of carbon dioxide.

Fins

These are not absolutely necessary, but they make swimming easier and let you dive deeper, and they give a margin of safety in currents. Fins either fit completely over your foot or have an open back with an adjustable strap around your heel, designed for use with wetsuit boots.

Shirt

A Lycra swim shirt or thin wetsuit top will protect against sunburn (a real hazard) and scratches from the coral or rocks. Even a T-shirt will help – but don't use a favourite as the sea water won't do the fabric any favours.

Snorkelling Safely

Don't snorkel alone, and always let someone else know where and when you'll be snorkelling. Colourful equipment or clothing will make you more visible. Beware of strong currents or rough conditions – wind chop and large swells can make snorkelling uncomfortable or even dangerous. In open water, carry a safety balloon and whistle to alert boats to your presence.

Surfing

Surfing has been slow to take off in the Maldives, but its popularity is on the increase. There's some great surf throughout the country, although only a few breaks are easily accessible from resorts, and they are only surfable from March to November. Surfers have a choice of basing themselves at a resort and taking a boat to nearby breaks, or arranging a live-aboard safari cruise. In either case, make arrangements in advance with a reputable surf travel operator who knows the area well. While traditionally the Maldives was definitely not the sort of place where a surfer can just turn up and head for the waves, the proliferation of new guesthouses on inhabited islands has made surfing in the Maldives far more appealing (and most importantly, far less expensive) than has been the case in the past.

The period of the southwest monsoon (May to November) generates the best waves, but March and April are also good and have the best weather. June can have bad weather and storms, and is not great for boat trips, but it is also a time for big swells. The best breaks occur on the outer reefs on the southeast sides of the atolls, but only where a gap in the reef allows the waves to wrap around.

Surfing in the Maldives was pioneered by Tony Hussein (also known as Tony Hinde), a Sydney surfer who was shipwrecked in the Maldives in the early 1970s. Before the first tourist resorts were opened, he discovered, surfed and named all the main breaks, and had them all to himself for many years.

North Male Atoll

This is where the best-known breaks are, and they can get a bit crowded, especially if there are several safari boats in the vicinity.

Chickens A left-hander that sections when small, but on a bigger swell and a higher tide it all comes together to make a long and satisfying wave. It's named for the old poultry farm onshore, not because of any reaction to the conditions here.

Cola's A heavy, hollow, shallow right-hander; when it's big, it's one of the best breaks in the area. This is a very thick wave breaking hard over a shallow reef, so it's definitely for experienced, gutsy surfers only. Named for the Coca-Cola factory nearby on the island of Thulusdhoo, it's also called Cokes.

Honky's During its season, this is the best wave in the Maldives. It's a super-long, wally left-hander that wraps almost 90 degrees and can nearly double in size by the end section.

Jailbreaks A right-hander that works best with a big swell, when the three sections combine to make a single, long, perfect wave. There used to be a prison on the island and the surrounding waters were off-limits, but now it's open to surfers.

Lohi's A solid left-hander that usually breaks in two sections, but with a big enough swell and a high enough tide the sections link up. You can paddle out there from the resort island of Lohifushi. Guests of that resort have exclusive access to the break.

Pasta Point A perfect left that works like clockwork on all tides. There's a long outside wall at the take-off point, jacking into a bowling section called the 'macaroni bowl'. On big days the break continues to another section called 'lock jaws', which grinds into very shallow water over the reef. It's easily reached from the shore at the Chaaya Island Dhonveli resort, whose guests have exclusive use of this break.

Piddlies A slow, mellow, mushy right-hander, a good Malibu wave. It's also called Ninja's because of its appeal to Japanese surfers. It's off the island of Kanifinolhu, home of the Club Med Kani resort, but it's very difficult to reach from the shore, and the wave is available to any boat-based surfer, not just Club Med guests.

Sultan's This is a classic right-hand break, and the bigger the swell, the better it works. A steep outside peak leads to a super-fast wall and then an inside section that throws right out, and tubes on every wave.

South Male Atoll

The breaks in South Male Atoll are smaller than those in North Male Atoll and generally more fickle. It will be harder here to find a boatman who really knows the surf scene.

Guru's A nice little left off the island of Gulhi; it can get good sometimes.

Kate's A small left-hander, rarely more than a metre.

Last Stops This is a bowly right-hander breaking over a channel reef. It's a Protected Marine Area, and can get very strong currents when the tides are running.

Natives A small right-hander, rarely more than a metre.

Quarters Another small right-hander, rarely more than a metre.

Outer Atolls

Only a few areas have the right combination of reef topography and orientation to swell and wind direction. Laamu and Addu both have surfable waves on occasions, but they're not reliable enough to be worth a special trip.

South of Male, Meemu Atoll has several excellent surf breaks on its eastern edge including Veyvah Point, Boahuraa Point and Mulee Point, which are gradually being explored by more adventurous surfers.

In the far south, Gaaf Dhaal has a series of reliable breaks that are accessed by safari boats in season. From west to east, the named breaks are Beacons, Castaways, Blue Bowls, Five Islands, Two Ways (also called Twin Peaks; left and right), Love Charms, Antiques and Tiger.

Resort-Based Surfing

The most accessible surf breaks are in the southeastern part of North Male Atoll. Half a dozen resorts and a few guesthouses are within a short boat ride, but check with them if you plan to surf, as only a few of them cater for surfers by providing regular boat service to the waves.

Chaaya Island Dhonveli (p71) is the resort that's best set up for surfers – the reliable waves of the 'house break', Pasta Point, are just out the back door, while Sultan's and Honky's are close by. A surfside bar provides a great view of the action. Surfing packages at Chaaya Island Dhonveli include unlimited boat trips to the other local breaks with surf guides who know the conditions well, leaving and returning on demand.

Adaaran Select Hudhuran Fushi (p68), a few kilometres northeast of Dhonveli, is a bigger, more expensive resort with more facilities and it also has its own, exclusive surf break at the southern tip of the island. A bar and a viewing terrace overlook the wave, which has hosted international surfing competitions.

Club Med Kani (p68) is the other resort island with an adjacent surf break, but you need a boat to reach it from the resort. There's no surfing program, no surf guides and no boats available for surfers. The nearby Four Seasons Kuda Huraa can arrange boat trips to the surf for guests.

Surfing Safaris

Most of the safari boats in the Maldives claim to do surfing trips, but very few of them have specialised knowledge of surfing or any experience cruising to the outer atolls. Ideally, a surfing safari boat should have an experienced surf guide and a second,

Surf Breaks

N

0 — 10 km
0 — 6 miles

Protected
Marine Area

Nakachchaafushi

Thulusdhoo

14

2

1

Kanifinolhu

16

11

8

Protected
Marine Area

Kanuhuraa

17

Huraa

15

Girifushi

10

Ihuru Vabbinfaru

5

Thaburudhoo

Baros

4

13

Kudabados

NORTH MALE ATOLL

Protected
Marine Area

Protected
Marine Area

Hulhumale

Protected
Marine Areas

Giraavaru

Hulhule

Male Ibrahim Nasir
International Airport

Viligili

KAAFU

☆ **MALE**

Vaadhoo Kandu

Velassaru

Vaadhoo

Embudhu Finolhu

Bolifushi

Protected
Marine Area

Emboodhoo

INDIAN

OCEAN

3

Gulhi

12

6

Veliganduhuraa

Maafushi

SOUTH MALE ATOLL

Biyadhoo
Viligilivaru

Kadoomafushi

Rannalhi

Guraidhoo

9

82m △ Fihalhohi

Protected
Marine Area

7

Bodufinolhu

Olhuveli

*Hathikolhu
Kandu*

Mahaana Elhi Huraa

Surf Breaks

smaller boat to accompany it, for accessing breaks in shallow water and getting in close to the waves. A surfing safari ('surfari') boat should also be equipped with fishing and snorkelling gear, for when the surf isn't working or you need a rest.

An inner-atolls surfari will just cruise around North Male Atoll, visiting breaks that are also accessible from resorts in the area. If the swell is big and the surf guide is knowledgeable, the boat may venture down to South Male Atoll to take advantage of the conditions. A one-week inner-atoll surf trip will start at around US$1000 per person. This might be cheaper than resort-based surfing, but it won't be as comfortable, and it won't give access to a handy and uncrowded house break.

An outer-atolls surfari is the only feasible way to surf the remote waves of Gaaf Dhaal or Meemu – an experienced outer-atoll guide is essential. If you're looking to surf in Meemu, the boat will probably pick you up in Male and then head south. If you're going surfing in Gaaf Dhaal, you'll normally take a Maldivian flight to the domestic airport on the island of Kaadedhoo, where the boat crew will meet you.

You need at least six people to make a safari boat affordable; the surfing specialists should be able to put together the necessary numbers. Don't book into a safari trip that is primarily for diving or cruising. Allow at least two weeks for the trip or you'll spend too much of your time getting to the waves and back. A 10-night surfari will cost from about US$2000 per person, including domestic airfares.

Surf Travel Operators

The following agents specialise in surf travel and book tours and safaris to the Maldives.

Atoll Travel (www.atolltravel.com) Australian and international agent for Atoll Adventures. It offers surfing packages to the Chaaya Island Dhonveli resort, premium surfing safari tours in Male Atoll and to the outer atolls.

Maldives Scuba Tours (www.scubascuba. com) Maldives dive travel agency and UK agent for Atoll Adventures. Offers Chaaya Island Dhonveli packages.

Surf Travel Company (www.surftravel.com. au) Venerable surf travel operator; it books surfers into Hudhuran Fushi, Four Seasons Kuda Huraa and Paradise Island. It also does boat-based tours throughout the country.

Turquoise Surf Travel (www.turquoise -voyages.fr) This agent offers surfing safaris in Gaaf Dhaal atoll as well as resort-based surfing at Adaaran Select Hudhuran Fushi.

World Surfaris (www.worldsurfaris.com) Offering tours to various surfing destinations, it books surfers into Dhonveli and also does boat-based trips in the inner atolls.

regions at a glance

Male

History ✓✓
Eating ✓
Shopping ✓

Mosques & Museums

Male has an array of ancient mosques and minarets to check out, as well as a brand new, first-class National History Museum that is unmissable for anyone interested in the unusual history of this small island nation. Make a point of seeing both the superb Old Friday Mosque with its intricate carvings and the impressive modern Grand Friday Mosque.

p44

Varied Dining

The capital has a great range of places to eat and drink (nonalcoholic only!). After being in a resort for a week or two, the low prices and wide choice will seem like thrills in themselves. The very best places to dine include international fusion at Aïoli and superb Thai at Sala Thai. Even if you're on a budget there's plenty to choose from: don't miss traditional Maldivian 'short eats' at Dawn Café or Irudhashu Hotaa – delicious!

Shop Till You Drop

Male is all about trade and commerce, and its mercantile atmosphere is infectious. Don't miss the catch being hauled in, cleaned up and sold off at the fish market, or the crowds at the produce market. But for a real slice of the shopping action, head down Chandhanee Magu for souvenir shops and then wander the main avenue of the city, Majeedee Magu, for clothes, bags and shoes.

North & South Male Atolls

Luxury ✓✓
Surfing ✓
Diving ✓✓

Superb Resorts

Few atolls have the concentration of excellent, world-class resorts that can be found in North and South Male Atolls. Whether it's small and romantic (Cocoa Island), super-glamorous (One & Only Reethi Rah) or back-to-nature luxury (Soneva Gili), you'll find the right resort here.

Surf Breaks

North Male has several excellent surf breaks on the eastern side of the atoll. There are a few nearby resorts and guesthouses that cater to surfers, and the best thing of all is that surf season coincides with Maldivian low season!

Underwater World

Don't forget your PADI certification or at least your mask and fins for some snorkelling in North and South Male Atolls. You'll see an incredible array of marine life on the reef, from sharks and moray eels to turtles and rays.

p60

Ari Atoll

Wildlife ✓✓✓
Island Hopping ✓✓
Beaches ✓✓

Whale Sharks & Hammerheads
There are two utterly amazing wildlife-watching opportunities in Ari Atoll, unfortunately at opposite ends of the atoll. In the south, swim with whale sharks, the largest fish in the world, while in the north, feed hammerhead sharks at Hammerhead Point.

Paradise Found
Ari has more than its fair share of uninhabited island paradises, and an island-hopping trip here is an amazing experience; swim in pristine waters and then enjoy a fresh fish barbecue on the beach.

Mind-Blowing Beaches
When it comes to beaches, you'll be spoiled for choice. Every single one of the dozens of resorts and guesthouses here has access to perfect white sand and amazing turquoise lagoon water.

p81

Northern Atolls

Diving ✓✓✓
History ✓
Beaches ✓✓✓

Pristine Underwater World
The lack of resorts and a new National Marine Park in Noonu Atoll makes the Northern Atolls one of the best places to dive in the country. Live-aboard dive boats can take you to even remoter locations than the resorts.

Maldivian Heritage
Take a trip to Utheemu in the country's very far north if you'd like to see some real Maldivian cultural heritage. The island is home to Utheemu Palace, a perfectly preserved nobleman's 16th-century mansion.

Perfect White Sand
The beaches in the remote Northern Atolls are some of the most extraordinarily perfect you'll ever come across. What's more, the relative lack of resorts means that even beyond your resort you'll find plenty of perfect uninhabited islands with equally brilliant sands.

p93

Southern Atolls

Snorkelling ✓✓✓
Fabulous Resorts ✓✓
Independent Travel ✓

Unbleached Corals
Addu Atoll managed to escape the ruinous coral bleaching that followed El Niño in 1997–98 and thus has the most dazzlingly colourful coral in the country. Don't miss snorkelling here.

Lap of Luxury
The Southern Atolls are home to some of the most impressive new luxury resorts, including the amazing Shangri-La Villingili, Six Senses Laamu, Jumeirah Dhevanafushi and Ayada Maldives, all setting new standards for pampering and style.

Culture
For the truly intrepid independent traveller, the south is a great place to explore alone. Check out the island of Fuvahmulah with its two inland lakes and traditionally isolated community, or visit the Maldives' second-largest city, Hithadhoo.

p106

> **Every listing is recommended by our authors, and their favourite places are listed first**

> **Look out for these icons:**

 Our author's top recommendation

 A green or sustainable option

 No payment required

See the Index for a full list of destinations covered in this book.

On the Road

Male

AREA 1.95 SQ KM / POP 103.693

Best Places to Stay

» Traders Hotel (p53)

» Sala Boutique Hotel (p53)

» House Clover (p50)

» Dacé Hotel (p52)

» Skai Lodge (p50)

Best Places to Eat

» Aïoli (p54)

» Sala Thai (p54)

» Royal Garden Cafe (p54)

» Shell Beans (p56)

» Irudhashu Hotaa (p55)

Why Go?

The pint-sized Maldivian capital is the throbbing, mercantile heart of the nation, a densely crowded and extraordinary place, notable mainly for its stark contrast to the laid-back pace of island life elsewhere in the country.

Male (*mar*-lay) offers the best chance to see the 'real' Maldives away from the resort buffet and infinity pool. Overlooked by brightly coloured tall buildings and surrounded by incongruously turquoise water, Male is a hive of activity, the engine driving the Maldives' economy and the forum for the country's political debate.

Male is pleasant and pleasingly quirky – its alcohol-free bars and restaurants jostle with its shops and lively markets and the general hubbub of a capital is very much present. This city island offers a chance to get a real feel for the Maldives and what makes its people tick and to meet Maldivians on an equal footing.

Male Highlights

» Gape at historic artifacts, giant fish and other quirky relics at the superb new **National Museum** (p45)

» Admire the beautiful exterior of the **Old Friday Mosque** (p45), the oldest in the country

» Watch the morning's catch being brought in, gutted and sold at the fascinating **Fish Market** (p47), one of Male's busiest places of trade

» Join locals for 'short eats' at any traditional **teashop** (p55), a delicious way to spend time outside the tourist bubble

History

Male has been the seat of the Maldives' ruling dynasties since before the 12th century, though none left any grand palaces. Some trading houses appeared in the 17th century, along with a ring of defensive bastions, but Male didn't acquire the trappings of a city and had a very limited range of economic and cultural activities. Visitors in the 1920s estimated the population at only 5000.

Growth began with the 1930s modernisation, and the first banks, hospitals, high schools and government offices appeared in the following decades. Only since the 1970s, with wealth from tourism and an expanding economy, has the city really burgeoned and growth emerged as a problem.

And a problem it has definitely become; despite extending the area of the city through land reclamation over the island's reef, Male is unable to extend any further and so the government is looking to projects such as nearby Hulhumale to accommodate the future overspill of the city.

Dangers & Annoyances

The main danger in Male is posed by the mopeds that seem to appear from nowhere at great speeds. Keep your wits about you and look around before crossing the road.

The principal annoyance in Male is the lack of alcohol. If you really want a drink, take the approximately hourly ferry from Jetty No 1 to the Hulhule Island Hotel (p53) near the airport, or take the airport ferry and walk the 10 minutes to the hotel for a cold beer by the pool.

◉ Sights

Male is more of an experience than a succession of astonishing must-sees. The best thing to do is enjoy a stroll and absorb the atmosphere of this oddest of capitals. That said, there are a few genuine sights to keep you occupied for a day.

Old Friday Mosque   MOSQUE
(Map p48; Medhuziyaarai Magu) **Hukuru Miskiiy** is the oldest mosque in the country, dating from 1656. It's a beautiful structure made from coral stone into which intricate decoration and Quranic script have been carved. Even though an ugly protective corrugated-iron sheet now covers the roof and some of the walls, this is still a fascinating place. The interior is superb and famed for its fine lacquer work and elaborate woodcarvings. One long panel, carved in the 13th century, commemorates the introduction of Islam to the Maldives. Visitors wishing to see inside are supposed to get permission from an official of the **Ministry of Islamic Affairs** (☑332 2266). However, most of the staff are officials of the ministry, and if you are respectful and well dressed, they will usually give you permission to enter the mosque on the spot.

The mosque was built on the foundations of an old temple that faced west to the setting sun, not northwest towards Mecca. Consequently, the worshippers have to face the corner of the mosque when they pray – the striped carpet, laid at an angle, shows the correct direction.

Overlooking the mosque is the solid, round, blue-and-white tower of the *munnaaru* – the squat minaret. Though it doesn't look that old, it dates from 1675. To one side of the mosque is a cemetery with many elaborately carved tombstones. Stones with rounded tops are for females, those with pointy tops are for males and those featuring gold-plated lettering are the graves of former sultans. The small buildings are family mausoleums and their stone walls are intricately carved. Respectably dressed non-Muslims are welcome to walk around the graveyard; you don't require permission for this.

National Museum   MUSEUM
(Map p48; Chandhanee Magu; adult/child under 12yr Rf50/15; ◷9am-5pm Sat-Thu, closed holidays) The brand new National Museum may be a ferociously ugly building gifted by China, but it nevertheless contains an excellent and well-labelled collection of historic artefacts that serve to trace the unusual history of these isolated islands.

The display begins downstairs with galleries devoted to the ancient and medieval periods of Maldivian history. Items on display include weaponry, religious paraphernalia and household wares as well as many impressively carved Arabic- and Thaana-engraved pieces of wood commemorating the conversion of the Maldives to Islam in 1153.

Upstairs is a display representing the modern period and including some prized examples of the lacquer-work boxes for which the Maldives are famous, and various pieces of antique technology including the country's first gramophone, telephone and a massive computer. Quirkier relics include the minutes of the famous underwater cabinet meeting held under President Nasheed in 2009 and an impressive marine collection, the highlight

Male

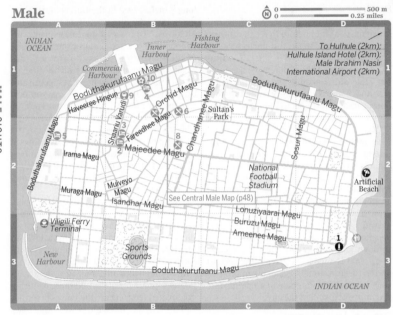

of which is the 6m-long skeleton of the very rare Longman's Beaked Whale, which is yet to have been sighted alive in the sea.

Rather annoyingly, despite nearly all items being safely behind glass, you're followed around the museum rather unsubtly by a guard, but that aside, this is an excellent and fascinating place to visit.

Grand Friday Mosque & Islamic Centre

MOSQUE

(Map p48; Jumhooree Maidan) The golden dome of this impressive but rather sterile mosque dominates the skyline of Male and has become something of a symbol for the city. Set back off the main square, Jumhooree Maidan, and opposite the National Security Service Headquarters, this is the biggest mosque in the country.

Opened in 1984, and built with help from the Gulf States, Pakistan, Brunei and Malaysia, the Grand Friday Mosque is striking in its plainness, built in white marble and virtually free from decoration. From a boat coming into Male's harbour, you can still see the gold dome glinting in the sun, although the gold is actually anodised aluminium. The *munnaaru,* with its space-age shape and distinctive zigzag decoration, was supposed to be the tallest structure in Male, but that title now goes to the telecommunications towers.

Visits to see the Grand Friday Mosque must be between 9am and 5pm, and outside prayer times. It closes to all non-Muslims 15 minutes before prayers and for the following hour. Before noon and between 2pm and 3pm are the best times to visit. Invading bands of casual sightseers are not encouraged, but if you are genuinely interested and suitably dressed, you'll be welcomed by one of the staff members who hang out by the entrance. Men must wear long trousers and women a long skirt or dress.

The main prayer hall inside the mosque can accommodate up to 5000 worshippers and has beautifully carved wooden side panels and doors, a specially woven carpet and impressive chandeliers. The Islamic Centre also includes a conference hall, library and classrooms.

Muleeaage & Medhu Ziyaarath
PRESIDENTIAL PALACE

Across the road from the Old Friday Mosque is Muleeaage (Map p48; Medhuziyaarai Magu), built as a palace in the early 20th century. The sultan was deposed before he could move in and the building was used for government offices for about 40 years. It became the president's residence in 1953 when the first republic was proclaimed, but lost the honour in 1994 to Theemuge (Map p48), a far more lavish residence on Orchid Magu favoured by President Gayoom. Muleeaage became the presidential residence again in 2009 when President Nasheed took power and decided to slim down the presidential residence and staff. The building became a focal point for both pro- and anti-Nasheed demonstrations before and immediately after the February 2012 political upheaval. At the eastern end of the building's compound, behind an elaborate blue-and-white gatehouse, the Medhu Ziyaarath (Map p48; Medhuziyaarai Magu) is the tomb of Abul Barakat Yoosuf Al Barbary, who brought Islam to Male in 1153.

Tomb of Mohammed Thakurufaanu
TOMB

(Map p48; Neelafaru Magu) In the back streets in the middle of town, in the grounds of a small mosque, is the tomb of Mohammed Thakurufaanu, the Maldives' national hero who liberated the country from Portuguese rule and was then the sultan from 1573 to 1585. Thakurufaanu is also commemorated in the name of the road that rings Male, Boduthakurufaanu Magu (*bodu* means 'big' or 'great').

National Art Gallery
MUSEUM

(Map p48; www.artgallery.gov.mv; Medhuziyaarai Magu; admission free; ⊗9am-6pm Sun-Thu) The Museum Building in one corner of Sultan's Park houses the National Library, various cultural centres from countries around the world and this exhibition space, which has regular displays of Maldivian art. There is sadly no permanent collection on display, but group and individual shows are regularly held and the biennial Maldives Contemporary exhibition is a great chance to see the varied art produced in the country, from photography to painting and conceptual works.

Markets
MARKET

The busy produce market (Map p48; Boduthakurufaanu Magu) gives a real flavour of the Maldives – people from all over the country gather here to sell home-grown and imported vegetables. Coconuts and bananas are the most plentiful produce, but look inside for the stacks of betel leaf, for wrapping up a 'chew'. Just wandering around, watching the hawkers and the shoppers and seeing the vast array of products on display is fascinating and as real a Maldivian experience as possible.

Nearby is the fish market (Map p48; Boduthakurufaanu Magu), which is not to be missed, although the squeamish may well object to the buckets of entrails or the very public gutting of fish going on all around. This is the soul of Male – and it's great fun watching the day's catch being brought in to the market from the adjacent fishing harbour. Look out for some truly vast tuna, octopus and grouper. Fishing and marketing are men's work here, and Maldivian women don't usually venture into these areas, although foreign women walking around won't cause any raised eyebrows.

Whale Submarine
SUBMARINE

(☎333 3939; www.whalesubmarine.com.mv; adult/child/family US$80/40/175) The Whale Submarine can hardly be described as a sight of Male, but it's a popular excursion. First things first, this is not a submarine for whale watching – its name is slightly misleading. It is, in fact, a submarine for looking at life on a reef. It's hard to recommend for divers, as the trip can't really compare to a real dive, but for kids (under-threes are not allowed) and those who don't dive, this is a great, if pricey, little excursion. As the submarine departs from a point off the coast, you have to get a boat either from the airport or Jetty No 1 (President's Jetty; Map p48). A boat picks up from both about 30 minutes before the scheduled departure of the submarine. You should ring ahead and book a place (there are several

Central Male

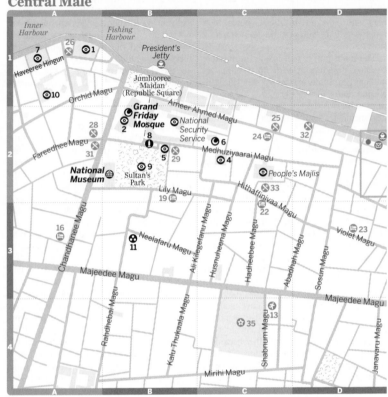

departures daily) so the boat can pick you up. At the submarine dock (the 'Whale House') you pay your money, have a cool drink and board the sub.

The sub takes a few minutes to get to its dive spot, and then descends to about 35m while passengers gaze out at the view through large, lenslike windows. A variety of fish come very close to the windows, attracted partly by the food that the sub dispenses and partly by the sub itself. Surgeonfish, blue-striped snapper and unicornfish are among the most commonly seen, but you will have an excellent view of smaller creatures as well, such as lionfish and anemonefish. The sub goes very close to a reef wall, and its lights illuminate crevices and show up colours that wouldn't be visible in natural light.

The total time spent underwater is about 45 minutes, but allow 1½ hours for the whole trip. Many people manage to

fit in a submarine trip if they have a few hours to spare at the airport before their departure flight. The sub maintains normal surface pressure inside, so it's quite safe to fly straight afterwards.

Artificial Beach   BEACH
(Map p46) The eastern seafront of Male is the city's recreational centre. Here a sweet little beach has been crafted from the breakwater tetrapods and there's a whole range of fast food cafes next to it as well as open fields for ad hoc games of soccer and cricket. Further up towards the airport ferry there are fairground attractions at the **Majeediyya Carnival** (Map p48), including a bowling alley and more eateries. The other way you'll see the charming **tetrapod monument** (Map p46), a local salute to the mini concrete structures that together form a life-saving breakwater for the city (see the box, p52).

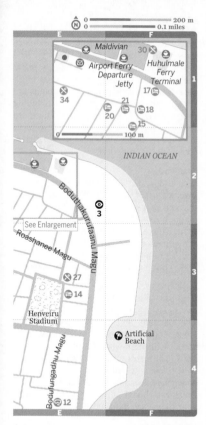

MALE ACTIVITIES

Activities

There is some excellent diving within a short boat ride of Male, even though the rubbish and pollution of the capital can be seen underwater.

Some of the best dives are along the edges of Vaadhoo Kandu (the channel between North and South Male Atolls), which has two Protected Marine Areas. There is also a well-known wreck.

Hans Hass Place (also called Kikki Reef; Map p59) is a demanding wall dive beside Vaadhoo Kandu in a Protected Marine Area. There is a lot to see at 4m or 5m, so it's good for snorkellers and less-experienced divers when the current is not too strong. There's a wide variety of marine life, including many tiny reef fish and larger species in the channel. Further down are caves and overhangs with sea fans and other soft corals.

Lion's Head (Map p59) is a Protected Marine Area that was once a popular place for shark feeding, and although this practice is now strongly discouraged, grey-tip reef sharks and the occasional turtle are still common here. The reef edge is thick with fish, sponges and soft corals; although it drops steeply, with numerous overhangs, to over 40m, there is still much to see at snorkelling depth.

The wreck of the **Maldive Victory** (Map p59) is an impressive and challenging dive because of the potential for strong currents. This cargo ship hit a reef and sank on Friday, 13 February 1981 and now sits with the wheelhouse at around 15m and the propeller at 35m. The ship has been stripped of anything movable, but the structure is almost intact and provides a home for a rich growth of new coral, sponges, tubastrea and large schools of fish.

Sea Explorers Dive School   DIVING

(Map p48; 331 6172; www.seamaldives.com.mv; Bodufungadhu Magu) The Sea Explorers Dive School is a very well-regarded operation that does dive courses and organises regular day trips to nearby dive sites.

Sirina Diving   DIVING

(Map p48; 330 6773; www.divesirinamaldives.com; Shabnum Magu) This new dive school offers PADI dive courses and does excursions to nearby dive sites. It also runs whale shark trips to South Ari Atoll during the whale shark season and organises live-aboard trips.

🛏 Sleeping

Male makes Hong Kong look spacious, and as you'd expect on this densely populated island, space is at a premium. Even top-end rooms are not large. Compared to the rest of Asia, prices are very high here, though a night in Male still costs peanuts compared to one in a resort. Many hotels offer 'day rooms' to people wanting a base in town while waiting for onward flights home or to a resort.

HAVE YOUR SAY

Found a fantastic restaurant that you're longing to share with the world? Disagree with our recommendations? Or just want to talk about your most recent trip?

Whatever your reason, head to lonelyplanet.com, where you can post a review, ask or answer a question on the Thorntree forum, comment on a blog, or share your photos and tips on Groups. Or you can simply spend time chatting with like-minded travellers. So go on, have your say.

BUDGET

Real Inn   BUDGET HOTEL $

(Map p48; 300 0822; realinn@dhinet.net.mv; off Ameer Ahmed Magu; s/d US$35/45; ❄🛜) The best deal in town at present is this place, tucked away on a side street just a block back from the airport ferry. The rooms are simple but have all you need, including fridge, cable TV and hot water. There are just two singles, so it's best to reserve in advance for these, although little English is spoken at the front desk.

Skai Lodge   GUESTHOUSE $

(Map p48; 333 7098; www.skailodge.com.mv; Violet Magu; s/d US$58/75; ❄🛜) This attractive and well-maintained town house full of plants boasts 13 clean and well-maintained rooms (those upstairs are bigger and brighter) with good bathrooms, hot water, phone and TV; some even have balconies, which makes this a good deal by local standards.

Park House   HOTEL $

(Map p48; 330 6600; www.theparkhouse.com.mv; Lily Magu; s/d incl breakfast US$62/75; ❄🛜) The pleasant and brightly painted Park House offers 20 large yellow-and-green rooms with dark-wood furniture and rock-hard mattresses. It's good value, though, with a pizza restaurant downstairs and a convenient location in the centre of town. Breakfast, though unexciting, is brought to your room each morning.

Maagiri Lodge   GUESTHOUSE $

(Map p48; 332 8787; www.maagirilodge.com.mv; Boduthakurufaanu Magu; s/d/tr US$63/73/83; ❄) This centrally located place is a tad overpriced for its level of accommodation, but its functional rooms are comfortable enough, albeit totally lacking in charm. Avoid the two dark downstairs rooms, where the drone of the lobby TV is audible at all times. English can sometimes be a problem at reception.

MIDRANGE

House Clover   GUESTHOUSE $$

(Map p48; 300 5855; www.houseclovermaldives.com; Shaheed KTM Hingun; s/d US$85/94; ❄@🛜) Set over several floors of a high rise building in the centre of the island, this innovative 20-room guesthouse is sparkling new, with bright and spacious rooms. The rooms have cable TV and decent bathrooms, while each floor shares basic kitchens and common areas. Staff members are super-helpful and reserving accommodation in advance is advised.

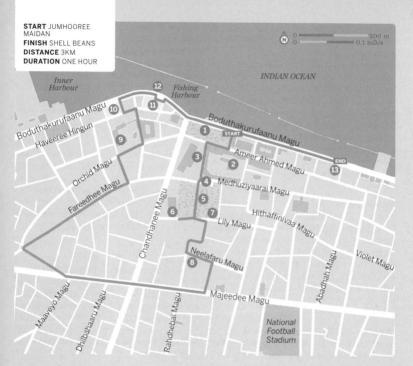

Walking Tour
Male

❭ Start from the waterfront near ❶ **Jumhooree Maidan**, the main square, conspicuous for the huge Maldivian flag flying on its eastern side. All around here is the apparatus of government and you'll notice that it's a well-guarded place, with the police station on one side and the white ❷ **National Security Service Headquarters** to the south.

To the right of the NSS is the ❸ **Grand Friday Mosque**. Walk down the gravel street past its main entrance and you'll arrive at the ❹ **Republican Monument**, a modern-style roundabout centrepiece unveiled in 1999 to commemorate 30 years of Maldivian independence. Cross over to the ❺ **Sultan's Park** and walk through noticing the new ❻ **National Museum** to your right. Exit the park and turn left, where you'll see a charming coral stone ❼ **mosque** at the corner of the park, typical of the intricate 17th-century Maldivian design. Continue south from here through streets that are far more typical of the crowd-

ed capital until you reach the ❽ **Tomb of Mohammed Thakurufaanu**, honouring the man who liberated the Maldives from the Portuguese in the 16th century.

Cut down to Majeedee Magu, the city's main thoroughfare, and absorb the shops, noise and bustle of the town's commercial heart as you walk west. Cut up through the good shopping streets of Fareedhee Magu and Orchid Magu, passing the striking ❾ **Theemuge**, previously the official residence of the president and now the seat of the supreme court.

From here head north towards the ❿ **produce market**. Continue along the seafront to the ⓫ **fish market**, which, along with the adjacent ⓬ **fishing harbour**, is a must-see for anyone in Male. Wander along the seafront, which is always fascinating as people crowd on and off boats. Finish up at ⓭ **Shell Beans** for a drink with a view of the harbour from the upstairs terrace.

Dacé Hotel
BOUTIQUE HOTEL $$

(Map p46; ☑766 3223; www.dacehotel.com; Jahaamuguri Goalhi; s/d $95/125; ❋☂) This tiny eight-room property on a side street looks anything but boutique from the outside, located as it is above a small café. The staff too seem rather clueless when you ask about the upstairs hotel, but providing you can make yourself understood, you'll find gleaming rooms here, each with minibar, safe and flat-screen TV. Not a place to consider if you're looking for a great front-of-house experience, but otherwise a decent choice.

Mookai Hotel
HOTEL $$

(Map p48; ☑333 8811; www.kaimoo.com; Meheli Golhi; s/d US$116/135; ❋☂⊠) With a good location just seconds from the waterfront, rooms with great views on the higher floors and a tiny but effective swimming pool to cool down in, the Mookai is a solid choice. Rooms are small but clean and well furnished, and the feel is upmarket.

Candies
GUESTHOUSE $$

(Map p48; ☑331 0220; www.candies.mv; Dheefuram Gholhi; s/d US$91/103; ❋☂) The 16 rooms here are comfortable, if rather worn, and not too cramped. They overlook a charming pool and popular garden cafe frequented by locals in the evening. Overall the whole place feels more like a large house than a hotel. A good breakfast costs an extra US$8. Booking is advised.

Mookai Suites
SUITES $$

(Map p46; ☑330 9911; www.mookaisuites.com.mv; Haveeree Hingun; s/d US$125/145; ❋☂) Although these business-oriented suites are sleekly furnished, they still feel rather sterile. Each room shares a sitting room and kitchen area with one other room, while rooms at the front have balconies and those on higher floors enjoy great harbour views.

Baani Hotel
HOTEL $$

(Map p48; ☑330 3530; www.baanihotels.com.mv; Filigas Hingun; s/d incl breakfast US$86/96; ❋☂) Overlooking one of Male's two football fields, the Baani offers spacious, bright rooms (avoid the dark ones at the back of the building) with pleasant views. The downside is that the breakfast sucks – eat out.

Relax Inn
HOTEL $$

(Map p48; ☑331 4531; www.hotelrelaxinn.com; Ameer Ahmed Magu; s/d/ste from US$100/114/123; ❋☂) The Relax Inn has two categories of rooms: on one side of the building the standard rooms are small and poorly furnished for their price and enjoy little natural light. The executive rooms on the other hand are far better appointed and have balconies and plenty of light.

Fuana Inn
GUESTHOUSE $$

(Map p59; ☑335 0610; www.fuana.net; Hulhumale island; s/d incl breakfast US$65/105; ❋☂) Staying on Hulhumale gives you the great combination of surreal and beachy. Surreal because this manmade island is a centrally planned

---

THE MAGNIFICENT TETRAPOD

The installation of tetrapod walls around much of Male saved it from potential devastation by the Indian Ocean tsunami in 2004. Tetrapods are concrete blocks with four fat legs, each approximately 1m long, sticking out like the four corners of a tetrahedron. These blocks can be stacked together in rows and layers so they interlock together to form a wall several metres high, looking like a giant version of a child's construction toy. A tetrapod breakwater has gaps that allow sea water to pass through, but collectively the structure is so massive and its surface so irregular that it absorbs and dissipates the force of the waves and protects the shoreline from the physical impact of a storm. As Male has expanded through land reclamation to cover its entire natural coral reef, its natural buffer from the force of strong waves has disappeared.

A severe storm in 1988 prompted the construction of the walls. Huge waves broke up tonnes of landfill that was part of a land-reclamation scheme, and much of this land was re-reclaimed by the sea. The solution was to protect the whole island with a rim of tetrapod breakwaters, constructed as part of a Japanese foreign-aid project. In some places the tetrapod walls are used to retain landfill, and have a path on top forming an attractive seaside promenade. In other places, tetrapod walls enclose an artificial harbour that provides a sheltered anchorage for small boats, and a safe spot for kids to swim. So beloved are these curious structures to locals, there's even a tetrapod monument (p52) in the southwestern corner of town.

MALE FOR CHILDREN

Male isn't particularly child-friendly, the narrow streets and rush of moped traffic make walking with kids or pushing a pram a fairly stressful experience; however, most hotels above two storeys have lifts and some restaurants have changing facilities. The Whale Submarine (p47) will appeal to kids of all ages (although be aware that those under three aren't allowed), while the Artificial Beach (p48) is also a great place for them to swim, and older kids might be able to join in soccer or cricket matches with local children at the recreational areas nearby. The nearby Majeediyya Carnival also has some fun activities for children, including the Slam Bowling Alley.

vision for 21st-century Maldives (see p58), but it's also on the beach and a snip at these prices. The rooms are modern and clean, and all doubles come with balconies over the sea.

Vilingili View Inn   GUESTHOUSE $$
(Map p46; 331 8696; www.tropicalisland.com.mv; Majeedee Magu; s/d US$64/85; ❄@☎) At the far west end of Majeedee Magu, this place is not conveniently located, and despite the name, views of the sea are hard to come by. But there's a bit of charm here, regardless of the flaking paint and damp in some rooms. Note: there's wi-fi in the lobby area only. There's also a popular restaurant that's perfect for a nonalcoholic sundowner.

TOP END

TOP CHOICE Traders Hotel   LUXURY HOTEL $$$
(Map p48; 330 0888; www.shangri-la.com/en/property/male/traders; Ameer Ahmed Magu; r from US$345; ❄☎❄) By far Male's best hotel is this superbly smart Shangri-La property a block back from the harbour. A little slice of glamour in the heart of Male, this stylish temple of orchids, doormen and minimalist furnishings has 117 very smart rooms, rooftop gym, bar and lap pool, spa and sumptuous breakfast buffet.

Sala Boutique Hotel   BOUTIQUE HOTEL $$$
(Map p48; 766 3223; www.salafamilymaldives.com; Buruneege; r $186; ❄☎) Set above Male's most celebrated restaurant, Sala Thai, these boutique rooms are of a very high standard, although like most Male non-high-rise hotels, there's little or no natural light in them. On the other hand there are real spring mattresses, mahogany furniture, flat-screen TVs, Nespresso machines and minibars. This is your best bet for affordable luxury in Male.

Beehive Nalahiya Hotel   HOTEL $$$
(Map p46; 334 6633; www.beehivehotels.com; Majeedee Magu; s/d US$125/150; ❄☎) Set in the centre of the island, this chic high-rise is an

oasis from the busy crossroads outside and one of the city's better hotels. The 42 rooms are tastefully furnished and feature local artwork, but they're short of charm and can be quite small. Don't miss the fantastic rooftop restaurant for great Male views.

Hulhule Island Hotel   HOTEL $$$
(Map p59; 333 0888; www.hih.com.mv; Hulhule island; s/d/ste incl breakfast US$341/377/450; ❄☎❄) Not actually in Male, but across the lagoon on the airport island, a 10-minute dhoni ride away, is this smart but fantastically overpriced hotel popular with people transiting between the airport and their resorts. It's mainly notable as the only place near Male that serves alcohol, for which expats in the capital frequently make the pilgrimage across the lagoon. The pool is another great attraction.

✖ Eating

You'll eat perfectly well in Male, with restaurants typically offering several different cuisines – most popular are Thai, Indonesian, Indian, Italian and American-style grills. Nearly everything is imported, including the prawns and the lobsters, which are the most expensive items.

Male restaurants don't serve alcohol, but many serve nonalcoholic beer. By contrast nearly every restaurant has now acquired an espresso machine, and you can get a good cup of coffee almost anywhere.

Local teashops are frequented by Maldivian men; it's not the done thing for local women to visit one. Some traditional teashops have broadened the menus, installed air-conditioning and improved service – you should feel quite comfortable in these places and they're a great way to meet locals. Foreign women may be an object of curiosity in teashops, but not unpleasantly so. A bigger and slightly better teashop might be called a cafe or 'hotel'.

Teashops have their goodies displayed on a counter behind a glass screen, and customers line up and choose, cafeteria style – if you don't know what to ask for, just point. Tea costs around Rf2 and the *hedhikaa* ('short eats'; finger-food snacks) from Rf1 to Rf3. You can fill yourself for under Rf10. At meal times teashops also serve 'long eats', such as soups, curried fish and *roshi* (unleavened bread). A good meal costs from Rf12 to Rf25.

Teashops open as early as 5am and close as late as 1am, particularly around the port area where they cater to fishermen. During Ramazan they're open till 2am or even later, but closed during the day. All restaurants are closed on Friday morning, which is a good time to avoid being in Male.

TOP CHOICE Aïoli   INTERNATIONAL $$$

(Map p48; Lotus Goalhi; mains Rf80-480; ☺9am-11.30pm Sun-Thu, 4-11.30pm Fri; ✴) Definitely the sleekest eating option in the capital, this large restaurant has the feel of a boutique hotel, decked out all in dark wood and cream furnishings. The menu is just as fabulous – choose from Black Angus filet steak, coconut chilli crab and baked mussels, for example – all served up on an attractive outdoor terrace or in one of two dining rooms.

Sala Thai   THAI $$$

(Map p48; ☎334 5959; Buruneege; mains Rf150-300; ☺noon-midnight Sat-Thu, 6pm-1am Fri; ✴) This very smart restaurant is generally held to be the best on the island, and it should be at these prices. The menu is sumptuous, though, with a huge choice of soups, noodles and curries. Booking is a good idea for evening meals. There's also an excellent Italian restaurant run by the same team in the same building with similar prices and opening hours.

Royal Garden Café   INTERNATIONAL $

(Map p48; Medhuziyaarai Magu; mains Rf50-115; ☺8am-1am Sun-Thu, 2pm-1am Fri; ✴) This great little place, with a charming garden and an air-conditioned, stylish dark-wood interior, is housed in a rare surviving example of a *ganduvaru,* a nobleman's house. The menu is a combination of Italian, Indonesian, American and Indian cuisines – try the delicious satay chicken.

Symphony   INDIAN $$

(Map p46; Athamaa Goalhi; mains Rf60-160; ☺11am-1am Sat-Thu, 6pm-1am Fri; ✴) This long-time favourite for Male residents, located off Majeedee Magu, has an exceptionally dark interior, chilly air-con and a smart look. The menu is comprehensive, and the Indian cooking is excellent and it boasts one of the best vegetarian selections in town.

Thai Wok   THAI $$

(Map p48; ☎331 0007; Hithaffivinivaa Magu; mains Rf75-180; ☺noon-3.30pm Sun-Thu, 7pm-midnight daily; ✴) The Thai food here is decent and authentic, though the best reason to visit is for the thrice-weekly buffet (R140 per person), where you can take your pick of lots of great dishes. Tables on the balcony are worth reserving.

Salsa Royal   INTERNATIONAL $

(Map p46; Orchid Magu; mains Rf50-100; ☺8am-1am Sat-Thu, 4pm-1am Fri; ✴) This airy, high-ceilinged place serves up Italian and Indian food from a large menu. There's also a huge range of snacks and drinks, and it's a popular spot for coffee.

Shell Beans   INTERNATIONAL $

(Map p48; Boduthakurufaanu Magu; mains Rf65-85; ☺8am-11.30pm Sun-Thu, 3pm-12.30am Fri; ✴🛜) This lifeline by the seafront serves up tasty sandwiches, full breakfasts, sandwiches, burgers, good coffee and pastries. It's a great spot for lunch on the run, although there's seating both upstairs (which includes a great balcony with harbour views) and downstairs for a less hurried meal.

Sea House   INTERNATIONAL $

(Map p48; Boduthakurufaanu Magu; mains Rf50-100; ☺24hr, closed 10am-1pm Fri) This breezy (and sometimes downright windy) place above the Hulhumale ferry terminal has expansive harbour views and a great menu that runs from pizza and sandwiches to full meals. It's very popular and a great place to meet friends. The food won't amaze you, but it's a reliable option and full of locals.

Seagull Café House   INTERNATIONAL $$

(Map p48; cnr Chandhanee Magu & Fareedhee Magu; mains Rf80-260; ☺8am-midnight Sun-Thu,

---

EATING PRICE RANGES

Male is the only place in the Maldives where there are 'standard' restaurants. Prices represent the price for an average main course.

Budget ($)	< Rf75
Midrange ($$)	Rf75-150
Top end ($$)	> Rf150

4pm-midnight Fri) The Seagull boasts a beautifully renovated space complete with a charming downstairs garden and a 1st-floor terrace with a tree growing through it. The menu is extensive and includes sandwiches, burgers, wraps, pasta, fish and grills. There's also a popular gelataria attached, serving up the city's best ice cream, perfect for dessert.

Olive Garden   PIZZA $$
(Map p48; Fareedhee Magu; mains Rf65-115; ⊙7.30am-1am, 2.30pm-1.30am Fri; ❋) This pizza joint doesn't do anything amazing, but it's a popular place for an evening meal or to meet friends for coffee. It has a fiercely air-conditioned and rather soulless downstairs dining room and a far more relaxed open-air terrace upstairs.

Irudhashu Hotaa   TEASHOP $
(Map p48; Filigas Hingun) Our favourite 'short eats' place in town is this perennially busy meeting place by the Henveiru football field. After prayers at the next-door mosque, it's always jammed, and the spicy fish curries and selection of *hedhikaa* are delicious.

Dawn Café   TEASHOP $
(Map p48; Haveeree Hingun; ⊙24hr) This is one of the best teashops in the area, and due to its fish-market location it's popular with fishermen and open around the clock. You can get a brilliant meal here. Try it on Friday afternoon when people come in after going to the mosque.

Watercress   TEASHOP $
(Map p48; Ameer Ahmed Magu) A popular place right in the centre of things, this friendly and somewhat upmarket teashop serves up delicious 'short eats'.

Fantasy Store   SUPERMARKET $
(Map p46; Fareedhee Magu; ⊙9am-10pm Sat-Thu, 2.30-10pm Fri; ❋) The city's best-stocked supermarket sells a great range of products, including fresh fruit and veg. It's handy for self-catering, which is a sensible option during Ramazan.

☆ Entertainment

Nobody comes to a dry town for nightlife, let's face it, but despite the sobriety of the Male populace, there's a surprising amount going on here. The evening is popular with strolling couples and groups of friends who promenade along the seafront and Majeedee Magu until late in the night. Thursday and Friday nights are the busiest, after prayers at

sundown. There are even sporadic club nights put on, although there's nothing regular. Keep your eye out for notices along the seafront, as such events are usually advertised.

Jazz Café   CAFE
(Map p46; Haveeree Hingun; ⊙7am-1am Sat-Thu, 2pm-1am Fri; ❋) This friendly cafe takes a thoroughly un-Maldivian concept (jazz) and marries it to another (good coffee) to create one of the capital's nicest hang-outs. It offers a full menu as well as good pastries to be enjoyed to the taped (and sometimes live) jazz accompaniment.

Hulhule Island Hotel   BAR
(www.hih.com.mv; Hulhule island; ⊙24hr; ❋) Most expats in town make the pilgrimage across the lagoon to the Hulhule Island Hotel bar for alcohol. There's a dedicated ferry service from Male run by the hotel, but it's usually faster to take the more frequent airport ferry (see p57) and then walk 10 minutes to the hotel from the airport.

Athena Cinema   CINEMA
(Map p46; Haveeree Hingun; ❋) Amid the bustle of the harbours, this popular cinema shows Indian films as well as the occasional Hollywood blockbuster.

National Stadium   SPECTATOR SPORT
(Map p48; Majeedee Magu) The National Stadium hosts the biggest soccer matches (tickets cost Rf15 to Rf50) and the occasional cricket match. More casual games can be seen any evening in the sports grounds at the east end of the island and near New Harbour.

🛍 Shopping

Shopping is at the frenetic heart of the Male experience, and sometimes it seems as if locals do nothing else – a walk down Majeedee Magu, the city's main avenue and shopping street, will reveal an endless parade of clothes, shoes and bag shops, although there's generally little that will excite seasoned international travellers here.

Shops selling imported and locally made souvenirs, which are aimed at tourists, are on and around Chandhanee Magu. Many of the tourist shops have a very similar range of tatty stock, and it's hard to recommend any in particular.

Male is definitely the best place to shop for more unusual antiques and Maldivian craft items – come here for old wooden measuring cups, coconut graters, ceremonial knives and finely woven grass mats.

ⓘ Information

Emergency

Ambulance (☏102)
Fire (☏118)
Police (☏119)
Police station (Boduthakurufaanu Magu) On the corner of Jumhooree Maidan (Map p48).

Internet Access

There are no internet cafes in Male – you'll need a laptop or smart phone to get online here, or ask at your hotel if you need to use a terminal. Nearly all hotels in Male have free wi-fi.

Wi-fi is also available at the following:

Bistro Jade (Boduthakurufaanu Magu; ⊗8am-11pm) A hub for expats, with lacklustre food.

Shell Beans (Map p48; Boduthakurufaanu Magu; ⊗8am-11.30pm Sat-Thu, 3pm-12.30am Fri) Thirty minutes access; after that you'll need to order another drink.

Laundry

Any hotel or guesthouse will take care of your laundry for anything up to a couple of dollars per item. A cheaper option is **Tip Top Laundry** (Orchid Magu), where you can drop laundry off and pick it up the next day.

Left Luggage

There are no dedicated left-luggage facilities in Male itself. The only option is taking a day room at a hotel, or asking nicely at reception if you can leave your bags. There is a left-luggage service at the airport that costs US$3 per item, per 24 hours.

Libraries

National Library (Map p48; Medhuziyaarai Magu; ⊗closed Fri) Has quite a few English titles. Nonresidents can't borrow books, but are welcome to sit and read in the library.

Medical Services

Both the following will make arrangements with travel insurance companies, and both have doctors trained to do a diving medical check. There are a large number of well-stocked chemists outside both establishments.

ADK Private Hospital (☏331 3553; www.adkhospital.mv; Sosun Magu) Private facility with Western-trained doctors and dentists, excellent standards of care and quite high prices.

Indira Gandhi Memorial Hospital (☏331 6647; www.mhsc.com.mv; Buruzu Magu) Modern public facility, well equipped and staffed with English-speaking doctors.

Money

International banks, including the State Bank of India, Bank of Ceylon and HSBC, all have premises near each other on Boduthakurufaanu Magu. All have ATMs that accept international cards.

More local banks are clustered near the harbour end of Chandhanee Magu and east along Boduthakurufaanu Magu. They all change travellers cheques, usually for a small transaction fee. Bank of Maldives doesn't charge a fee if you change travellers cheques for Maldivian rufiyaa, but does charge if you want US dollars.

Post

Main post office (Map p48; Boduthakurufaanu Magu; ⊗8.15am-9pm Sun-Thu, 3-9pm Fri, 9.15am-9pm Sat) The main post office is just opposite the airport ferry dock. There's a post office at the airport too.

Telephone

Anyone staying in the Maldives for a long time will save a lot of money by getting a local SIM card for their mobile phone (see p175). Go to either of the following:

Dhiraagu (☏123; www.dhiraagu.com; Chandhanee Magu)

Wataniya (☏929; www.wataniya.com.mv; Majeedee Magu)

Toilets

The most conveniently located public toilet (Rf2) is on the back street between Bistro Jade and the small mosque on Ameer Ahmed Magu. However, you can also pop in and use the toilets of

---

HOUSE NAMES

Street numbers are rarely used in Male, so most houses and buildings have a distinctive name, typically written in picturesque English as well as in the local Thaana script. Some Maldivians prefer rustic titles like Crabtree, Forest, Oasis View and Banana Cabin. Others are specifically floral, like Sweet Rose and Luxury Garden, or even vegetable, like Carrot, or the perplexing Leaf Mess. There are also exotic names like Paris Villa and River Nile, while some sound like toilet disinfectants – Ozone, Green Zest, Dawn Fresh.

Some of our quirkier favourite house names include Hot Lips, Subtle Laughter, Remind House, Pardon Villa, Frenzy, Mary Lightning and Aston Villa.

Shop names and businesses, on the other hand, often have an overt advertising message – People's Choice Supermarket, Bless Trade, Fair Price and Neat Store. Premier Chambers is not a pretentious house name – it's where you'll find Male's first barrister.

most cafes or restaurants; the owners are almost universally polite and don't seem to mind.

Tourist Information

There is a tourist information desk at the airport, which is supposedly open when international flights arrive, but sometimes this isn't the case. Even when it's not staffed, look on the shelf out the front for some useful booklets. Otherwise, the best places to start are the following:

www.lonelyplanet.com/maldives/male For planning advice, author recommendations, traveller reviews and insider tips.

www.visitmaldives.com The country's official tourism portal.

Travel Agencies

Few travellers use a travel agency in the Maldives, as most people book their holidays from home and have little need to arrange anything in the country. However, anyone travelling independently can try the following agencies, which vary enormously in terms of services offered. If you're an independent traveller looking for a resort or a safari tour, be prepared to do some shopping around – ask in town, or call one or more of those listed below. A full list of Male travel agents can be found at www.visitmaldives.com.

Crown Tours (Map p48; ☑ 332 9889; www. crowntoursmaldives.com; 5th fl, Fasmeeru Bldg, Boduthakurufaanu Magu) Can book resorts and organise live aboards, diving and transfers.

Elysian Maldives (☑ 773 8889; www.elysian maldives.com; Viligili) Elysian specialises in independent travel and guesthouses, but can also arrange surf cruises, live aboards and book resorts. The company's office is on the island of Viligili, so everything is done by phone or email.

Inner Maldives (Map p48; ☑ 300 6886; www. innermaldives.com.mv; Ameer Ahmed Magu) Highly regarded local operator with plenty of experience with independent travellers.

Sultans of the Sea (Map p48; ☑ 332 0330; www.sultansoftheseas.com; ground fl, Fasmeeru Bldg, Boduthakurufaanu Magu) Charters yachts of all sizes.

Voyages Maldives (Map p48; ☑ 332 2019; www.voyagesmaldives.com; Chandhanee Magu) Specialises in live-aboard dive boats, sailing and surfing trips, but can also book resorts and arrange transfers.

Getting There & Away
Air

Nearly all international flights to the Maldives use Male's **Ibrahim Nasir International Airport** (www.airports.com.mv), which is on a separate island, Hulhule, about 2km east of Male island. Domestic flights and seaplane transfers to resorts also use the airport, although the seaplane

terminal is on the far side of the island, involving a free five-minute bus ride around the runway. Male is linked by daily flights to Colombo, Doha, Dubai, Kiev, Kuala Lumpur and Trivandrum, and regular flights to Abu Dhabi, Bangalore, Bangkok, Frankfurt, Hong Kong, Kuala Lumpur, London, Milan, Moscow, Muscat, Paris, Shanghai, Singapore, Tokyo, Vienna and Zurich.

Boat

Male is the boat transport hub for the entire country, and with the introduction of a public ferry system under President Nasheed, it's now easier than ever to connect by boat with atolls that were previously only accessible to travellers by seaplane.

Nearly all national ferry services depart from the New Harbour on the southwest corner of Male, including those to nearby Viligili, but some ferries depart from the Hulhumale Ferry Terminal on the city's northeastern corner, and various other services go from different jetties along the waterfront between the Hulhumale Ferry Terminal and the produce market, so always check where exactly any ferry you're supposed to be taking leaves from. Ferries to the airport depart from outside the main post office on Boduthakurufaanu Magu.

In terms of reaching resorts, the airport harbour functions as the biggest transport hub in the country. In general, if you want to travel by boat to a resort from Male, you'll usually need to take the airport ferry and get a transfer from the harbour. You'll need to book your accommodation and the transfer in advance – it's not generally possible to take transfers to resorts without planning to stay there, though some resorts allow visitors to come for dinner or go diving.

Safari boats and private yachts usually moor between Male island and Viligili, or in the lagoon west of Hulhumale. Safari-boat operators will normally pick up new passengers from the airport or Male and ferry them directly to the boat.

Getting Around
To/From the Airport

Dhonis shuttle between the airport and Male all day and most of the night, departing promptly every 10 minutes. At the airport, dhonis leave from the jetties just north of the arrivals hall. In Male they arrive and depart from the landing at the east end of Boduthakurufaanu Magu. The crossing costs Rf10 per person or US$1 if you don't have any local cash.

Bicycle

A bicycle or scooter is a good way to get around, but there's no place to rent one. Your guesthouse might be able to arrange something, but if you make a local friend, be prepared to be given a high adrenaline ride through the city.

Taxi

The numerous taxis in the city offer a few minutes of cool, air-conditioned comfort and a driver who can usually find any address in Male. Many streets are one way and others may be blocked by construction work or stationary vehicles, so taxis will often take roundabout routes.

Fares are the same (Rf20) for any distance, rising to Rf25 after midnight. Taxis may charge Rf10 extra for luggage. You don't have to tip. There are various taxi companies, but don't worry about the names – just call one of the following numbers: ☏ 332 3132, ☏ 332 5757 or ☏ 332 2454.

AROUND MALE

Viligili

Probably the most obvious day trip from Male is the short ferry ride to Viligili, the closest thing Male has to a suburb, just 1km from the western shore of the capital. The short boat ride takes you into a different world. Far more relaxed than Male, Viligili has something of a Caribbean feel, with its brightly painted houses and laid-back pace. Here Male residents come to enjoy some space, play soccer and go swimming (usually fully clothed in the local conservative fashion – this is no place to be seen in a bikini). While it's still a great deal more cosmopolitan than most inhabited islands in the Maldives, if you only visit Male and resorts, this is perhaps the best chance you'll have of seeing everyday life. There are several shops, restaurants and places to go for a drink. To get here just catch one of the frequent dhoni ferries from New Harbour on the southwest corner of Male (Rf3, 10 minutes, every five minutes).

Hulhule

Better known as the airport island, Hulhule was once densely wooded with very few inhabitants – just a graveyard and a reputation for being haunted. The first airstrip was built here in 1960, and in the early 1980s it had a major upgrade to accommodate long-distance passenger jets. Airport facilities have expanded to keep pace with the burgeoning tourist industry and a brand new world-class terminal is due to open in 2014.

As well as being the country's main international airport, Hulhule also accommodates the seaplane terminal on the lagoon on the east side of the island. Everyone passes through this island on their way in and out of the country, but it's also a serious leisure option from Male due to both the excellent swimming pool and the availability of alcohol at the Hulhule Island Hotel. The hotel runs a free transfer boat 14 times a day, from beside the President's Jetty (Jetty No 1) in Male. Day membership that allows use of the swimming pool costs US$20.

Hulhumale

A fascinating trip from Male is to the easily accessible Hulhumale – or, as many people see it – the future of the Maldives. Here, on the other side of the airport, 1.8 sq km of reef has been built up to create a manmade island – the first phase of an ambitious project to relieve the pressure of growth on Male. Sand and coral were dug up from the lagoon and pumped into big heaps on the reef top. Then bulldozers pushed the rubble around to form a quadrilateral of dry land about 2km long and 1km wide, joined by a causeway to the airport island. It's built up to about 2m above sea level to provide a margin of protection against the possibility of sea-level rises.

This utopian project began in 1997 and now the northern section (about an eighth of the island's total area) is a fully functioning town, complete with rather Soviet-looking apartment blocks, a school, a pharmacy, an array of shops and a huge mosque – the golden glass dome of which is visible from all over the southern part of North Male Atoll. There's even a surprisingly attractive artificial beach down the eastern side of the island. Coming here makes a fascinating contrast to the chaotic capital – the planning is so precise and mathematical you could be on the set of *Brave New World*. Walking across the hectares of land that has yet to be built upon towards the tiny conurbation on the far side is an eerie experience and a bewildering glimpse into the future of the Maldivian nation if sea levels continue to rise.

When the first-phase land is fully developed by 2020 it will accommodate 50,000 people and have waterfront esplanades, light industrial areas, government offices, shopping centres, boulevards of palm trees, a marina and a national stadium. The basic layout has been carefully planned, but the details are still flexible, allowing for some natural, organic growth through multiple private developments. The second phase, a long-term proposal, involves reclaiming a

Around Male

further 2.4 sq km of land (engulfing all of Farukolhufushi, currently the Club Faru resort) and bringing the total population of Hulhumale to around 100,000 people.

To visit Hulhumale from Male, take the ferry (Rf5, 20 minutes, every 30 minutes) from the terminal next to the airport ferry jetty and opposite the Maagiri Lodge. On the island a bus service connects the ferry terminal to the settlement, but it's an easy 10-minute walk if there's not one waiting when you arrive.

Other Islands

With so many small islands in the Maldives, some are allocated for particular activities or a specific use. One example is **Funadhoo**, between the airport and Male, which is used for fuel storage – it's a safe distance from inhabited areas, and convenient for both seagoing tankers and smaller boats serving the atolls.

One of the fastest-growing islands in the country, west of Viligili, is **Thilafushi**, also known as 'Rubbish Island'. It's where the capital dumps its garbage. The land is earmarked for industrial development, and its three conspicuous, round towers are part of a cement factory. It's perfectly possible to visit Thilafushi, though you'll need to hire a launch or get a lift there – a cruise around its

post-apocalyptic rubbish mountains is a sobering flipside to more conventional images of the country. While the truly ghastly part is the south part of the island, the north part is a small township of migrant workers tending various industrial plants – you're free to wander about if you can get here.

The island of **Dhoonidhoo**, just north of Male, was the British governor's residence until 1964. The house was used during the Gayoom era for detaining political prisoners, all of whom have now been set free.

Slightly further north, **Aarah** is a small island that was used as the president's holiday retreat during the Gayoom era and as such was a heavily fortified installation complete with bunkers on the beach. Under President Nasheed the island was used to host the Hay Festival Maldives, an offshoot of the famous British literary festival, as well as to host some big beach parties featuring international DJs for the youth of Male.

Another 3km further north, the island of **Kuda Bandos** was saved from resort development and became the Kuda Bandos Reserve, to be preserved in its natural state for the people's enjoyment. It has a few facilities for day-trippers, but is otherwise undeveloped. Tourists come to Kuda Bandos on 'island-hopping' trips from nearby resorts.

North & South Male Atolls

Best Places to Stay

» One & Only Reethi Rah (p63)

» Cocoa Island (p76)

» Soneva Gili (p64)

» Jumeirah Vittaveli (p76)

» Meeru Island Resort (p69)

Why Go?

These atolls boast remote-feeling desert-island paradises and many of the country's most famous island resorts, despite also being home to the Maldives' main international airport.

Excellent dive sites pepper both sides of Vaadhoo Kandu, the channel that runs between North and South Male Atolls. At the outer edge of the atolls, dive sites can be explored from only a few resorts or by safari boat, and you'll probably have them all to yourself. Gaafaru Falhu Atoll, north of North Male Atoll, has at least three diveable shipwrecks. And some of the Maldives' best surf breaks are also in North Male Atoll, which is home to a small, seasonal surfer scene.

North and South Male Atolls will be where most people experience the Maldives, and both atolls are stunning visions of cobalt-blue water, white sand and island idyll – both worthy introductions to this extraordinary paradise.

North Male Atoll

Tourism is well developed in North Male Atoll, and as well as having lots of resorts, there are several fledgling guesthouses here too. Male itself isn't the atoll capital, as it's considered to be its own administrative district. Instead, the atoll capital is **Thulusdhoo**, on the eastern edge of North Male Atoll, with a population of about 1150. Thulusdhoo is an industrious island, known for the manufacture of *bodu beru* (big drums), for its traditional dancing and for its salted-fish warehouse. It is also unique for its Coca-Cola factory, the only one in the world where the drink is made from desalinated water.

The island of **Huraa** (population 750) is well used to tourists visiting from nearby resorts, but it retains its small-island feel. Huraa's dynasty of sultans, founded in 1759 by Sultan Al-Ghaazi Hassan Izzaddeen, built a mosque on the island.

Many tourists visit **Himmafushi** (population 855) on excursions arranged from nearby resorts. The main street has two long rows of shops, where you can pick up some of the least expensive souvenirs in the country. Carved rosewood manta rays, sharks and dolphins are made locally. If you wander into the back streets, you quickly get away from the tourist strip to find an attractive, well-kept village and an attractive cemetery with coral headstones. There's a drug rehabilitation centre here and part of the island is off-limits due to this.

A sand spit has joined Himmafushi to the once separate island of **Gaamaadhoo**, where there used to be a prison. The surf break here, aptly called **Jailbreaks**, is a great right-hander, accessible by boat from nearby resorts.

Further north, **Dhiffushi** is one of the most appealing local islands, with around 1000 inhabitants, three mosques and two schools. Mainly a fishing island, it has lots of greenery and grows tropical fruit. Tourists from Meeru Island Resort are regular visitors.

🏊 Activities

North Male Atoll has been well explored by divers and has some superb dive sites. Some are heavily dived, especially in peak seasons, due to the many resorts in the atoll. The following is just a sample of the best-known sites, listed from north to south.

Helengeli Thila DIVING
Famous for its prolific marine life, Helengeli Thila, also called Bodu Thila, is a long narrow thila on the eastern edge of the atoll. Reef fish include surgeonfish, bannerfish, butterflyfish and dense schools of snapper and fusilier. Larger fish and pelagics (fish that inhabit the upper layers of the open sea) are also common – sharks, tuna, rays and jacks. Soft corals are spectacular in the cliffs and caves on the west side of the thila at about 25m. The large hard coral formations here are recovering from coral bleaching quite quickly, possibly because of the strong, nutrient-rich currents.

Shark Point DIVING
Also called Saddle, or Kuda Faru, Shark Point is in a Protected Marine Area and is subject to strong currents. Lots of white-tip and grey-tip reef sharks can be seen in the channel between a thila and the reef, along with fusiliers, jackfish, stingrays and some impressive caves.

Blue Canyon DIVING
The alternative, less-picturesque name of Blue Canyon is Kuda Thila, which means 'small thila'. A canyon, 25m to 30m deep and lined with soft, blue corals, runs beside the thila. The numerous overhangs make for an exciting dive; this is one for experienced divers.

Bodu Hithi Thila DIVING
Bodu Hithi Thila is a prime manta-spotting site from December to March, with a good number of sharks and many reef fish. The soft corals on the sides of the thila are in excellent condition. If currents are moderate, this site is suitable for intermediate divers, and the shallow waters atop the thila offer superb snorkelling. Nearby, the **Peak** is another great place to see mantas in season; it is also home to some large Napoleon wrasse.

Rasfari DIVING
The outer-reef slope of Rasfari drops down to a depth of more than 40m, but a couple of thilas rise up to about 25m. Grey-tip reef sharks love it here – you might see 20 or 30 of them, as well as white-tip sharks, barracuda, eagle rays and trevally. It's a Protected Marine Area.

Colosseum DIVING
A curving cliff near a channel entrance forms the Colosseum, where pelagics do the performing. Sharks and barracuda are often seen here. Experienced divers do this as a drift dive, going right into the channel past ledges and caves, with soft corals and the occasional turtle. Even beginners can do this one in good conditions.

Aquarium DIVING
As the name suggests, Aquarium (a coral rock formation about 15m down) features a large variety of reef fish. A sandy bottom at 25m can have small sharks and rays, and you might also see giant wrasse and schools of snapper. It's an easy dive and is suitable for snorkelling.

Kani Corner DIVING
Across the kandu from the Aquarium, Kani Corner is the start of a long drift dive through a narrow channel with steep sides, past caves and overhangs decorated with soft corals. Lots of large marine life can be seen, including sharks, barracuda, Napoleon wrasse and tuna. Beware of fast currents.

HP Reef DIVING
Also called Rainbow Reef or Girifushi Thila, HP Reef sits beside a narrow channel where currents provide much nourishment for incredibly rich growths of soft, blue corals, and support a large variety of reef fish and pelagics. The formations include large blocks, spectacular caves and a 25m vertical, swim-through chimney. It is a Protected Marine Area.

North Male Atoll

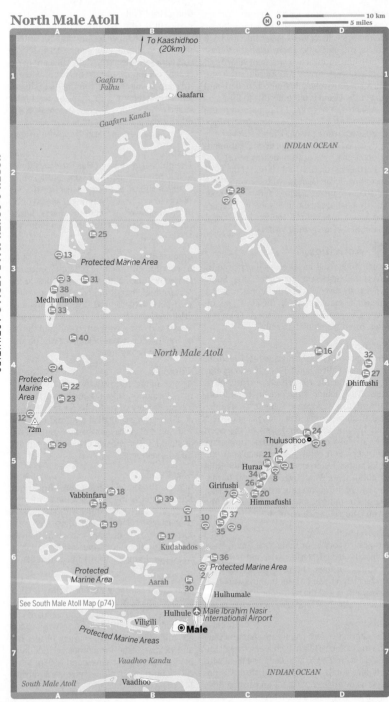

N
0 — 10 km
0 — 5 miles

To Kaashidhoo
(20km)

*Gaafaru
Falhu*

Gaafaru

Gaafaru Kandu

INDIAN OCEAN

28
6

25

13

Protected Marine Area

3 31
38
Medhufinolhu
33

40

North Male Atoll

16
32
27
Dhiffushi

4
*Protected
Marine
Area*
22
23

12
72m

29

24
5
Thulusdhoo

21 14
Huraa 1
34 8
26
Girifushi 20
7 Himmafushi

Vabbinfaru 18
15

39
11 10 37
35 9

19

17
Kudabados
36
2
Protected Marine Area
Aarah
30

Hulhumale

See South Male Atoll Map (p74)

*Protected
Marine Area*

Hulhule Male Ibrahim Nasir
International Airport

Viligili
Male

Protected Marine Areas

Vaadhoo Kandu

South Male Atoll
Vaadhoo

INDIAN OCEAN

North Male Atoll

Okobe Thila DIVING

Also called Barracuda Giri, the attraction of Okobe Thila is the variety of spectacular reef fish that inhabit the shallow caves and crannies, including lionfish, scorpionfish, batfish, sweetlips, moray eels, sharks and big Napoleon wrasse.

Nassimo Thila DIVING

The demanding dive at Nassimo Thila follows the north side of a fine thila, also known as Paradise Rock, which has superb gorgonians and sea fans on coral blocks, cliffs and overhangs. Numerous large fish frequent this site.

Manta Point DIVING

The best time to see the mantas for which Manta Point is famous is from May to November. Coral outcrops at about 8m are a 'cleaning station', where cleaner wrasse feed on parasites from the mantas' wings. Cliffs, coral tables, turtles, sharks and numerous reef fish are other attractions, as are the nearby **Lankan Caves**.

Banana Reef DIVING

The Protected Marine Area of Banana Reef has a bit of everything: dramatic cliffs, caves and overhangs; brilliant coral growths; big predators such as sharks, barracuda and grouper; and prolific reef fish, including jackfish, morays, Napoleon wrasse and blue-striped snapper. It was one of the first dive sites in the country to become internationally known. The reef top is excellent for snorkelling.

Sleeping

One advantage of staying on North Male Atoll is the proximity to the airport. All resorts here can be reached by speedboat from the airport in under an hour.

TOP CHOICE One & Only Reethi Rah LUXURY RESORT $$$

(664 8800; www.oneandonlyresorts.com; r/wv incl breakfast from US$1840/2055;) One & Only Reethi Rah is still king of the Maldivian resorts. There may be plenty of resorts that cost more, but none have surpassed this extraordinary place, which remains the most famous and gossiped about in the country.

Reethi Rah is about glamour and style, and shamelessly so. If you aren't comfortable with almost mind-boggling pampering and fly anything other than first class, this probably isn't the place for you. Rooms are some of the most enormous in the country, with high ceilings and beautifully furnished Asian interiors. Some have their own pools, and those that don't enjoy direct access to the lagoon or beach.

The most controversial thing about Reethi Rah is also ones of its biggest draws – though you would never guess it, the island is largely made from reclaimed land, which means there's an unusual number of beaches, all in perfect crescents around the island (if you arrive by seaplane its atypical geography is clearly apparent). From its original 15.8 hectares, the island now stands at an incredible (for the Maldives, at least) 44 hectares, which gives the island a spread-out feel, meaning plenty of privacy, empty beaches and guaranteed tranquillity.

All guests get around by bicycle, although those unable to ride can call club cars from reception to take them around – the island is too large to be covered comfortably on foot. Other unique features include a charming canal that was built for the sea to flow through the island (a unique example of this in the Maldives), a sumptuous lap pool built out over the ocean and a reception like a Balinese palace. Vegetation is thick and the spotless white-sand beaches truly alluring.

There are three restaurants on the island: the main one, Reethi Restaurant; a chic Japanese restaurant, Tapasake; and perhaps the most magical, the open-air Fanditha, at the northern tip of the island, an informal Middle Eastern–style restaurant where meals are served on the beach.

The huge ESPA-run spa focuses on Asian treatments, including Balinese and Thai massage. Other attractions include two tennis courts and a pro-tennis trainer, a superb diving school, a kids club and a full watersports program.

Book as far in advance as you can; it can be impossible to get a room at short notice. Reethi Rah remains the most talked about resort in the Maldives, not least as it's alleged behind-the-scenes shenanigans are subject of a popular holiday paperback called *Beach Babylon* – set in a place easily recognisable as Reethi Rah.

Soneva Gili   LUXURY RESORT **$$$**
(☑664 0304; www.sixsenses.com; wv incl breakfast US$1750; ✳@☎☀) Consistently rated one of the Maldives' very best resorts, astonishingly impressive Soneva Gili is essentially Swiss Family Robinson meets stylish travel magazine, and we're smitten. All villas (for there are no mere rooms here) are over water, ranging from the 'standard' Villa Suite, which has three rooms as well as a sea garden, a sun deck and a bed on the roof for stargazing, to the incredible Private Reserve, a free-standing lagoon complex sleeping nine people in the lap of luxury, a short boat ride from the main island.

All the buildings are made from natural materials – most woods are imported from sustainable forests elsewhere in Asia – and all villas are as open to the elements as possible (it's only the bedroom that is air-conditioned; the rest of the villa is essentially open-air). The attention to detail is incredible, with luxurious treats hidden away under natural fibres in what is one of the Maldives' most environmentally conscious resorts.

The island itself is very pretty, crisscrossed with sand paths, along which guests can cycle to the main communal areas: the infinity pool overlooking the beach, the charming bar and the beachside restaurant, where elaborate buffets and à la carte menus are equally impressive.

The diving school allows you to dive from a luxury dhoni complete with waiters. The water-sports centre offers all nonmotorised sports for free, and the lagoon is great for snorkelling a little further out to 'one palm island' – a desert island belonging to the resort.

Foodies will appreciate the wine cellar, a sumptuous subterranean space for private degustation dinners and wine tasting around a huge driftwood table, although the three further restaurants on the island are also excellent and helmed by international chefs creating sumptuous dishes.

Staff magically appear to know your name and are positively obsequious – this is not a good place for those who don't like to be fussed over. But this is the only gripe we could have with this intelligent, sumptuous place.

Huvafen Fushi   LUXURY RESORT **$$$**
(☑664 4222; www.huvafenfushi.com; r/wv incl breakfast US$1690/2150; ✳@☎☀) Huvafen Fushi set a new standard for stylish, sophisticated luxury when it opened almost a decade ago and has inspired countless imitators elsewhere in the Maldives and beyond. While Huvafen Fushi can rightly be cited as the resort that standardised private plunge pools, few imitators come close to this place in terms of the less-tangible signs of luxury – namely style, atmosphere and service.

Understated and more than a little fabulous, Huvafen Fushi is all about unfussy luxury, relaxed style and hassle-free glamour. The rooms are stunning in their simplicity, space and design savvy, all somehow still managing to feature 40in plasma-screen TVs, Bose surround systems, iPod plug-in points, espresso machines and remote-control everything.

The water villas that have been so widely copied remain some of the most impressive in the country – each with its own sizeable plunge pool on an enclosed deck overlooking the sea, with access to the lagoon down a staircase. The bedrooms and bathrooms are massive, boasting luxuries such as rain showers and some of the largest king-sized beds we've ever come across. Linen is from Frette and furniture by names such as Frank Gehry – the vibe is architect designed through and through.

Despite this, the atmosphere within the resort is informal and relaxed. The international clientele is made up mainly of honeymooners and couples, who spend the day by the enormous infinity pool overlooking the sea, lunching in one of the four superb restaurants (Celsius for international, Salt for fish and seafood, Raw for Japanese and Fogliani's for pizza) and being treated at the spa – unique for having an amazing underwater treatment room, so you can be massaged while schools of fish swim by the windows. For entertainment there's Vinum, one of the largest wine cellars in the Maldives, the funky sand-floored UMBar and regular international DJs.

Diving and water sports are catered for amply, and the entire place feels eerily empty even at full capacity, such is the way in which the resort has been laid out. This is a great place for a luxurious honeymoon or a romantic break with a funky feel.

Banyan Tree Vabbinfaru   LUXURY RESORT **$$$**
(☎664 3147; www.banyantree.com; full board r US$1345; ✳@🤶) A wonderful mix of shameless outright luxury, romantic destination and ecotourism project, Banyan Tree's main Maldives resort feels totally original and worlds away from being part of a hotel chain. Located far enough from Male to feel like a true desert island experience, the island offers a refreshing take on the top-end experience given that it doesn't have many of the features (such as a swimming pool) that many lesser resorts would take for granted. This is intentional and ties in with

the overall guiding policy that tourism must be sustainable and ecofriendly.

This is a romantic resort, extremely quiet and popular with couples. The rooms are huge and beautifully appointed with the use of lots of wood imported from Indonesia; they have a gorgeous feel with terrific and unusual outdoor bathrooms.

The house reef is excellent for snorkelling and diving, but the very best dive sites are some distance away on the edges of the atoll. The five-star PADI dive centre offers a very luxurious diving experience, while it also has a 24-hour gym and a water-sports centre for those who can't get enough strenuous activity.

By far the resort's distinguishing feature is the marine laboratory on the island, run by a charming team of marine biologists. Guests are able to help out in various capacities – from planting their own coral in the coral garden, helping with reef cleans and even monitoring the sharks and turtles kept under observation in cages just off the island shore. All of these activities are free, and marine biology lessons are given twice a week to any guest whose interest in the sea has suddenly been piqued.

The restaurant and bar are both casually elegant, open-sided spaces with sand floors and quality furniture, and the superb buffet meals cater to all tastes. For special meals, in-villa dining and sandbank dining are both available, which appeals to the many honeymooners who come here.

This was one of the first resorts to have a spa, and it's one of the best in the country, with Thai-trained therapists offering everything from a turmeric and honey body cleanser to a Hawaiian Lomi Lomi for two.

Angsana, Banyan Tree's 'little sister' resort, is just across a small channel next door – a boat goes back and forth every half-hour, allowing guests at each resort to enjoy the other's facilities.

Four Seasons
Kuda Huraa   LUXURY RESORT **$$$**
(☎664 4888; www.fourseasons.com/maldiveskh; r/wv incl breakfast from US$1100/1200; ✳@🤶⛵🪴) The smaller of the two Four Seasons properties in the Maldives, Four Seasons Kuda Huraa is also the more intimate and laid-back. The style here is apparently that of a Maldivian village, although you'd be hard pressed to find many Maldivians living in this amount of luxury. It's actually somewhat less luxurious than its sister resort, but

still a very comfortable and stylish place to spend time.

The charming rooms range from beach bungalows with quaint brick walls and high thatched roofs to glamorous water villas on the far side of the resort. The furnishings combine tropical luxury with modern design and are sleek and attractive. All categories of rooms have private plunge pools, save the water villas.

The beaches on the island are lovely and there's an enormous curved infinity pool around which the main restaurant is curled. There's always something going on here, and there's the feel of glamorous country club about the place.

The unique feature of the gorgeous and well-run spa is its location on a smaller island a short boat ride across the lagoon. The trip is done on a mini-dhoni that goes back and forth whenever guests want to get there. A kids club and a teens club are both free and make this a great option for a family holiday. Wi-fi on the island is charged, but there is a terminal in the library that can be used for free by guests. All nonmotorised water sports are free, and the gym is excellent.

The island itself is long and very attractive, and the nearby inhabited island of Bodhu Huraa is a short hop away by boat, and is popular with guests for its many craft workshops, where souvenirs can be bought.

Four Seasons Kuda Huraa is a glamorous and stylish place with friendly staff and a laid-back approach to luxury. It has a different feel to its grander sister island Landaa Giraavaru (see p101), and consequently is often combined with it on a two-centre holiday.

Angsana Ihuru   LUXURY RESORT $$$
(☏664 3502; www.angsana.com; r incl breakfast US$810; ✳@⊛) Just across the water from its sister resort Banyan Tree, Angsana Ihuru has an innovative management team who combine romantic luxury and thoughtfulness.

With its canopy of palm trees and surrounding gorgeous white beach, Angsana conforms exactly to the tropical-island stereotype and often features in photographs publicising the Maldives. The house reef forms a near-perfect circle around the island, brilliant for snorkelling and shore dives. Look near the jetty for the 'barnacle', the oldest of several metal structures on which a small electric current stimulates coral growth.

The stylish rooms are decorated in contemporary style, with black furniture, lime-green fabrics and designer bathrooms. There's a modern look in the restaurant too, but most guests prefer to eat dinner on the deck overlooking the sea. The luxurious spa consists of eight treatment rooms, almost all doubles, perfect for romantic pampering à deux.

All nonmotorised water sports are free, including all snorkelling equipment. While there is some decent shore diving to be done, the best dive sites are some distance away on the edges of the atoll. Boats take divers out each morning and afternoon.

Overall Angsana offers a very Banyan Tree mix of cuisine, comfort and indulgence, but it's more relaxed and informal, and great for upscale romance.

Baros   LUXURY RESORT $$$
(☏664 2672; www.baros.com; r/wv incl breakfast US$1072/1496; ✳@⊛) Understated, sophisticated class jumps out at you from the moment you arrive at Baros, the jewel in the crown of Universal Resorts, one of the country's largest resort groups. Refitted in 2005, Baros reopened as a magnificently rejuvenated place the same year and is a classic luxury resort at surprisingly decent prices.

The centrepiece of the resort is the impressive Lighthouse Restaurant, a fine-dining and cocktail-bar establishment, which has a shapely circus-tent roof and the feel of an exclusive yacht club. Other dining can be had at the far less formal Cayenne Grill overlooking the reef, where you can have your food cooked any way you choose by the fleet of chefs, or the all-day Lime Restaurant, where buffet breakfasts and à la carte lunch and dinner are served. All guests are on a bed-and-breakfast basis, allowing them to enjoy the variety of eating opportunities throughout their stay (although this does add up quickly).

The atmosphere is intimate and quiet, with children under six not allowed – this is upmarket European honeymoon territory. There's 'gentle' jazz and Maldivian music three times a week, and that's about the scope of the nightlife. As well as diving, snorkelling and swimming, there's a luxurious spa popular with couples. The three room categories on the island are all beautiful. Even the standard 'deluxe villa' is an 89-sq-metre work of gorgeous refinement with a sumptuous outdoor shower and garden, while the water bungalows are proper holiday-of-a-lifetime stuff.

Baros is one of many upmarket resorts that has made a conscious decision not to have a swimming pool. It's an excellent resort and has rightly earned a loyal following. This is a great choice for a luxurious and romantic getaway.

Coco Palm Bodu Hithi
LUXURY RESORT $$$
(☏334 5555; www.cococollection.com.mv; s/d/wv incl breakfast US$1010/1070/1230; ✳@🌐☎🏊🍴) Totally remodelled in a luxurious post-tsunami facelift, Coco Palm Bodu Hithi is now right up there with the big names of the Maldivian luxury market. A large resort, Bodu Hithi nevertheless manages to impress with its excellent rooms and wide variety of activity, even if it's hardly an isolated or particularly quiet spot.

The rooms come in several different categories. The island villas are sublimely stylish, with a big bathtub central to the room and lots of designer-fabulous touches. The top categories are the Escape villas and residences, a mini resorts-within-a-resort found on their own private over-water pier. These are gorgeously sleek, with huge windows onto the sea, private lap pools and enormous bathrooms stuffed with Molton Brown goodies. Escape guests also have their own buggy chauffer service to take them anywhere on the island.

The rest of the island ticks every box – there are five superb restaurants, a magnificent wine collection, a water-sports centre offering everything from wakeboarding to windsurfing, a top-notch dive school with easy access to a host of excellent sites, a large and beautiful spa, free wi-fi, great beaches and one of the most interesting pools in the Maldives (an infinity pool with glass sides in front of the main restaurant).

Along with its new look comes a progressive environmental policy – Coco Palm plans to be the first carbon-neutral resort in the country and offers excellent educational activities through its marine biology department.

Makunudu Island
ROMANTIC RESORT $$
(☏664 6464; www.makunudu.com; half board s/d US$374/452; ✳@) Makunudu Island is wonderful, and an old favourite of ours. Just 2.4 hectares in area, the tiny island almost looks like it might sink under the sheer weight of lush vegetation on it – and the surrounding reef is so big that it's hard for speedboats unfamiliar with the island to find their way into the dock through the shallow lagoon.

Things are extremely tasteful here and almost unbelievably low-key, with individual thatched-roof bungalows hidden amid the jungle-like foliage. All rooms face the beach and feature natural finishes, varnished timber, textured white walls and open-air bathrooms, and have all facilities except the purposely excluded TV. The service and food are both excellent. Breakfast and lunch are buffets, while most dinners are a choice of thoughtfully prepared set menus, served in the delightful open-sided restaurant. Communal beach barbecues are a weekly event.

Guests are nearly all European couples who come to relax, get away from it all or enjoy a low-key and tranquil honeymoon, evidenced by the trees planted by newlyweds all over the island, each marked by memorial plaques. In keeping with the laid-back ethos, there is no wi-fi on the island, but there's a cybercafe, where 30 minutes' access costs US$5.

There are excellent dive sites in the area, the house reef is great for snorkelling, and the Dive Ocean (www.dive-ocean.com) dive school is very experienced after over a decade running dives from the island. Dive groups tend to be small and friendly. Windsurfing and sailing are free, as are shorter excursions. This unaffected place won't appeal to travellers wanting pampering, water villas or cutting-edge design, but if a small, exclusive, natural-style resort appeals, Makunudu is one of the best choices in the Maldives.

Sheraton Maldives
Full Moon Resort & Spa
LUXURY RESORT $$
(☏664 2010; www.starwoodhotels.com; r/wv incl breakfast US$636/990; ✳@🌐☎) Magnificently laid out with real style and class, Sheraton Maldives Full Moon Resort & Spa has the ambience of an upmarket country club rather than a remote tropical island. This is in part due to its proximity to the capital, but that aside everything here is aimed at the sophisticate, from the gorgeously understated public areas to the luxurious spa, housed on its own island and linked to the resort by a footbridge.

The second Maldives property of the innovative Starwood Hotels group, which also runs it-resort W Resort Maldives, this place offers midrange luxury in its 176 refurbished rooms, including its state-of-the-art water villas and beachfront deluxe rooms, all of which feature thatched roofs, shuttered windows and private gardens or terraces.

For dining, choose between an excellent Thai restaurant; the al fresco Sand Coast, which serves up international cuisine; and the beachfront Sea Salt, where steaks and seafood are the order of the day. Feast, the main restaurant, also serves high-quality buffets three times a day.

A full range of facilities is squeezed onto this small island, including an inviting swimming pool that has its own waterfall, tennis courts, a gym, a gorgeous spa and a business centre. There are no motorised water sports, and the lagoon is unsuitable for snorkelling, but sailing, windsurfing and snorkelling trips are offered. There's a full and well-run dive centre, and big-game fishing is also available. With lots to do and a glamorous, urbane feel, Full Moon is a great choice for an upscale break.

Vivanta by Taj Coral Reef   LUXURY RESORT $$
(✆664 1948; www.tajhotels.com; r/wv incl breakfast US$655/828; ❈@⧢⧢⧢) Totally remodelled in 2009, heart-shaped Taj Vivanta is a glamorous midrange luxury resort that manages nevertheless to feel laid-back and unpretentious. Although cheaper than its sister resort Taj Exotica, it's not a large step down in service and quality, with all 62 rooms brand new and very plush, including 32 water villas with large terraces and direct access to snorkelling in the lagoon. Rooms feel thoroughly modern and smart, if a bit anonymous and Ikea-like in their art choices. However, there are great touches such as iPod decks, DVD players and outside showers.

The resort centres on the large Latitude restaurant, which has a great beachside position and serves up three buffet meals per day. Nearby are a pizza station and a teppanyaki bar next to the large infinity pool. The beach isn't the best here, somewhat narrow, rocky in part and held in place by wired rocks, though the sand is wonderfully soft elsewhere.

Other facilities include Jiva Spa, which focuses on Indian massage, Ayurvedic therapies and other treatments and pampering from the subcontinent. You'll find a watersports centre and a dive school, and snorkelling around the island is excellent (and equipment is free). A reliable number of manta rays turns up at 5pm every day to be fed, an incredible spectacle and one that visitors from nearby resorts sometimes come over to see. Overall, Taj Vivanta is a recommended choice for small, smart, luxury without any fuss.

Helengeli Island Resort   DIVING RESORT $
(✆664 4615; www.helengeli.net; full board s/d/tr US$261/291/356; ❈@⧢⧢) Blissfully isolated at the top of North Male Atoll, Helengeli is quite simply a paradise for divers. There are some 40 dive sites easily accessible from this charming and laid-back island, and most are used exclusively by Helengeli guests and the occasional passing safari boat. It's a European diving resort, with 85% of the guests from Switzerland and the remainder from Germany, Austria and the UK.

Accommodation is in two-room blocks, which are simple, clean and pleasant, all with minibar, safe and basic outdoor bathrooms. The rooms are far from luxurious, but that's not why people come here. The public areas have sand floors, so you can leave your shoes in your luggage. The focus of the resort is on the swimming pool and bar-restaurant area, where all meals are served up as buffets.

The 2km-long house reef is excellent, so you need not venture far for snorkelling, and qualified divers can do unguided scuba dives from the beach. Nearby Helengeli Thila is considered one of the best dive sites in the country. Dive costs start at US$50 for a boat

---

ALSO IN NORTH MALE ATOLL

Coco Palm Kuda Hithi (www.cococollection.com) The smaller of the two islands run by Coco Collection in North Male Atoll, Coco Palm Kudahithi, a short distance away from Coco Palm Bodu Hithi, is a private island for one single couple staying in mind-blowing luxury.

Adaaran Select Hudhuran Fushi (www.adaaran.com) A family-oriented resort that offers tonnes of activities. It's particularly good for water-sports fanatics and has a popular surf break. There's also a sleek resort-within-a-resort here, the upmarket Ocean Villas.

Club Med Kani (www.clubmed.com) A perennially popular all-inclusive resort near the airport, Club Med Kani keeps its guests busy from morning to night with an endless array of activities. No extra charges.

dive with tanks and weights, or US$315 for a package of five dives with all equipment provided. An open-water course costs US$698. The **Ocean-Pro dive base** (www.oceanpro-diveteam.com) aims for personalised service and tries to keep guests with the same dive guides for their whole stay.

Windsurfing, sailing and other water sports aren't offered, but a few excursions are, including dolphin watching and trips to the inhabited island of Gaafaru nearby. There's also a small spa. Evening entertainment is very low-key, consisting mainly of a few drinks at the delightful beachfront bar, and an early night in preparation for the next day's diving activity. Internet access is available, but is pricy: wi-fi is available at the bar for US$5 per hour, while 30 minutes of internet access from the library terminal costs US$10.

TOP CHOICE Meeru Island Resort

ALL-INCLUSIVE RESORT $

(☑664 3157; www.meeru.com; full board s/d/tr/w US$220/260/350/455; ❈@🛜🌊) Meeru Island Resort will have you smitten at first sight – it's a beautiful long, verdant stretch of land with a dazzling white beach. The resort is enormous, the third largest in the country, and offers almost every conceivable activity. Indeed, so large is the resort that for convenience there are two receptions and two buffet restaurants, to avoid guests overexerting themselves on the way to dinner.

That said, the resort is only for a certain type of guest. With a minimum six-night stay required – and the only options being full board, all inclusive or all inclusive plus – this will suit those happy to spend all their time in the resort unwinding.

Rooms come in a startling number of categories, from prefab timber-clad self-contained units that are very cosy and sweet to the 87 water villas. The latter range from rustic-style older rooms in bright colours with open-air bathrooms and Jacuzzis to newer, sleeker but perhaps less charming water villas, all in dark wood and with extra luxuries such as espresso machines and direct water access.

All nonmotorised water sports are included here. There are two excellent spas, the newest of which is entirely over water, and two swimming pools. Other amenities include a nine-hole golf course, two tennis courts, a gym and a golf driving range. Even more unusual is the extraordinary blue-whale skeleton on display in the middle of

the island, and a small and rather neglected museum of Maldivian history and traditions above the barnlike main reception.

Meerufenfushi actually means 'Sweet Water Island' in Dhivehi, and the island's wells were used to replenish passing dhonis in the past. The unusual retention of ground water here has created a large amount of natural vegetation and now some of the 28-hectare island is used for growing fruit and vegetables. There's a massive range of activities and excursions, and the evenings can be lively in the various bars, as many guests are on all-inclusive packages.

The house reef can only be reached by boat and these leave every two hours to take snorkellers and divers off to the outer reef, where the aquatic life is fantastic. All the usual water sports are offered, fishing trips are popular, and the vast lagoon is perfect for learning sailing and windsurfing. Meeru has its own safari boats, and two- or three-day cruises can be taken from the resort. Inexpensive excursions go to the fishing village on neighbouring Dhiffushi.

Ocean-Pro (www.oceanpro-diveteam.com) is the large diving centre. Diving quickly adds up here, however; while a single dive with equipment is US$50 with tank and weights only, there's a boat charge of US$19/31/36 for one/two/three boat trips. An open-water course costs US$698. A whole slew of great dive sites are accessible in the channels within 5km.

Overall, Meeru gets great reviews from guests. It caters to a wide variety of interests and budget levels – it's a big resort but it's not crowded and has retained its personal, friendly feel.

Palma Guesthouse

GUESTHOUSE $

(☑794 0123, 775 2008; www.maldives-guesthouse.com; Huraa; full board s/d US$110/158; ❈🛜) The project of a Franco-Maldivian couple, this charming, modern and comfortable house operates with very pleasant Gallic flair and dubs itself a *chamber d'hôte* (homestay), rather than anything as formal as a hotel. Rooms all have good bathrooms with hot water, and guests are actively invited to participate in preparing the meals, giving the place a real community feel. As well as full board, the price includes an activity each day, ranging from fishing to snorkelling.

Kurumba Maldives

ACTIVITIES RESORT $$

(☑664 2324; www.kurumba.com; r incl breakfast from US$448; ❈@🛜🌊🍴) Established in 1972,

Kurumba Maldives was the first resort in the country. It was refurbished in 2003 and reopened as a high-quality place that continues to be extremely popular, combining a huge range of facilities, ease of access from the airport, family friendliness and quality accommodation. Some may feel the overly manicured gardens and relentlessly modern architecture make the resort feel a little sterile; others, however, will like its grand country-club style – golf buggies rule the roads here and the resort is big enough for this to be justifiable.

Kurumba is the closest resort to Male, and as such it regularly caters for business conferences and conventions as well as day-trippers from the capital, who come for the renowned restaurants. There are eight restaurants to choose from (more than on any other resort island in the country), including those serving up Indian, Italian, Chinese and Japanese.

The rooms come in a huge range of categories, the pool villas being especially impressive, each with its own pool in a private back garden. For those wanting to splurge there are presidential villas and the Royal Kurumba Residence, which should satisfy even the most demanding international jet-setters. There are no water villas here, and few villas have direct beach access, but it's never too far to the water.

There's no end to the facilities available, from a huge and well-equipped dive school to a water-sports centre offering every conceivable discipline, tennis courts, babysitters, a gorgeous spa, two gyms and two pools. Kurumba is a place for scale and grandeur and not for hiding away on a desert island, but it remains a hugely popular choice for both couples and families.

Thulhagiri RUSTIC RESORT **$$**
(☑664 5930; www.thulhagiri.com.mv; half board r/ wv US$350/442; ✳@☎) Small, intimate and low-key, Thulhagiri is as laid-back as it is pretty. Its wide, sloping white beaches and thick palm vegetation greet you as you arrive at its small jetty, beyond which two rows of water villas jut out over the turquoise lagoon. The resort itself is rustic, with a charming open-air reception area and other nice touches, including a lily pond among the dense foliage. Thulhagiri represents a great choice for its price range. It's small and less expensive, but its size gives it a more exclusive feel than some of the bigger budget places.

The Sub Aqua Dive Centre offers a full program of courses and activities, including Nitrox. There's a good water-sports centre with catamarans and waterskiing available. The small, rather murky swimming pool is the only real evidence that this is a budget resort.

Rooms are in a rustic style, featuring thatched roofs and wooden interiors. The older 17 water villas have four-poster beds, colourful fabrics and coffee-making facilities – they're decent, but not especially great value at their high-season price, while the 17 newer water villas are far smarter and enjoy a more contemporary feel.

There's also the new Coconut Spa, offering a full range of treatments. Wi-fi is charged and available at a hotspot around the bar only. All meals are buffets, and they're very good for a resort in this range.

Asdu Sun Island DIVING RESORT **$**
(☑664 5051; www.asdu.com; full board s/d US$140/280; @) Perhaps the least self-conscious resort in the country, the delightfully laid-back Asdu Sun Island is about as far away from the luxury super resorts as can be imagined. As such, it's a great place to feel you're meeting locals, while enjoying some of the perks of life on a resort island. All the staff on the island are members of owner Ahmed's family, whose quarters are not hidden away out of sight as is the norm in Maldives, but instead enjoy equal status on the island to those of the guest rooms. Chickens run around freely and reception's own computer is yours to use for checking your email.

The tiny island is thickly forested and has a stunning white beach around much of it, though erosion is a problem on one side. Most guests come from Italy, but there's a wide range of nationalities here, all drawn by the cheap and excellent diving. Accommodation is in two- and three-unit white-painted concrete huts, all terribly simple and rather worn, free of air-con, TV and glass windows, but clean. The **Submaldive diving school** (www.submaldive.com) offers comprehensive daily excursions and courses at reasonable rates, with dives costing $37 each, or $32 each if you pay for 10.

Summer Island Village ALL-INCLUSIVE RESORT **$**
(☑664 1949; www.summerislandvillage.com; all-inclusive s/d/tr/wv US$209/302/385/376; ✳@) Summer Island Village is a long, thin island that's all about affordable fun. It's popular with repeat visitors from Germany and Britain who enjoy the laid-back approach and

profit from the good-value, all-inclusive packages. The once rather sparse vegetation on the island has improved enormously in recent years, and the beaches are excellent.

Accommodation is a little spartan but clean and adequate, all rooms being on the beach and having an extra bed and a spacious outdoor bathroom. The units are tightly packed together, and some rooms are in two-storey units. The modern-style water bungalows at the island's southern end are a recent addition. They're nothing fancy, with no direct access to the water and just a small hole in the floor looking into the sea, but they're bigger and more comfortable than the standard rooms.

Sand floors in the public areas and friendly staff give the whole place a relaxed feel. Meals are buffets with a modest selection of curry, fish, salads and vegetables. Weekly theme nights feature Asian and international cuisine.

The lagoon is wide and shallow, so the resort is more suited to windsurfing, waterskiing and sailing than to snorkelling or swimming. While the beaches on both sides of the island are good, some stretches are protected by somewhat unattractive breakwaters.

There are some great dive sites within about 5km. The **Diverland dive centre** (www.diverland.com) offers a single dive with equipment for US$64 or an excellent deal on 10 dives, starting at just US$470 including tanks and weights; a NAUI scuba diver course costs US$620. A daily snorkelling trip is included in the package (excluding equipment), as are table tennis, volleyball and badminton. There's also the Serena Spa if you'd like to pamper yourself with a range of massages and other treatments. This is a decent choice if you'd like to combine diving with a beach holiday.

Eriyadu
DIVING RESORT $

(☎664 4487; www.eriyadumaldives.com; half board s/d/tr US$265/340/450; ✳@) Located right at the top of North Male Atoll, Eriyadu is pleasantly remote, which is a major incentive for divers who come here for the uncrowded waters that surround the resort. It's also a wonderfully mellow place where you're left to your own devices.

The island is full of repeat visitors – the vast majority of whom are German. Children aren't really encouraged, as there are no facilities tailored to them, and this leads to a very quiet and undisturbed atmosphere.

The island is an oval shape, and sadly suffers from bad erosion, but the beaches are still attractive, with a beautiful sandbank sometimes created by the changing current. There's a good reef, great for snorkelling, with turtles and dolphins regular fixtures just metres from the beach. There's no pool but there is a spa.

The **Euro-Divers** (www.euro-divers.com) dive centre offers a single lagoon dive for US$52, while a six-day no-limit dive package costs US$492 – making it a great deal. An open-water course is also good value at US$480.

The rooms are divided into two categories. Most are in two-room units on the beach, each with its own sea-facing patio, though views can be blocked by the island's thick foliage. The six cheaper rooms (euphemistically called 'garden villas') are in a two-storey block set back from the beach. Rooms have polished timber floors, TV and minibar. The island is quite heavily developed, but the buildings are interspersed with lots of shady trees and shrubbery. The sand-floor restaurant serves most meals in buffet style, with a varied selection of European dishes, curries and seafood.

The usual water sports and excursions are available, as is some low-key evening entertainment, but this economical resort is mainly for diving, snorkelling and relaxing on the beach.

Chaaya Island Dhonveli
BUDGET RESORT $

(☎664 0055; www.chaayahotels.com; half board s/d/tr/wv US$250/300/370/360; ✳@🛜🏊) Following full-scale devastation in the 2004 tsunami when its water bungalows were washed away, this old timer was rebuilt and then later became part of the Chaaya group. It's now a well-run if rather crowded resort with a great pool, its own surf break and tennis courts.

There are six categories of room catering for everyone from honeymooners to groups of surfers who come here in big numbers from June to September. The charming-looking new water villas are painted blue, have thatched roofs and Indian-style carved wood frames, although they are more impressive outside than in, where furnishings are rather garish and cheap. The older water villas that survived the tsunami are a bit poky and similarly garish. Better value are the cheaper rooms on the island itself, which are simple but attractive.

While having some attractive beaches, the island is quite sparse in places, and beach erosion is a real problem, with some unsightly sandbags in sight. The beach on the north side of the island is great for swimming and sunbathing, and is safe for children. All meals are buffet style and feature a fair selection of good food. Dhonveli is not a big diving destination, but there are lots of good dive sites nearby (the Protected Marine Area at HP Reef is very close).

Diving is done through the new **Meredis Diving Centre** (www.meridis.de), where dives start at US$55 without equipment and boat fees ($14) and an open-water course costs US$598. Discounts are available if you pay in advance. Surfers, who come here in the summer to enjoy the island's private surf break, a consistent left-hander called Pasta Point, are well catered for too, with board hire through **Atoll Travel** (www.atolltravel.com) ranging from US$25/145 per day/week. All in all, there's a lot going for Dhonveli, as it offers a good standard of service and facilities for the price.

Paradise Island   ACTIVITIES RESORT **$**
(☑664 0011; www.villahotels.com; half board s/d/tr/wv US$264/321/354/650; ✴@🛜🏊♨) Paradise Island is one of the Maldives' biggest resorts, and offers some great deals for people seeking a huge range of facilities and services at a bargain price. The beaches are gorgeous, the lagoon an incredible colour even by local standards and the whole place is well run and friendly. It's a great choice if you like endless activities options and plenty going on. The atmosphere, though, is hardly intimate: you're crowded onto one of the country's biggest island resorts. If you want seclusion and true escape, perhaps move on.

A recent addition is the Haven, a luxury resort within a resort, which aims to satisfy the apparently limitless appetite for water villas, though given its prices are comparable to other more intimate, less mass-market resorts, its appeal is rather limited.

Rooms in Paradise proper are simple, with white tiles, white walls, air-con and satellite TV. They are absolutely fine, but unlikely to be places you'll want to spend much of your time. By contrast, the 62 brand new rooms in the Haven come in four categories. They are very sleek, stylish and rather minimalist, the higher categories coming with enormous slate pools and all having large sun terraces with direct access to the water.

Packages with meals at the resort are definitely worth it: you get a decent buffet for every meal and the other three restaurants are nothing to shout about, so you won't find yourself wanting to eat elsewhere that much.

Guests staying at the Haven have two restaurants for their exclusive use.

The island is well landscaped and has good beaches and a swimming pool. Some rooms are a long way from the restaurant, and many don't have much of a view. Activities include gym, squash, badminton, tennis and billiards, all at extra cost, while darts and table tennis are free. There's a huge spa here too. Snorkelling is excellent in the lagoon and on the house reef, which is full of fascinating marine life. The **Dive Oceanus dive centre** (www.diveoceanus.com) is very friendly and offers boat dives to the many excellent dive sites nearby.

Bandos Island Resort   ACTIVITIES RESORT **$$**
(☑664 0088; www.bandosmaldives.com; s/d/wv incl breakfast US$360/455/1310; ✴@🛜🏊♨) One of the largest resorts in the country, Bandos Island Resort has developed and expanded enormously since it opened as the second resort in the Maldives in 1972. It has an enviable range of facilities – 500-seat conference centre, coffee shop, several restaurants, disco, tennis courts, billiard room, sauna, gym, swimming pool, beauty salon and spa-massage service. The child-care centre is free during the day, and babysitters are only US$8 per hour in the evening, so in general the resort is one of the most child-friendly in the country, with many families choosing it for its combination of facilities, activities and child-care options.

The island is highly developed and resembles a well-manicured town centre rather than a typical tropical island. Many love it for that reason, though you may be disappointed if you're yearning to get away from it all.

Sailing and windsurfing are available, along with a full range of motorised water sports and an active big-game-fishing centre. Fine, narrow beaches surround the island, and the house reef is handy for snorkelling and diving. Lots of fish and a small wreck can be seen here. The state-of-the-art dive centre does trips to about 40 dive sites in the area, and offers a full range of courses, including nitrox and rebreather training. A single boat dive costs US$72, including all equipment and boat charges, or US$58 with your own equipment. The diving health clinic here has a decompression chamber. An open-water course costs US$580.

Bandos caters for evening visitors and day-trippers from Male, but currently does not provide a regular boat – call the resort if you want to arrange something. As well as guests from all over Europe and Asia, many airlines use Bandos for layovers, so there can be a very mixed group here.

Rooms are modern, with red-tiled roofs, white-tiled floors, air-con, hairdryer, minibar and phone. Other categories include the Jacuzzi Beach Villa and the luxurious Water Villas, which include services such as a private butler, although they're a lot more expensive.

The main Gallery Restaurant does three international high-quality buffet meals daily. Other restaurants include the 24-hour Seabreeze Café for à la carte pasta and curries, and the Harbour Restaurant for Asian fusion cuisine. The Sand Bar hosts live bands, discos and karaoke several nights a week and is one of the most boisterous bars in the Maldives. Bandos is great for families and those who like big resorts where there's potential to meet lots of new people and to have a huge range of activities available.

Cola's Guesthouse GUESTHOUSE $
(☑777 7366; www.islandlifemaldives.net; Thulusdhoo; s/d from US$50/100; ✱☎) This budget 12-room option is very popular with surfers who come here between April and October to enjoy the nearby breaks at Coke's and Chicken's. All rooms are comfortably furnished, with fridges and private bathrooms. A range of good-value meal plans are available.

Happy Life Safari Lodge GUESTHOUSE $
(☑977 4151; www.guesthouses-in-maldives.com; Dhiffushi; s/d US$70/80; ✱@) On one of North Male Atoll's most pleasant inhabited islands, this friendly guesthouse has four comfortable if rather small rooms, all of which have open-air bathrooms and enjoy sea views. The downstairs sand-floor restaurant serves up good meals, and there's an impressive list of activities available, from yoga and snorkelling to spa treatments and night fishing.

❶ Getting There & Away

Nearly all resorts in North Male Atoll collect their guests from the airport by launch, as even the furthest island is less than an hour away. All the inhabited islands are connected by ferry from Male's Viligili Ferry Terminal. Ferries go in both directions every day except Friday.

Kaashidhoo

Though in the Kaafu (Male) administrative district, the island of Kaashidhoo is way out by itself, in a channel north of North Male Atoll. The island has a clinic, a secondary

school and over 1900 people, which makes it one of the most populous in Kaafu. Some of the ruins here are believed to be remains of an old Buddhist temple. Local crops include watermelon, lemon, banana, cucumber and zucchini, but the island is best known for its *raa* – the 'palm toddy' made from the sap of a palm tree, drunk fresh or slightly fermented.

Local boats going to or from the northern atolls sometimes shelter in the lagoon in Kaashidhoo in bad weather. Dive boats on longer trips might stop to dive Kaashidhoo East Faru, a good place to see large pelagic marine life.

Gaafaru Falhu

This small atoll has just one island, also called Gaafaru, with a population of 1100. The channel to the north of the atoll, Kaashidhoo Kuda Kandu, has long been a shipping lane, and several vessels have veered off course and ended up on the hidden reefs of Gaafaru Falhu. There are three diveable wrecks – SS *Seagull* (1879), *Erlangen* (1894) and *Lady Christine* (1974). None is anywhere near intact, but the remains all have good coral growth and plentiful fish. Dive trips are possible from Helengeli and Eriyadu, but most visitors are from live-aboard dive boats.

South Male Atoll

Crossing the Vaadhoo Kandu, the choppy channel between North and South Male Atolls, you'll quickly notice that South Male Atoll has a very different feel from its busy northern neighbour. This is partly due to the lack of people – there are only three inhabited islands here, all of which are on the eastern edge of the atoll and have small populations – and partly to do with the fact that the uninhabited islands are spread out and so you really feel that you're remote from the hustle and bustle of Male and its surrounding islands.

The biggest island in South Male Atoll is charming and friendly **Maafushi** (population 1200), which hosts the country's largest prison and a reformatory. The island is also a fast-growing independent tourism destination with four functioning guesthouses and a dive school under construction at the time of research.

Nearby **Guraidhoo**, more populous than the bigger Maafushi with around 1800 people, is the atoll's largest town. Its lagoon has a

South Male Atoll

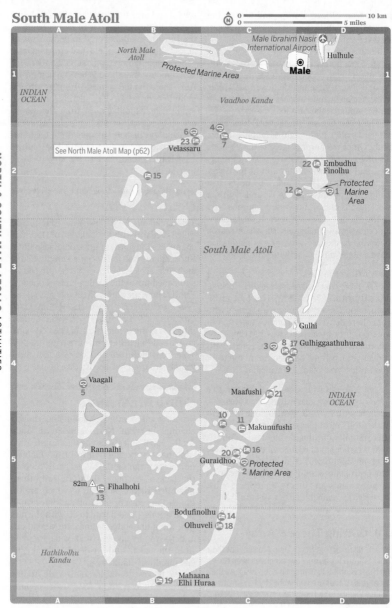

good anchorage and it's a busy port used by both fishing dhonis and passing safari boats. Sultans from Male sought refuge here during rebellions from as early as the 17th century, while today it's popular with budget travellers who stay at the cheap guesthouses, and with visitors from nearby resorts (it's actually possible to walk across the lagoon to Kandooma resort at low tide!). As tourists have been visiting for years, the island is well used to foreigners, and there are plenty of souvenir shops along the town's sandy main street.

South Male Atoll

The island of **Gulhi**, north of Maafushi, is not large but is inhabited by around 750 people. Fishing is the main activity, and there's also a small shipyard, but there are no guesthouses yet.

🏃 Activities

Some of the best dive sites are around the Vaadhoo Kandu, which funnels a huge volume of water between the North and South Male Atolls. Various smaller kandus channel water between the atoll and the surrounding sea, and also provide great diving. Some typical, well-known sites are listed following.

Velassaru Caves DIVING
The rugged Velassaru Caves and overhangs, on the steep wall of the Vaadhoo Kandu, have very attractive coral growth. You may see sharks, turtles and rays on the bottom at around 30m. This dive is not for beginners, but if the current isn't too strong there's excellent snorkelling on the reef edge.

Vaadhoo Caves DIVING
Vaadhoo Caves consists of a row of small caves, plus a bigger one with a swim-through tunnel, as well as excellent soft corals, gorgonians, jackfish and the odd eagle ray. If the current is strong, this is a demanding dive; if not, it's great for snorkelling.

Embudhoo Express DIVING
Embudhoo Express is a 2km drift dive through the Embudhoo Kandu, which is a Protected Marine Area. With the current running in, rays, Napoleon wrasse and sharks often congregate around the

entrance. The current carries divers along a wall with overhangs and a big cave. The speed of the current makes for a demanding dive, but also provides the ideal environment for soft corals and a large variety of fish. The reef top is good for snorkelling.

Kuda Giri DIVING
Also called Yacht Thila, the attraction of Kuda Giri is the hulk of a small freight ship, deliberately sunk here to create an artificial reef. Sponges and cup corals are growing on the wreck, and it provides a home for morays, groupers and large schools of batfish. A nearby thila has recovering coral growth and lots of reef fish can be seen at snorkelling depths. Sheltered from strong currents, this is a good site for beginners and for night dives.

Vaagali Caves DIVING
Vaagali Caves is an exciting dive and not too demanding. It's in a less exposed location and has many caves on its north side, at around 15m, filled with sponges and soft corals. There's also good coral regrowth and lots of fish on the top of the reef.

Guraidhoo Kandu DIVING
A central reef splits Guraidhoo Kandu into two channels, with many possibilities for divers, even those with less experience. There are numerous reef fish, larger pelagics near the entrance and mantas when the current is running out. The kandu is a Protected Marine Area.

🛏 Sleeping

South Male Atoll is easily reached by speedboat transfer from the airport, and there are now also a good range of guesthouses on inhabited islands in the atoll to choose from.

TOP CHOICE Cocoa Island   LUXURY RESORT $$$

(☑664 1818; www.cocoaisland.como.bz; wv incl breakfast from US$1350; ❄@🌐🏊) Cocoa Island is one of the very few resorts that manages to get everything so right with such little fuss. This wonderful place is one of the most unique Maldivian resorts, and since its lavish refit at the hands of the COMO group, Cocoa has consistently impressed.

First of all, the small island has no rooms on it at all – they're all built over water in a shape that mirrors that of the island itself. And what rooms they are – built in the shape of traditional Maldivian dhoni boats, their interiors straight out of a glossy magazine spread – all clean lines, white cotton and dark wood. Newer two-floor loft villas are furnished with white timbers and are even more stunning. Other great touches include outdoor showers, direct sea access from the rooms, free wi-fi and gorgeous COMO Shambhala bathroom products.

On the island proper there is nothing superfluous. A large infinity pool, cracking beaches the entire way around the island, a superb restaurant with a large range of dishes, a smart cocktail bar, a sumptuous spa, a gym, and the excellent and friendly dive centre. Everything is luxurious, but nothing is over the top. All in all, a great recommendation for unpretentious and low-key luxury.

Jumeirah Vittaveli   LUXURY RESORT $$$

(☑664 2020; www.jumeirah.com; r/wv incl breakfast from $1815/2045; ❄@🌐🏊) One of two super-smart new Jumeirah resorts in the Maldives, Jumeirah Vittaveli, which opened in 2012, is a stunning state-of-the art luxury destination. Everything here displays plenty of thought, fusing several of the country's best resorts.

The island is beautiful, with gorgeous stretches of beach and plentiful thick vegetation (the island was an established resort called Bolifushi for a long time before Jumeirah redeveloped it). The public areas are beautiful, all crafted in gorgeous timbers and sublimely decorated without being over the top, but the real highlights are the rooms, which across the board are simply stunning.

Even the starting category, the Beach Villa, is a palatial 184 sq metres, and all rooms have their own private swimming pools as standard, up to and including the 800-sq-metre Presidential Suite, which is astoundingly luxurious. As well as being spacious, rooms are tall, with wonderful beamed ceilings and distinctive thatched roofs, while decor combines timeless tradition with modern touches such as flat-screen TVs, free wi-fi, iPod docks and rain showers.

Facilities on the island include the magnificent Talise Spa, a gym, a water-sports centre and a very smart diving centre with brand new equipment. The resort has two L-shaped communal pools, one for families, the other restricted to adults, so there's peace and quiet even though kids are welcome on the island. There are three restaurants to choose from: Samsara for Pan-Asian cuisine; Mediterranean Fenesse; and steak and seafood at the candlelit Mu Beach Bar & Grill.

Overall Jumeirah is one of the hottest new resorts in Maldives and a perfect choice for the discerning luxury traveller.

Rihiveli Beach Resort   RUSTIC RESORT $$

(☑664 3731; www.rihiveli-maldives.com; full board r US$368; 🌐) Rihiveli Beach Resort is the personal creation of a Frenchman who lived here for 20 years. While he has now moved on, his legacy remains, and this almost exclusively French and Swiss resort retains its ecofriendly, laid-back credentials. Indeed, this was the resort that coined the phrase 'no news, no shoes' – now used across the country – and you'll get funny looks if your shoes remain on for long after arrival.

Accommodation consists of just 48 seafacing bungalows, all built in a rustic style from now-illegal coral stone and with traditional thatched roofs. They have all the basics for comfort such as hot water but nothing considered superfluous, such as air-con, fridges, phones or a TV. This is the secret of its success and as such Rihiveli (Silver Sand) will never be overrun with your run-of-the-mill package group.

The open-air bar has a sand floor and shady trees overhead, while the restaurant is built over the lagoon and has a lovely view as well as excellent food. A conch shell is blown to call guests to meals, and everyone is invited to take tea with the staff daily at 5.30pm: yes, this is not your typical Maldivian resort! The usual water sports and tennis are all included in the room price, as is a daily excursion, so there's no chance of boredom here. You can wade across the lagoon to two uninhabited islands where the resort organises regular barbecue lunches. Frequent boat trips to other reefs make up for the lack of snorkelling sites next to the resort. The main diving destinations are around nearby Hathikolhu Kandu, and there's a small wreck to explore. Wi-fi is available at the lobby for free, but elsewhere it's just you and nature, so there's no need to take your iPhone to the beach.

With its relaxed ambience, French style and natural appeal, Rihiveli is a unique and special resort for those who appreciate the simple things and want a totally laid-back and unfussy beach and activities holiday.

Taj Exotica   LUXURY RESORT **$$$**
(☑664 2200; www.tajhotels.com; r incl breakfast from US$1060; ❄@🛜🏊) This elegant, understated resort is all about quiet luxury and indulgence and is the flagship Maldivian resort of the Indian Taj Group. Its super-stylish public areas and gorgeous rooms make it perfectly suited to romantic beach holidays, making it very popular with honeymooners.

Within easy striking distance of the airport, yet still feeling pleasantly secluded, Embudhu Finolhu island is long and thin, with a beach on the lagoon side and water villas on the atoll edge. The public areas include a DVD and book library, a well-stocked games room, a gorgeous infinity pool and, at the far end of the island, the breathtaking Jiva Grande Spa. There's a gym and free yoga classes each morning.

All categories of rooms are very smart, many of them with their own plunge pools overlooking the beach. The bathrooms in the lagoon villas have wonderful bathtubs next to huge windows allowing you to contemplate the sea as you soak.

Taj Exotica was one of the original pioneers of fine à la carte dining in the Maldives – the main Asia-Pacific restaurant here wouldn't know a buffet if it hit it in the face – and it's safe to say you'll eat excellently here, with everything ordered and individually cooked from a sumptuous and expensive menu. This is one place where full board would come in handy – the meals here are far from budget. One feature of the second restaurant, which is built out over the lagoon and is open in the evenings, is an open hole over the water, where fish flock in the evening, attracted by the light.

Overall this small but perfectly formed island is a real treat for honeymooners or couples looking for a perfect high-style escape.

Naladhu   LUXURY RESORT **$$$**
(☑664 1888; www.naladhu.com; villa incl breakfast from US$2412; ❄@🛜🏊) Naladhu is the third island around the lagoon at Anantara and is operated by the same management, but marketed as a completely separate resort. Its concept is simple – an exclusive place where the rich and famous can remain unseen and totally private living in one of 19 large villas. This place is popular with security-conscious Russian millionaires, and though it's linked by a bridge to Anantara Veli, there's no access for non-Naladhu guests to the island. The villas are sumptuous, with huge pools and either beach access in the six beach houses or views to the ocean in the ocean houses where there's no sand. The resort, unsurprisingly, has little community feel – a large pool and a smart restaurant are all there really are to the communal areas – this is a place to celebrate privacy in style.

ALSO IN SOUTH MALE ATOLL

Velassaru (www.velassaru.com) A large upmarket property from local giant Universal Resorts, this place was totally refurbished in 2009 and offers stylish accommodation, including very smart new water villas.

Fun Island Resort (www.funislandmaldives.com) The name of this 50-room budget resort is a bit misleading, as it's actually a quiet diving and family holiday resort, rather than one that packs in the activities. But it's a decent choice for a no-frills beach holiday.

Adaaran Prestige Vadoo (www.adaaran.com) This upmarket resort has all 50 of its rooms over water, including four honeymoon suites that are only reachable by boat from the pretty, beach-ringed island. It's renowned for superb diving and is conveniently near to the airport.

Fihalhohi Resort (www.fihalhohi.net) Low prices and a fantastic reef make Fihalhohi a good choice for a budget diving holiday. The island itself is charming, with beaches all the way around, although erosion is a problem and sandbags are in evidence. But overall, this resort is great value for money.

Anantara Dhigu &
Anantara Veli
LUXURY RESORT $$$

(☑664 4100; www.anantara.com; Dhigu r/wv incl breakfast US$1188/1510, Veli wv US$979; ❋@ ☎≊⚒) This high-end Thai-owned resort is draped over three islands. All are officially their own resorts, and while in reality they're all centrally managed, we've listed Naladhu separately, as it's a 'six-star' property that's out of bounds to guests staying at the lowlier resorts. Not that Dhigu or Veli could ever be considered budget destinations.

Dhigu is the main resort, where guests arrive and where the majority of the facilities, such as diving school and water-sports centre, are housed. It's a relatively crowded island featuring beach villas and large, very glamorous water villas decorated in classic Asian styles and with spacious sun decks. It has a big pool by the beach, a kids club, and a gorgeous over-water spa for all your pampering needs.

Crossing the lagoon to next-door Veli by a shuttle boat, there's more of the same. Veli, where all the accommodation is over water, nevertheless has the lowest-priced rooms at the resort, though even in the bottom category they're a good size – 62 sq metres each. Veli feels slightly over-developed in places, with seemingly endless over-water pathways to yet more water bungalows – despite the minimalist aesthetic in some of the rooms, the architects here clearly didn't agree that less really is more.

Veli has its own large pool, restaurants and spa, and is connected by a walkway to Naladhu. There are a variety of eateries here – seven in total across the three islands, including an excellent Thai restaurant on a walkway between Naladhu and Veli. This means that you're unlikely to get bored with the food, or with the huge amount of activities available. There's free wi-fi at Dhigu's reception area, but elsewhere wireless access is charged.

Olhuveli Beach & Spa
ACTIVITIES RESORT $$

(☑664 2788; www.olhuvelimaldives.com; s/d/wv incl breakfast US$400/435/650; ❋@≊) Olhuveli Beach & Spa is a big upmarket resort that somehow manages to feel very intimate. This is largely due to a stylish post-tsunami refit, which has kept the place looking stylish and smart several years on, and the size of the island, which accommodates its 129 rooms without feeling crowded.

The main market is Italians, followed by Germans and a smattering of Japanese and British visitors. The rooms are spread along beaches in two-level blocks, but are tastefully done, furnished throughout with dark-wood four-poster beds and all featuring balconies or patios that lead straight out to the gorgeous beaches on either side of the island. There are also two rings of swish but rather identikit water bungalows stretching over the lagoon.

Although they're narrow in places, the beaches are attractive, and the wide lagoon is good for sailing and windsurfing, while kitesurfing lessons and equipment are also on offer. Snorkelling is excellent off the end of the jetty, at the edge of the reef, where turtles are common. The dive school runs drift dives in nearby channels, as well as wreck and night dives. Food is excellent, served at the main restaurant buffet, but with several alternatives such as pan-Asian restaurant Four Spices, the poolside Island Pizza and the beachfront Lagoon Restaurant. The Sun Spa offers a huge range of treatments, massage and other therapies, and is a great place for a spot of pampering.

Overall, Olhuveli offers excellent value. It's an great compromise between budget prices and high standards and between romance and activities.

Summer Villa
GUESTHOUSE $

(☑795 4445, 775 5812; www.summervillamaldives. com; Maafushi; s/d incl breakfast US$68/84; ❋☎) This popular guesthouse is situated a couple of blocks back from the port and is a great choice. Run by an enthusiastic team of young locals, Summer Villa organises lots of activities and has a fun and friendly communal vibe. The six rooms are smart and comfortable, and meals are served in the sandy garden.

Arena Lodge
GUESTHOUSE $

(☑798 5142; www.arenalodgemaldives.com; Maafushi; s/d incl breakfast US$72/79; ❋☎) Opening in early 2012 opposite Summer Villa, Arena offers four similar standard rooms with tiled floors and modern bathrooms set in a pleasant house with a sandy courtyard, all tastefully done.

Kandooma
ACTIVITIES RESORT $

(☑664 0511; www.kandooma-maldives.com; r/wv incl breakfast US$336/675; ❋@☎≊⚒) Kandooma, which reopened in 2008 after a long refurbishment that saw the entire place rebuilt following terrible tsunami damage, is a funky, fun resort that feels more like Ibiza or Miami than your typical Maldivian honeymoon bunk hole. The most noticeable feature is the cluster of buildings around reception that from the landing dock look like giant coconuts (apparently they're inspired by barnacles!). Inside, however, the reception area sets the tone for the revamped place – light, bright and with avant-garde light fittings.

The rooms are just as luminous: all white with the odd splash of tropical colour, they are definitely some of the coolest in the country in this price range. We especially love the duplex villas, with a bedroom, bathroom and balcony upstairs and an open-air downstairs sitting room with a sand floor facing the beach. There are 19 very smart water villas too, ideal for romantic sojourns.

There's an impressive COMO Shambhala spa, complimentary wi-fi in the rooms and free PC use above reception. The wide choice of food ranges from excellent buffets in the main restaurant to à la carte dining elsewhere. As the island is on the atoll edge the sea can be very rough and beaches are rocky by local standards, which is where the huge pool comes in handy. Children are well catered for, with a kids club and plenty of activities, including all water sports and a dive school. The local island of Guraidhoo is so close that you can walk to it across the lagoon at low tide.

Overall, this is a young and friendly resort that makes a great choice for people who want all the usual Maldivian treats in a sociable and outgoing atmosphere.

Embudu Village BUDGET RESORT **$**

(☎664 4776; www.embudu.com; full board s/d/tr/wv US$132/232/312/330; ❄@) Embudu Village is a very popular and enduring budget resort with a heavy focus on divers and couples. It's as relaxed as its sand-floor reception suggests, and has lots of thoroughly unpretentious charm. This is a resort where people make friends and socialise without it really being a party island – it's just a friendly and straightforward place. The island has lots of shady trees, some gorgeous beaches and a very accessible house reef.

All accommodation is on a full-board basis, with buffet meals. The standard rooms are fan-cooled, and don't have heated water but are still very acceptable. There are also 16 deluxe over-water bungalows, although budget water bungalows are always something of a letdown – these are bare and functional and you may be disappointed if you're after romance.

The food is decent enough for an inexpensive resort, with a varied selection and fresh fruit and vegetables daily. Entertainment is organised one night per week, but the main attraction is watching the sunset from the casual beach bar.

Diving is popular here, thanks to the very professional **Diverland** (www.diverland.com) and the great dive sites in the area (over 90 different sites are reached on a regular basis). Diving is excellent value and there are discounts for multidive packages. If you're not looking for luxuries but an unpretentious beach and diving holiday, Embudu Village is an excellent and enjoyable resort.

Biyadhoo DIVING RESORT **$**

(☎333 6611; www.biyadhoo.com.mv; full board s/d US$240/280; ❄@) An attractive diving island, Biyadhoo has thick foliage, high palms and lovely beaches in parts. It attracts a crowd of loyal divers, many of whom are repeat visitors and love the good deal it's possible to get here. The in-house dive operation charges guests at the end of their stay for the best overall package based on the number of dives they did, so there's no need to book anything in advance.

However, be aware that at this price, you're getting a no-frills experience. All 96 rooms are standards, housed in 16-room blocks. All have air-con and a minibar, but the rooms are pretty tired, so don't come expecting modernity (mould is visible in some rooms – the management know it's a problem, but they seem to be fighting a losing battle).

Request a room on the west side of the island for beach proximity – beaches on the east side have been badly affected by erosion and as such are not good for sunbathing, often visibly covered in sandbags. While the main beach on the west side is wide and flat, it can feel crowded.

Most people here are on full-board deals, with buffets served up for each meal in the resort's one restaurant. Other facilities include a football pitch, badminton and volleyball facilities, and a spa. The resort has a friendly and relaxed feel and won't disappoint anyone looking for a good base for diving.

Rip Tide Vacation Inn GUESTHOUSE **$**

(☎777 6272; www.guesthouses-in-maldives.com; Guraidhoo; r incl breakfast US$135; ❄📶) The first guesthouse established on Guraidhoo is this seven-room place on the beach facing the resort of Kandooma across a shallow lagoon. The rooms are comfortable with large bathrooms and satellite TV, and there's a pleasant sand-floored restaurant. Wi-fi costs US$5 per day, which adds up and makes this place rather overpriced.

Yellow Rehendi Inn　　　　GUESTHOUSE **$**
(☑974 7006, 974 6655; www.miniconmaldives.com; Maafushi; r incl breakfast US$75; ❄️🛜) Something of a focal point for the island, this busy restaurant right on the harbour also has a four-room guesthouse upstairs. Rooms are on the small side with no windows, but are decently furnished.

White Shell Beach Inn　　　GUESTHOUSE **$**
(☑778 7099; www.thewhiteshell.com; Maafushi; r incl breakfast from US$95; ❄️🛜) The only guesthouse on Maafushi that is actually on the beach, the White Shell offers two types of room, the cheapest of which have no hot water or TV. It's a bit overpriced for what it is (although the rooms are decent) and the beach is rather scrappy, with sandbags blighting the view.

❶ Getting There & Away

Nearly all resorts in South Male Atoll collect their guests from the airport by launch, as even the furthest island is less than an hour away. All the inhabited islands can be reached by ferry from Male's Viligili Ferry Terminal. Ferries go in both directions every day except Friday.

Ari Atoll

Best Places to Stay

» W Retreat & Spa (p86)
» Banyan Tree Madivaru (p86)
» Mirihi (p86)
» Conrad Maldives Rangali Island (p87)
» Kuramathi (p83)

Why Go?

A vast, sumptuously inviting oval lagoon dotted with reefs, Ari Atoll sits to the west of the capital. Like Male Atoll, Ari is known by its traditional name rather than its official name of Alif, a usage we have followed.

While the atoll is one natural entity, it's large enough to have been split into two districts – North and South Ari Atoll. North Ari includes tiny Rasdhoo Atoll and Thoddoo, which aren't naturally part of Ari, but just northeast of it.

Abundant marine life in the atoll creates nutrient-rich water that flows out through channels, attracting large creatures from the open sea and divers from all over the world – South Ari remains one of the best places in the world to see whale sharks, the world's largest fish, which are spotted year-round on the outer reef.

The atoll hosts some of the most famous and exclusive resorts in the country, but its exceptional diving means there are a host of cheaper diving resorts and beach resorts.

Thoddoo

Though administratively part of Ari Atoll, Thoddoo is actually a single, separate, oval island about 20km from the northern edge of the main atoll. It's about 1km across, and has a population of 1400. The principal activity is fishing, but Thoddoo is also known for its market-garden produce (watermelons and betel leaf especially) and its troupe of traditional dancers, who perform in nearby resorts.

Thoddoo is believed to have been occupied since ancient times. A Buddhist temple here contained a Roman coin minted in 90 BC, as well as a silver bowl and a fine stone statue of Buddha, the head of which is now in the National Museum in Male.

To get to Thoddoo, there's a daily ferry from nearby Rasdhoo (Rf20, 1¼ hours), from where it's possible to connect to Male (see p84).

Ari Atoll

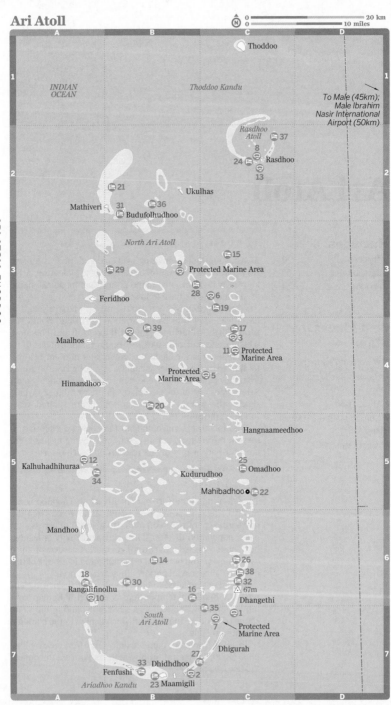

N
0 _____ 20 km
0 _____ 10 miles

Thoddoo

INDIAN
OCEAN

Thoddoo Kandu

To Male (45km);
Male Ibrahim
Nasir International
Airport (50km)

Rasdhoo
Atoll

37

8

24   Rasdhoo

13

Ukulhas

21

Mathiveri   31   36
Budufolhudhoo

North Ari Atoll

15

29   9   Protected Marine Area

28   6

Feridhoo   19

17

3

Maalhos   39   11   Protected
4   Marine Area

Protected   5
Marine Area

Himandhoo

20

Hangnaameedhoo

25

Kalhuhadhihuraa   12   Omadhoo

34   Kudurudhoo

Mahibadhoo 22

Mandhoo

14   26

18   38
30   32
Rangalifinolhu   16   67m
10   Dhangethi

35

South   7
Ari Atoll   Protected
Marine Area

Dhigurah

27   Dhiguraah

33   Dhidhdhoo

Fenfushi   2

Ariadhoo Kandu   23 Maamigili

Ari Atoll

Rasdhoo Atoll

The small atoll of Rasdhoo lies off the northeastern corner of Ari Atoll proper. The atoll's main island, also called **Rasdhoo** (population 850), is the administrative capital of North Ari Atoll, despite not being within the natural atoll itself. Rasdhoo is an attractive little town with a junior secondary school, a health centre, several mosques and a score of souvenir shops – it's often visited as a day trip from the nearby resorts. The island has been settled for many centuries and there are traces here of a Buddhist society predating the arrival of Islam.

 Activities

The medical centre at Kuramathi has a decompression chamber and trained hyperbaric specialists.

Kuramathi House Reef   DIVING
Accessible from the shore, Kuramathi House Reef is good for beginning divers and snorkellers. A small dhoni and a 30m freighter have been sunk off the island to provide an attraction for divers. Sea fans and featherstars decorate the reef wall, and sharks, stingrays and turtles are also frequent visitors.

Rasdhoo Madivaru   DIVING
Also known as Hammerhead Point, Rasdhoo Madivaru is a more demanding dive on an outer reef where hammerhead sharks, mantas and other large pelagics are frequent visitors. Outside this reef the depth drops rapidly to over 200m and the water is exceptionally clear. It's a fine snorkelling site if conditions permit.

🛏 **Sleeping**

Kuramathi   ACTIVITIES RESORT **$$**
(☏666 0527; www.kuramathi.com; full board r/wv from US$470/842; ❄@🛜🌊🏠) Fully renovated in 2009, Kuramathi is now one of the biggest resorts in the country, with 290 rooms. Previously run as three separate resorts for three separate types of visitor, it's now a unified super-resort and continues to offer something for everyone.

The island itself is huge by Maldivian standards, 1.8km long, meaning that it has the luxury of thick vegetation and plenty of undeveloped areas, which makes it perfect for long walks. The beaches are excellent, and there's a gorgeous and improbably long sandbank at one end of the island, which is great for a sunset stroll. Throughout the island signs tell you about the flora and fauna, forming a nature trail through the undergrowth, which is a good touch.

The rooms are what you'd expect from a place at the top of the midrange bracket, all brand new and beautifully furnished in an elegant and understated style with four-poster beds, plenty of wooden furniture, iPod docks and stylish outdoor bathrooms. The nine different categories run from the 45-sq-metre beach villas to the honeymoon pool villas, which check in at an insane 310 sq metres and include their own 10m lap pools.

For dining there's a suitably enormous choice too, though if you're on the simplest full-board option, you'll only eat at the main buffet; if you'd prefer greater variety and à la carte options, opt for a pricier meal plan that will allow you to eat in different places. The restaurants include the Reef seafood restaurant, Thai at Siam Garden, a pizzeria and gelataria, and a popular Indian restaurant, the Tandoor Mahal.

The island's list of activities is enormous – it has a huge and gorgeous spa, several swimming pools, a gym, a dive school, a watersports centre and the excellent Bageecha children's club, which keeps kids under 13 busy with games, treasure hunts, nature walks and other activities all day long. There's also a dedicated Eco Centre, which runs projects such as a hydroponic garden (from which the restaurants' salads come) and has a resident marine biologist monitoring coral growth around the island and educating visitors about what can be seen while diving or snorkelling. There's a popular feeding of giant rays each evening, which shouldn't be missed. Overall the island distinguishes itself with excellent and attentive customer service.

Veligandu ACTIVITIES RESORT $$
(☏666 0519; www.veliganduisland.com; full board r & wv from US$700; ❇@🛜🌊🏊) A charming island fringed with white beaches and featuring a huge 80m sandbank at one end, Veligandu is a great midrange option with good accommodation for its price following a full refit. Rooms are attractive and stylish, and nearly all of them are over water. The Jacuzzi Beach Villas are the lower category and are nestled among the trees on the beach, while the very smart Jacuzzi Water Villas feature outdoor Jacuzzis and semi-open-air bathrooms and have steps down into the lagoon for easy swimming directly from the sun deck. Guests are generally on

full board, although all-inclusive packages are also possible. The main Dhonveli restaurant serves up buffets three times a day, while the à la carte Madivaru restaurant is open in the evenings for a quieter and more romantic dinner.

The island is rightly famous for its great beaches and is located on a beautiful lagoon within Rasdhoo. There are a couple of excellent dive sites nearby, with hammerhead shark sightings very common. The Swiss-run **Ocean-Pro dive base** (www.oceanpro-diveteam. com) charges reasonably. The edge of the house reef is not very accessible and is not great for snorkelling, so most diving and snorkelling is done by boat at a wide range of nearby sites. Overall this is a popular and smart midrange resort with superb beaches and comfortable over-water accommodation.

❶ Getting There & Away

Guests at resorts in Rasdhoo arrive by Trans Maldivian Airways seaplane charters from Male airport. There's a ferry from Male to Rasdhoo every Sunday, Tuesday and Thursday (Rf50, three hours 10 minutes), while the same boat makes the trip in the opposite direction every Saturday, Monday and Wednesday. Rasdhoo is also connected by daily ferries to Thoddoo (Rf20, 1¼ hours) and to Ukulhas (Rf20, one hour) in Ari Atoll.

Ari Atoll

The geographic entity of Ari Atoll (as opposed to the administrative regions of North and South Ari) is about 80km from north to south and 30km wide and contains 18 inhabited islands out of a total of 81. The most populous island is **Mahibadhoo**, the capital of South Ari, with some 2000 people. Fishing and fish processing are the main industries – there's a cold storage and processing plant here. There is now a guesthouse on Mahibadhoo and several more in the planning and building stages.

Other inhabited islands, typically with a population of a few hundred, are dotted around the edges of the atoll. Quite a few islands have ruins or artefacts of ancient Buddhist and Hindu settlements.

Maamigili, in the south of the atoll, has over 1600 people, many of whom work in nearby resorts, or in tourist shops that cater to island-hopping visitors. There's a new airstrip here and Villa Air runs daily flights from Male several times a day.

The island of **Fenfushi** (population 825), on the southwest corner of the atoll, is noted for coral carving.

◉ Activities

All of the resorts have diving operations and Ari is a top pick for those who love underwater activities, being the best place in the Maldives to see large pelagics such as hammerheads and whale sharks. The following is a brief description of some well-known sites (from north to south), to give an idea of the possibilities.

Maaya Thila   DIVING
Maaya Thila is a classic round thila known for the white-tip reef sharks that circle it. Caves and overhangs around the thila have lots of gorgonians, soft corals and schools of reef fish. It's a Protected Marine Area.

Halaveli Wreck   DIVING
The well-known Halaveli Wreck was created in 1991 when a 38m cargo ship was deliberately sunk. It's famous for the friendly stingrays enticed here by regular feeding – keep your fingers away from their mouths.

Fesdu Wreck   DIVING
Fesdu Wreck is a 30m trawler with a good covering of corals at a depth of 18m to 30m. Moray eels and grouper live inside the hull, which is easily entered and has good growths of soft corals and sponges. Divers can also check the adjacent thila, which has hard and soft corals as well as lots of fish.

Ellaidhoo House Reef   DIVING
Only accessible to Ellaidhoo's guests, the excellent Ellaidhoo House Reef has a long wall just 25m from the beach. It has a row of caves with sea fans, whip corals, schools of bannerfish, Napoleons, stingrays and morays, and even a small wreck. This reef is popular with night divers.

Orimas Thila   DIVING
Overhangs, caves, crevices, canyons and coral heads make Orimas Thila an exciting dive. Marine life includes good growths of soft corals, sea fans, anemones and clown fish. The top of the thila is only 3m down, and can be easily enjoyed by snorkellers if the conditions are calm. It is a Protected Marine Area.

Fish Head   DIVING
Also called Mushimasmingali Thila, Fish Head is one of the world's most famous dive sites. Its steep sides are spectacular, with multi-level ledges, overhangs and caves supporting many sea fans and black corals; its top is heavily encrusted with anemones. Beware of stonefish. The prolific fish life at this Protected Marine Area includes fusiliers, large Napoleons, trevally and schools of hungry barracuda. The main attractions, however, are the numerous grey-tip reef sharks, which can be seen up close. Strong currents can make this a demanding dive, and extreme care should be taken not to damage the superb but heavily used site.

Panetone   DIVING
The north side of Kalhuhadhihuraa Faru is subject to strong currents, so the caves and overhangs of Panetone are thick with soft coral growth. As well as the many reef fish, there are giant trevally, sharks, barracuda and turtles. From December to April, mantas feed around the outside of the channel; March to November are the best months to see sharks. There's excellent snorkelling in light currents.

Manta Reef   DIVING
Also called Madivaru, Manta Reef is at the end of a channel where powerful currents carry plankton out of the atoll during the northeast monsoon (December to April) – fast food for manta rays. Mantas also come to be cleaned. Reef fish include Napoleon wrasse, snapper and parrotfish, while pelagics such as turtles, tuna and sharks visit the outer reef slope. It's for advanced divers only, and is great for snorkellers in the right conditions.

Kudarah Thila   DIVING
Kudarah Thila is a very demanding but exciting dive – if there is a current running, this is strictly for experienced divers. There are gorgonians, whip corals, black corals and a whole field of sea fans swaying in the current, surrounded by sharks and trevally from the open sea. In the gaps between large coral blocks, bluestriped snapper, tallfin, batfish, goby and other unusual small fish can be seen. It's a Protected Marine Area.

Broken Rock   DIVING
In the mouth of the Dhigurashu Kandu, Broken Rock is bisected by a canyon up to 10m deep and only 1m to 3m wide. Swimming through the 50m canyon is unforgettable, but extreme care is needed not to damage the coral formations on either side. Rock formations around the thila are decorated with sea fans and superb corals, and are inhabited by abundant marine life.

Dhidhdhoo Beyru DIVING
From May to September, whale sharks cruise almost continually along the 10km-long Dhidhdhoo Beyru on the southwestern edge of the atoll, which extends from Ariyadhoo Kandu north to the tip of Dhigurah island. However, even out of season there are consistent whale shark sightings here, which increase during a full moon when the currents become faster.

🛏 Sleeping

While some resorts nearer to Male operate speedboat transfers to and from the airport, the majority of resorts use seaplane transfers due to the distances involved. These take anything from 20 to 45 minutes, and are more expensive than speedboat transfers. Bear in mind that seaplanes do not fly at night. If you arrive after 4pm at Male airport, you'll have to stopover in Male until the next morning for your seaplane transfer.

TOP CHOICE W Retreat & Spa LUXURY RESORT **$$$**
(✆666 2222; www.wretreatmaldives.com; r/wv incl breakfast US$1400/1825; ❄@🛜🌊) W Retreat & Spa, in the middle of Ari Atoll, is sleek and imaginative, a boutique luxury venture loaded with more cool than any other in the country. W manages to get it right on all levels – staff are informal and friendly, the reception area is so efficient you'll rarely see anyone even needing to be there and the resort itself is stunning.

To start with, tiny Fesdhoo island is gorgeous, with some lovely beaches and a great house reef packed with turtles, rays and reef sharks. On the island itself are the standard rooms – and even in the starting categories they're wonderful – each with its own private plunge pool and, perhaps their most charming feature, a thatched-roof 'viewing deck' above the room, complete with daybeds. Higher categories are over water, culminating in four vast suites that would satisfy even the most demanding Saudi prince. All rooms are staggeringly cool, with clean lines, Bose surround-sound system and huge private terraces.

The activities and facilities are just as good – from free nonmotorised water sports and an excellent diving school to a superb spa that looks a world away from any other in the Maldives. It also has a nightclub (one of the few in the country and definitely the best looking), which is open three times a week and comes with a dangerously wide-ranging vodka collection. Add to this three excellent restaurants, three glamorous bars, a vast swimming pool and even a private desert island for guests to use, and it's easy to see why this is the choice of the discerning, wealthy cool.

Banyan Tree Madivaru LUXURY RESORT **$$$**
(✆666 0760; www.banyantree.com; r incl breakfast US$3520; ❄🛜🌊) Banyan Tree Madivaru is the second venture for the famous luxury chain in the Maldives. This latest addition to the crowded top end of the hotel market is a beautiful but thoroughly simple concept that works extremely well.

Beyrumadivaru island is tiny even by local standards and here Banyan Tree has created a mini-resort that manages to combine simplicity with luxury. The six residences on the island are 'tented pool villas', large, beautifully appointed collections of three tents, all with timber floors, wooden furniture and gorgeous design features, surrounding a large private swimming pool. Other features include an outdoor shower, a vast indoor bathroom and even two twin beds for receiving spa treatments in your own room.

With fleets of staff hidden away far from your eye line in the island's thick foliage, you'll want for nothing. For those who actually wish to leave their tented villa for food (in-villa dining is the norm here) there's a choice of sandbank dining, the main restaurant, Boa Keyo, or the Madi 'Dining Experience', which is dinner on a yacht that sails around nearby islands. Diving (with a choice of excellent local sites) can be arranged, as well as almost any excursion or activity. Overall this a great place for a trip-of-a-lifetime romantic escape and complete luxury.

Mirihi LUXURY RESORT **$$$**
(✆668 0500; www.mirihi.com; s/d/tr/wv incl breakfast US$960/1000/1380/1035; ❄@🛜) Tiny Mirihi seems to go from strength to strength if rave traveller feedback is anything to go by. This gem of a resort takes its name from the yellow flower that grows around the island, and its philosophy is keeping it simple and natural. The wonderful beach that rings the thick vegetation in the centre of the island and the fantastic house reef beyond are both first class. Redeveloped in classy, contemporary style, Mirihi is a tiny island, but 30 of the rooms are built over the water, so it's not too crowded – in fact, if anything, it feels positively spacious.

The beach villas have eye-catching decor, polished timber finishes, white linen furnishings, rich red and brown accents and every amenity, including a CD player, TV and espresso machine. The over-water rooms have all this plus water views and very private sun decks. The main restaurant presents a lavish gourmet buffet for nearly every meal, usually eaten on a sun deck or on the sand. Some nights feature à la carte specials or theme dinners.

The main buffet is a sand-floor affair with excellent food and attentive staff. The other option is the romantic Muraka restaurant, on a jetty over the water, which specialises in grills and seafood and is a great place for romantic sunset drinks.

In addition, it has a gym, a small spa, and activities such as board games, windsurfing and kayaking. Divers come here for access to sites all over South Ari Atoll. The Ocean-Pro dive centre (www.oceanpro-diveteam.com) charges US$52 per dive without equipment and a package of 10 dives with all equipment is US$660. Free wi-fi ensures you're never out of touch with the world, even though most guests spend their days here barefoot and phoneless. Overall Mirihi is remarkable for making the most of a small island without overdeveloping it. It's equally attractive as a stylish luxury resort, a rustic romantic retreat or a top-end dive island.

Conrad Maldives
Rangali Island   LUXURY RESORT $$$

(📞666 0629; conradhotels3.hilton.com; r/wv incl breakfast US$1640/2510; ✳@☎✍⛱) Sumptuous barefoot luxury is the name of the game at the Conrad Maldives Rangali Island, the Hilton Group's long-standing Maldivian resort, which was rebranded into a Conrad, one of the groups most exclusive brands, in 2007. Famous throughout the Maldives for its incredible undersea restaurant, Conrad Maldives is an excellent choice for couples and families wanting to escape in style.

The property occupies two islands connected by walkway across a broad lagoon, a charming touch that gives you a large choice of beaches (all superb) and plenty of space. The heart of the resort, with the main lobby, restaurants, bars, water sports, dive centres and 100 beach villas, is on Rangalifinolhu; on the second island, Rangali, which is only for adults, there are two other restaurants plus a bar, a separate reception area, and 50 water villas in their very own class of exclusivity.

The rooms are varied and beautifully conceived in all 11 categories; with even the standard beach villas checking in at an incredible 150 sq metres. All rooms have outdoor terraces and outdoor bathrooms as well as sea views from the bath. The spectacular water villas all enjoy their own private terraces, gorgeous wooden interiors and, in the more luxurious ones, glass floors.

With seven restaurants running the whole gamut of cuisines from local Maldivian to Japanese and European, you have plenty of choice. Most amazing, of course, is the Ithaa Undersea Restaurant, where diners eat in a glass-domed restaurant underwater, an experience quite unlike any other in the country. There's also a resident sommelier whose climate-controlled cave contains some 5000 bottles of selected wines. There are four bars at the resort, so you'll be in no danger of going dry.

Diving, water sports, excursions, a fantastic kids club and light entertainment are all on offer, as are three spas (including one exclusively for children!). But the real attraction at the Conrad is the unobtrusive, efficient and friendly service and the incredible selection of food and wine.

Centara Grand Island
Resort & Spa Maldives   ACTIVITIES RESORT $$$

(📞668 8000; www.centarahotelsresorts.com; r/wv incl breakfast US$1500/1600; ✳@☎✍⛱) This newly remodelled place is a very good all-round resort from the Thai Centara Group. Its 112 suites and villas offer a great choice for everyone from couples to families and it's particularly child-friendly, with an ethos of welcoming families that extends far beyond the kids club and daily children's activities on offer.

Gorgeous beaches can be found all around the island, while rooms are stylishly modern in decor with grand country-club style and anonymously smart furniture. The two-storey water villas are particularly great, with their two sundecks and thatched roofs overlooking the lagoon.

The resort has all the amenities you'd expect at this price: a good pool, three restaurants (Thai and Italian à la carte places supplement the excellent and varied buffet where most guests eat), a dive school, a water-sports centre, a gym, a great spa and plenty of excursions. This is a top choice for a smart, family holiday where everyone will have plenty of options for how to spend their days.

LUX* Maldives
LUXURY RESORT $$

(☑668 0901; www.luxislandresorts.com; r/wv incl breakfast from US$727/1092; ❄@🛜🌊🏊) This beautiful and large island is a solid top-end choice where stylish, largely over-water rooms complement an already stunning island. At 2km long the island is one of the bigger ones in the Maldives, but the resort doesn't feel too big, and is still very manageable on foot.

Rooms range from beach pavilions, which at 65 sq metres are a good size, and go up to a giant 360 sq metre LUX* villa. There is a large set of water villas on each side of the island, both quite some distance from the island itself, which can either make you feel like you have a long walk to the main restaurant, or that you're lucky enough to enjoy some seclusion. Water villas do not have plunge pools, but the cheaper beach pool villas do, which makes them good value for money. All rooms have the usual luxuries you'd expect at this level, including DVD players, wi-fi and outdoor showers. The rest of the island is equally well equipped for entertainment and activities, featuring no less than seven restaurants, multiple bars, a great spa, a PADI five-star diving school, a full water-sports centre and the usual host of excursions.

The island enjoys luscious vegetation and long white sandy beaches that won't disappoint even the most demanding Maldivian old hand. The lagoon is wide on all sides, and a good place to learn windsurfing or catamaran sailing. There's no snorkelling to be had from the shore: take one of the free boat trips to the reef edge – these go every afternoon. The island has always been popular with divers, especially for the whale sharks that cruise the outside edge of the atoll here from May to November, and the mantas on the west side of the atoll from December to May, and many guests are here to enjoy the high standard of sites on offer combined with luxurious accommodation and high-quality drinking and dining.

Chaaya Reef Ellaidhoo
DIVING RESORT $

(☑666 0669; www.chaayahotels.com; r/wv incl breakfast from US$220/380; ❄@🛜🌊) Chaaya Reef Ellaidhoo has a reputation as the most hard-core diving destination in the Maldives, with over 100 dive sites within a half-day trip. It has what many consider to be the country's finest house reef (quite an accolade given the competition!), with a 750m wall, lots of caves, corals, rich marine life (turtles, sharks, mantas and eagle rays) and even a small shipwreck.

Indeed, it's hard to choose a better base for divers, not least since a 2008 refit by the Chaaya Hotel group, which has seen smart villa-style accommodation and large two-storey water bungalows on the lagoon replace the older, budget rooms. Yet despite this, prices have remained comfortably low.

The island isn't the most picturesque in the country by a long shot, with a fairly small beach, but it offers enough of an all-round holiday to attract non-divers as well as divers, and the friendly staff consistently get rave reviews.

Angaga
DIVING RESORT $

(☑666 0510; www.angaga.com.mv; half board r/wv US$290/390; ❄@) Angaga was Ari Atoll's first resort and has been operating since 1989. It's a gorgeous and obvious-choice island, fringed by amazing, wide and white beaches and with a superb house reef for snorkelling. The thatch-roofed bungalows, with a traditional *undholi* (swing seat) at the front and rustic furnishing inside, show a little more character than many of the midrange resorts available, while the 20 newer water villas, complete with glass walls and private sun decks, are good for this price range.

The spacious sand-floored bar and restaurant serves up large but medium-quality buffets and is the only eating option. All-inclusive deals are popular and ensure that there's always a crowd enjoying the house beer and wine. Most guests are here to dive, snorkel and enjoy the beaches, though, and there's a good-value dive school as well as water sports and excursions on offer, making this a great budget choice for those wanting to enjoy both beach and reef in unfussy surroundings.

Madoogali
ACTIVITIES RESORT $$

(☑332 7443; www.madoogalimaldives.com; half board s/d US$522/533; ❄@) An almost implausibly perfect island, Madoogali is richly verdant, has gorgeous beaches all the way around its circular shore and is set on a stunning lagoon. The ethos here is rustic Maldivian relaxation – the coral-walled architecture with thatched roofs and wooden interiors may have air-con, but that's one of the few concessions to the modern world. There are no fancy features such as water villas or private pools here (in fact, there's not even a communal swimming pool!), just the beaches and perfect tranquillity.

However, as the vast majority of guests are Italian, you can expect to feel a little left out if you're not an Italian speaker yourself. That said, the house reef is excellent for snorkelling, and as Madoogali is the only resort in this part of the atoll, there is easy access to lots of little-used dive sites. The dive centre charges reasonable rates.

Vilamendhoo
ACTIVITIES RESORT **$$**

(☑644 4487; www.vilamendhooisland.com; full board r from US$310; ✳@☎☒) Vilamendhoo is a very lush, well-vegetated island that offers a solid midmarket experience to visitors who usually come on all-inclusive deals. The beaches are narrow around most of the island, but there's a big sandy area at one end, or both ends, depending on the season. The house reef is particularly good for snorkelling, and marked channels make it easy to reach the reef edge. The whole place can feel rather crowded, especially since a recent renovation has added some water villas, meaning that there are even more guests on the island.

The rooms are divided into four categories; all are spacious, clean and comfortable, with a toupee of thatch as a concession to natural style. There are two buffets where most all-inclusive guests eat, but also the choice of several other à la carte restaurants open to all (which cost extra). The main bar is the heart of the resort, and the guests on all-inclusive packages make sure it keeps beating. There are over 40 accessible dive sites in the area, including some of the very best in the Maldives. For non-divers there are numerous excursions, a tennis court, spa, windsurfing and water sports.

Velidhu Island Resort
DIVING RESORT **$$**

(☑666 0595; www.velidhu.com.mv; half board r/wv US$435/590; ✳@☎) Velidhu Island Resort is a sizeable island with some great beaches and a good house reef. While its architecture is not stunning, the rooms are fine, despite ordinary, rather tired interiors. The newer water bungalows have charming conical thatch roofs and are much better. The island is delightfully simple – what most guests here want – with no pool and just one restaurant and bar for the entire island.

The **Euro-Divers dive centre** (www.eurodivers.com) is very professional and enthusiastic about the diving in this part of the atoll. A single reef dive is US$52 with tank and weights, making it a reasonable deal. Even better is the 10-dives package for US$440. Velidhu is a good choice for keen divers who are not looking for luxury, and its low-season prices can be great value.

Nika Island
RUSTIC RESORT **$$**

(☑666 0515; www.nikaisland.com.mv; full board r/wv US$685/820; ✳@☎) Nika Island is a majority Italian and Russian resort and one whose innovative approach to environmentally friendly and back-to-nature tourism has influenced resorts throughout the country. While Nika is now booked exclusively by a Milanese company, there is still an international clientele here, many of whom have been regulars since the 1980s.

Individual villas are spacious and imaginatively designed in a seashell shape, with thatched roofs and handcrafted timber furniture, although they can be rather dark inside. Each villa has a private garden and its own private slice of the island's plentiful beach, a novel idea that we've not seen elsewhere in the Maldives. The concept is also genuinely ecofriendly, with no pool and no air-conditioning outside some of the bedrooms – just the sea and natural ventilation through wooden louvre windows. The effect

ALSO IN ARI ATOLL

Constance Halaveli Resort (www.halaveli.constancehotels.com) A high-end Constance 'six-star' property following a long closure and a total refit. The resort boasts a great spa, sumptuous rooms and beautiful white beaches.

Ranveli Beach Resort (www.ranvelivillage.com) A rather crowded, Italian-flavoured resort with great diving and snorkelling and some cracking beaches.

Thudufushi (www.thudufushibeach.diamonds-resorts.com) A fully refurbished Italian-flavoured resort, Thudufushi is not unlike its sister island Diamonds Athuruga in offering smart, midrange all-inclusive accommodation, a great beach and lots of activities.

Vakarufalhi Island Resort (www.vakaru.com) Following a total refurbishment that has brought it into a higher category of resort with the addition of smart water bungalows, this place is popular mainly with Italian and Chinese travellers.

is that it looks spookily like a traditional Maldivian fishing village populated by well-heeled Europeans. Water villas are a later addition and are innovatively designed over three split levels.

The average meals are Italian/international style and are served in the sand-floored dining room or outside on a seaside deck.

Dive costs here are higher than at other resorts, but groups are small and the attention is personal. Fishing, windsurfing, tennis and most other activities are included.

Diamonds Athuruga
Beach & Water Villas   ACTIVITIES RESORT $$

(☏666 0508; www.planhotel.com; all-inclusive r/wv from US$620/925; ❄@🖥) Athuruga is one of two Planhotel properties in Ari Atoll (Thudufushi is the other one). It's an all-inclusive resort, including most drinks, excursions and nonmotorised water sports in the daily rate, and following a recent renovation is now an upmarket midrange resort with lots of white, minimalist fittings across the island.

The rooms are spacious and comfortable, and those on the island face the superb beach. The 25 water villas are sumptuous, enjoy wonderful views and are furnished strikingly all in white. The house reef offers easy snorkelling and a lot to see, and there are some good dive sites nearby, though it's an hour by boat to the exciting dives on the western rim of the atoll. There are three restaurants, a gorgeous rustic-style spa and perfect beaches.

Gangehi Island Resort   RUSTIC RESORT $$

(☏666 0505; www.gangehi.com; full board s/d/wv US$490/600/760; ❄@🖥🏊) Gangehi Island Resort is an intimate, upmarket Italian-oriented resort that nevertheless delights its non-Italian guests with its warm service, good food, superb beaches and waters teeming with marine life. Following a total renovation in 2008, the place is looking excellent, with eight new deluxe water villas to complement the older eight.

The new-look rooms combine rustic wooden exteriors with sleek and contemporary style and Asian furnishings. Stays are all full board here and the Veli buffet restaurant, where most people eat, is supplemented by the à la carte over-water Thari Restaurant. Other new additions include a beautiful new spa, where the treatments are carried out in 19th-century Keralan style, a brand new dive school and a new gym.

The island is pretty, with lots of palm trees, but unfortunately has suffered from sand movements, so the seafront rooms have very limited beaches and the over-water villas are sometimes surrounded by a sandbar. This is a great choice for a relaxed, upmarket resort with excellent diving nearby.

Lily Beach Resort   ALL-INCLUSIVE RESORT $$$

(☏666 0013; www.lilybeachmaldives.com; all-inclusive d/wv from US$989/1824; ❄@🖥🏊) After a total refit in 2009, Lily Beach Resort reopened with a brand new concept: an upscale all-inclusive resort. This was a first for the Maldives and it has proved exceptionally popular in a destination where the 'extras' at a resort can quickly add up to rival the amount you paid for your accommodation.

Here guests pay for few or no extras, as everything is included in the 'platinum plan' – from unlimited cocktails (with brand-name spirits, no cheapo versions) to free snorkelling, excursions and even (weirdly) free cigarettes. It's a recipe that has worked well, and as with any all-inclusive resort, it attracts people looking for a good time who are going to use the facilities and enjoy the supplies of food and alcohol to the max.

The rooms come in five categories and are all very smart, ranging from the beach villas at 68 sq metres to the sunset water suite at 182 sq metres. The style is modern, sleek and perhaps rather anonymous, but the rooms are spacious and extremely comfortable. As well as the main Lily Maa open-air restaurant on the lagoon, there's a fine dining à la carte restaurant, Tamarind, which serves Chinese and Indian cuisine and at which all guests are entitled to have one meal per week. As with most all-inclusive places, the numerous bars are the centre of resort life, and all three bars here are busy all day long.

The house reef is very good, with turtles commonly spotted and easily accessible for snorkelling. Diving costs extra, and is very popular, with a number of superb diving sites nearby. It also has a spa, where all treatments are extra, and free wi-fi across the island. If you're looking for an upscale yet affordable activities holiday, this is a great option.

Kuri Inn   GUESTHOUSE $

(☏753 3737; www.kuriinn.com; Omadhoo; all-inclusive r US$120; ❄🖥) This sweet four-room guesthouse on the charming fishing island of Omadhoo, just north of South Ari's capital, Mahibadhoo, is one of the few places to stay independently on an inhabited island in this most popular of atolls. Each simple but comfortable and modern room has its own private bathroom, and the house has its own common areas where guests can relax and socialise. The enthusiastic and young team keep the activities coming – snorkelling, island hopping, beach barbecues, big-game fishing and water sports are organised daily. Highly recommended for a slice of real island life.

Goby Lodge
GUESTHOUSE $

(☎778 7073; www.gobylodge.com; Mahibadhoo; full board s/d US$88/114; ✹🛜) The only guesthouse located on South Ari's capital, Manhibadhoo, this is a great place to stay to see some local provincial life, while still being able to partake in all the activities that you'd associate with an independent trip around the Maldives. The modern rooms are comfortable and spacious, each with their own private bathroom and twin beds. The team here keeps visitors occupied with trips to local islands, as well as fishing, snorkelling and diving trips.

Sun Island
ACTIVITIES RESORT $$

(☎666 0088; www.villahotels.com; half board r/wv from US$375/550; ✹@✹) Sun Island is the largest resort in the country, and while it will appeal to anyone wanting lots of activities and plenty of socialising, it's no place for re-enacting Robinson Crusoe fantasies.

The rooms themselves are large and have decent indoor-outdoor bathrooms, bidets and minibars. Everything is very modern, although it's hardly cutting-edge style.

The Sun Island Diving School is quite a big operation, with reasonable prices. Most dives are done at nearby sites, and groups can be pretty big. Snorkelling isn't really possible here; you'll have to take a special trip to nearby reefs. The lagoon is wide, and good for swimming and water sports, however.

If you want an activities-packed holiday with endless choices, Sun is a good option. There are multiple bars, five restaurants, and the fullest possible choice of water sports, diving, spa treatments, excursions and sports (including a putting green and tennis court), a video arcade and a good gym.

Holiday Island
ACTIVITIES RESORT $$

(☎668 0011; www.villahotels.com; half board s/d/tr US$364/372/495; ✹@🛜✹) Villa Hotels has a habit of giving its resorts such corny names that they seem half before you even arrive, which is a real pity, as Holiday Island is beautiful. Wide beaches, lush vegetation and a gorgeous lagoon make this every bit the picture-perfect Maldivian island. Like most of Villa Hotels' places this is a mid-level resort. The accommodation is basic despite consistent attempts to upgrade the mustier rooms, without ever undertaking a full refurbishment. Perhaps more of a gripe is that the whole place can feel rather crowded; indeed, the main buffet restaurant at dinnertime is quite a sight to behold!

The rooms are in blocks of two (some with interconnecting doors for families), surrounded by little gardens and fitted out with TV and hot water. Meal selection can be limited, but the quality is generally OK. The entire place is geared towards people who want to have fun, meet others and party. It's certainly not a place to escape from life and the omnipresent loud music may annoy you unless you're looking for it.

Recreational activities such as table tennis, badminton, billiards, tennis and use of the gym are free, while windsurfing, catamaran sailing and motorised water sports are extra. The beaches are lovely around most of the island, but snorkelling is not good in the lagoon, and boat trips out to the reef edge and beyond are also charged as an extra. Diving is well catered for by the Villa Diving dive school; there are lots of good dive sites around and costs are average to low. Holiday Island is quite pricey for the quality of its accommodation and meals. However, its great beaches and plentiful activities will appeal to families and anyone wanting an action-packed break.

Maayafushi
DIVING RESORT $

(☎666 0588; maaya@dhivehinet.net.mv; full board r from US$260; ✹@) Maayafushi is a largely Italian resort that offers good-value diving holidays and plenty of fun courtesy of an enthusiastic team that gets guests busy with daily activities, evening shows and the like.

The island is small and quite intensively developed, but is ringed by perfect sandy beaches and has a beautiful house reef. Rooms all have the basic furnishings and some enjoy beach frontage, but none are more special or functional than the others.

As well as the majority of Italians, most of the guests are divers from Germany, Switzerland or Austria, nearly all of whom are here to dive or to simply relax on the beach. The dive school is cheap and the choice of sites is excellent. Night dives are available and trips to the famous Maaya Thila dive site are very popular and a great way to see sharks.

ARI ATOLL ARI ATOLL

If good food is a priority, then Maayafushi isn't the right resort for you. Like most cheap diving resorts, the buffets here are simple and can be repetitive after a few days. Think lots of pasta, instant coffee and little variety in the vegetables available.

Maayafushi can only be booked through tour operators (it doesn't even have its own website!), so it's not a great option for independent travellers. However, if cheap and cheerful diving and a good beach is what you seek, you'll be happy here.

ⓘ Getting There & Away

Nearly all resorts in Ari Atoll fly in their guests direct, using seaplane charters from Maldivian Air Taxi and Trans Maldivian Airways. A small private airport on the island of Maamigili is served by several Villa Air flights a day from Male airport, which can work out cheaper than seaplane transfers and is a popular way to reach some nearby resorts.

For independent travellers, there are regular ferry connections from Male's Viligili Ferry Terminal to the South Ari capital of Mahibadhoo (Rf50, 4¼ hours), which continue to Maamigili (Rf50, seven hours). These leave Male at 9am on Saturday, Monday and Wednesday and return from Maamigili and Mahibadhoo on Sunday, Tuesday and Thursday. There's also another inter-atoll ferry service connecting Male to Ukulhas (Rf50, 4½ hours) in North Ari, which leaves Male at 9am on Sunday, Tuesday and Thursday, returning from Ukulhas at 10.30am on Saturday, Monday and Wednesday.

ⓘ Getting Around

The 18 inhabited islands of Ari Atoll are connected to each other by a number of daily ferries. Route 304 connects Ukulhas to Himandhoo via all the inhabited islands along the atoll edge in North Ari. Route 306 connects Mandhoo to Mahibadhoo and the other islands along the eastern atoll edge in South Ari. Finally, Route 307 connects Mahibadhoo to all the inhabited island in the south of South Ari Atoll, going as far as Fenfushi.

Northern Atolls

Includes »

Best Places to Stay

» Four Seasons Landaa Giraavaru (p101)

» Soneva Fushi (p102)

» Waldorf Astoria Maldives (p95)

» Dusit Thani Maldives (p102)

» Asseyri Tourist Inn (p97)

Why Go?

The least developed region of the Maldives, the northern atolls remain almost unknown to foreigners, and that makes them a great place to experience untouched, traditional Maldivian life. Maldivian history owes much to this part of the country – national hero Mohammed Thakurufaanu, the man who drove the Portuguese out of the Maldives in the 16th century, was born on the island of Utheemu in Haa Alifu Atoll. The island is today a place of pilgrimage for Maldivians, who come to see his small wooden 'palace'.

There's also huge diving potential throughout the region; there are wrecks along the western fringe of the atolls, many only now being properly explored and documented. Anyone lucky enough to visit can expect to have the place pretty much to themselves. With just a handful of resorts (including some of the country's most exclusive), the northern atolls are a great destination for escape and solitude.

Haa Alifu

Traditionally known as Ihavandhippolhu and North Thiladhunmathee Atolls, the very northern tip of the Maldives is generally known to one and all as Haa Alifu Atoll, even though this refers to an administrative district that actually comprises the small, trapezoid-shaped Ihavandhippolhu Atoll and the northern tip of North Thiladhunmathee Atoll.

Haa Alifu contains the island of Utheemu (population 900), by far the most interesting and historic island in the Northern Atolls, if not the entire country. The birthplace of Sultan Mohammed Thakurufaanu, who, with his brothers, overthrew Portuguese rule in 1573, the island is centred around a memorial to this Maldivian hero, with a small museum and library, opened in 1986. Thakurufaanu's well-preserved wooden palace has been restored and Utheemu is a popular destination for Maldivians paying homage to their national hero. Visitors are escorted around the small complex by a member of staff from the museum (admission Rf 25;

Northern Atolls

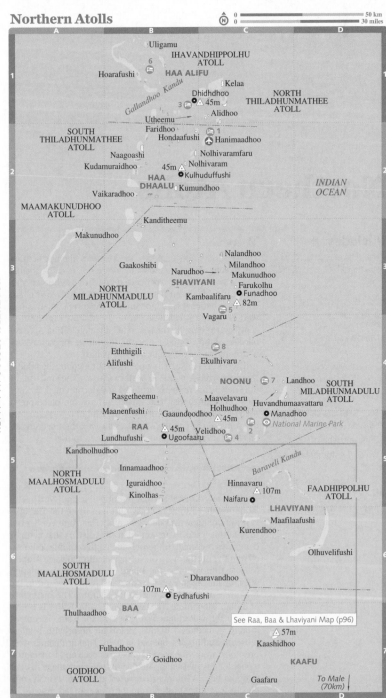

0   50 km
0   30 miles

Uligamu

IHAVANDHIPPOLHU ATOLL

HAA ALIFU

Hoarafushi

Gallandhoo Kandu

Kelaa

NORTH THILADHUNMATHEE ATOLL

Dhidhdhoo
45m
Alidhoo

Utheemu

Faridhoo

SOUTH THILADHUNMATHEE ATOLL

Hondaafushi
Hanimaadhoo

Nolhivaramfaru

Naagoashi

Kudamuraidhoo
45m
Nolhivaram

Kulhuduffushi

HAA DHAALU

Vaikaradhoo
Kumundhoo

INDIAN OCEAN

MAAMAKUNUDHOO ATOLL

Kanditheemu

Makunudhoo

Nalandhoo
Milandhoo

Gaakoshibi
Narudhoo
Makunudhoo

SHAVIYANI

Farukolhu

NORTH MILADHUNMADULU ATOLL

Kambaalifaru
Funadhoo
82m

5
Vagaru

8

Eththigili
Ekulhivaru

Alifushi

NOONU
7
Landhoo

SOUTH MILADHUNMADULU ATOLL

Rasgetheemu

Maavelavaru
Holhudhoo
Huvandhumaavattaru

Maanenfushi
Gaaundoodhoo
45m
Manadhoo

RAA
45m
Velidhoo
National Marine Park

Lundhufushi
Ugoofaaru
4

Kandholhudhoo

Baraveli Kandu

NORTH MAALHOSMADULU ATOLL

Innamaadhoo
Iguraidhoo
Kinolhas

Hinnavaru
107m

FAADHIPPOLHU ATOLL

Naifaru

LHAVIYANI

Maafilaafushi

Kurendhoo

Olhuvelifushi

SOUTH MAALHOSMADULU ATOLL

Dharavandhoo

107m
Eydhafushi

Thulhaadhoo

BAA

See Raa, Baa & Lhaviyani Map (p96)

57m
Kaashidhoo

Fulhadhoo
Goidhoo

KAAFU

GOIDHOO ATOLL

Gaafaru

To Male (70km)

Northern Atolls

🕙 Sun-Thu) and are able to see the fascinating 500-year-old wooden interiors, including swing beds (used to keep cool in the heat), lamps that burn coco palm oil, elaborate wooden carvings and a large palm-thatch shed used as a sleeping room. Elsewhere on the island is the Kandhuvalu Mosque, a short walk beyond the palace. It's a tiny place with a beautiful teak interior that can be glimpsed from the entrance, as entering is not possible for non-Muslims. There's a gorgeous beach here, and a guesthouse is planned.

Elsewhere in the atoll, the capital island is **Dhidhdhoo** (population 4500), which offers good anchorage for passing yachts. **Hoarafushi**, the next largest island (population 2780), is noted for its music and dancing. **Kelaa** (population 2205) was the northern British base during WWII, mirroring Gan at the other end of the archipelago. The mosque here dates from the end of the 17th century.

At the very top of Haa Alifu, **Uligamu** (population 490) is the 'clear-in' port for private yachts – it has health and immigration officers, so yachts are able to complete all formalities here (see p179).

🛏 Sleeping

If you're arriving in the Maldives after a long-haul flight, bear in mind that selecting a resort in the far north of the country will add on at least two hours to your journey each way – often even more, depending on flight timings. This can come as a shock to travellers, so be prepared.

Waldorf Astoria Maldives   LUXURY RESORT **$$$**
(📞650 0400; www.waldorfastoria.com; r/wv incl breakfast US$1298/1182; ✴@🤖☀️👶) The most northerly resort in the country, Waldorf Astoria is an exclusive place that now rubs shoulders with the very best hotels in the country. Part of the Hilton group, it's often combined with one or both of the brand's other Maldivian resorts, though this resort is the top of the pile.

The island itself is gorgeous, with superb soft, white-sand beaches all around, thick vegetation and dazzling turquoise waters. The rooms are stylishly designed, albeit in an anonymous international style, with the starting category alone being an enormous 152 sq metres, going up to the 693-sq-metre Grand Beach Pavilion. Each room on the island has its own private plunge pool and the look is minimal but stylish, with Asian touches such as dark wood fittings and rattan chairs. A large causeway of top-quality water villas fans out from each side of the island.

The resort has all the facilities you'd expect of a top-end property, including two pools, an enormous spa in huge gardens, several excellent restaurants, a kids club with its own infinity pool and mini-loungers, a good gym, an excellent diving school, a full water-sports centre and even a wine cellar with a choice of some 3500 bottles of wine, which are paired by a sommelier with degustation meals. The island also owns two nearby desert islands, which are perfect for picnics.

Overall the Waldorf Astoria is a great choice for those wanting a glamorous but understated break on a luxuriously appointed island with dazzling beaches.

Island Hideaway   LUXURY RESORT **$$$**
(📞650 1515; www.island-hideaway.com; r/wv incl breakfast from US$1275/1950; ✴@🤖☀️👶) Island Hideaway is certainly true to its name – located about as remotely as you can imagine in the Maldives' most northerly atoll. But while some resorts might blanch at the idea of being so far removed from Male and the busy international airport, Island Hideaway has effortlessly capitalised on it, attracting those truly wanting to escape, and indeed this resort has a less communal feel than most, with many guests keeping to themselves in their villas, often even taking their meals there.

Set on a gorgeous crescent-shaped island with beaches 1.5km long on both sides, Island Hideaway is breathtaking and thickly vegetated. On arrival, you'll be given ice tea, a garland of flowers and a back massage – definitely one of the best welcomes in the country – before being taken to your villa by golf buggy.

The 49 villas all share a rustic style – think curved, mottled white walls topped by palm frond roofs, stylish wooden furniture and Maldivian decor and fittings. All have huge outdoor bathrooms and enjoy splendid isolation from one another. They're sprinkled around the island and most enjoy their own direct beach access.

The pampering extends to the Mandara Spa, the infinity pool, two excellent restaurants and a charming over-water bar, which also has its own menu. The pristine reefs around the island provide superb snorkelling and the untouched sites further afield make diving with the **Meridis Diving School** (www.meridis.de) another great reason to come here. The resort is totally child-friendly, has a great kids club, and many of the villas are designed to accommodate entire families, so space isn't a problem. However, while the beaches are beautiful, the reef comes all the way up to the beach on one side, making swimming from the beach on one side of the island tricky, but this is a small gripe with an otherwise superb resort. Finally, if you're travelling by yacht, Island Hideaway has its own Walcon Marine Marina, with 30 berths for yachts up to 80m. Look no further for total seclusion.

ⓘ Getting There & Away

There is no airport in Haa Alifu, but the main airport of the northern Maldives, Hanimaadhoo (see p98), is just a short distance away in Haa Dhaalu. Most resorts arrange for their guests to take scheduled Maldivian flights to Hanimaadhoo and collect them by launch.

Haa Dhaalu

Haa Dhaalu is an administrative district spread over 16 inhabited islands and made up of South Thiladhunmathee Atoll and the far smaller Maamakunudhoo Atoll. The capital island, **Kulhuduffushi** is the most

Raa, Baa & Lhaviyani

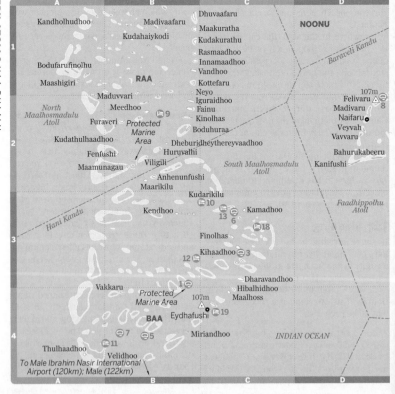

populous, with a population of around 8500 people. It's the most important island in the northern Maldives and has a hospital, secondary school and plenty of shops, although no airport. The traditional specialities here are rope making and shark fishing, though a national ban introduced in 2009 by the Maldivian government has forced local shark fishermen to hunt for other fish.

The regional airport is on **Hanimaadhoo** (population 1800). Maldivian has multiple daily flights to and from Male, but as this is the only runway in all the Northern Atolls, flights are busy. It's now possible to stay on Hanimaadhoo with the opening of an excellent guesthouse in 2012.

Elsewhere in Haa Dhaalu, there's a stone circle that is thought to be the base of a Buddhist stupa on the island of **Kumundhoo,** and *hawitta* (artificial mound) remains can still be seen on **Vaikaradhoo.**

The area around Haa Dhaalu suffers severe storms, and quite a few vessels have gone down in these waters. Maamakunudhoo Atoll is the graveyard of several ships, including the English ships *Persia Merchant,* wrecked here in 1658, and the *Hayston,* which ran onto a reef in 1819. In each instance, survivors were rescued by local people and treated with kindness, a source of great local pride.

🛏 Sleeping

There are currently no resorts in Haa Dhaalu Atoll, but travellers can stay at the new guesthouse on Hanimaadhoo.

TOP CHOICE **Asseyri Tourist Inn**　　GUESTHOUSE **$**
(☑790 1142; www.asseyri-inn.com; Hanimaadhoo; r incl breakfast from US$85; ❄🛜) Opening in early 2012 and run by a young local couple, this six-room guesthouse is a charming place set in a gorgeous tropical garden just a stone's throw from the town beach. Rooms are large, with low-slung beds and quirky wooden interiors cheered up by bright splashes of colour. The owners are trying to negotiate with the town council for the formation of a 'Western' beach, where guests can swim without offending local sensibilities. They are also planning a water-sports centre on the beach. In the meantime, everything from snorkelling trips, fishing trips, bike hire and island hopping can be arranged. There's

NORTHERN ATOLLS HAA DHAALU

a good restaurant here too, serving three meals a day, and as it's the only restaurant on the island, it's worth taking out a full-board package. Around 70% of the building materials used for the lodge are recycled, and at reception locally made soap and coconut oil are sold, which brings money into the local community.

ℹ Getting There & Away

The main airport in the northern Maldives is on Hanimaadhoo in Haa Dhaalu. There are five flights a day between Hanimaadhoo and Male (one hour, US$275 return) on **Maldivian** (www.maldivian.aero). Ferries connect the inhabited islands in Haa Dhaalu and also run to islands in Haa Alifu and Shaviyani. The main hubs are the capital Kulhuduffushi and the airport island Hanimaadhoo.

Shaviyani

Shaviyani administrative district comprises 16 inhabited islands and is made up of the natural atolls Miladhunmadulu and Thiladhunmathee. Still totally untouched by tourism, the atoll is most famous today as a major breeding ground for turtles, which lay their eggs very successfully on its pristine beaches.

Since 2009, the atoll's capital has been the island of **Milandhoo** (population 2145), an island that was uninhabited until 1997, when it was quickly settled to relocate the population of the nearby Makunudhoo, whose water supply had become contaminated. Much of the island has been cleared for plantain growing, the island's main industry.

The former atoll capital is **Funadhoo** (population 2900), a pretty island with the ruins of an ancient mosque and 13th-century tombstones. **Narudhoo** (population 473) is a tiny island with a natural freshwater lake on it – one of the very few places in the whole country where water collects above ground.

The main mosque on the island of **Kanditheemu** (population 1300) incorporates the oldest known example of the Maldives' unique Thaana script – it's an inscription on a doorframe, which notes that the roof was constructed in 1588.

The beautiful crescent island of Dholhiyadhoo was in the process of being converted into the first resort in the atoll, the luxury 100-room **Zitahli Resort & Spa Dholhiyadhoo Maldives** (www.zitahlidholhiyadhoo.com) at the time of writing. A further four islands

in the atoll have been earmarked for development into resorts, including Vagaru Island, which was also nearing completion as **Viceroy Maldives** (www.viceroyhotelsandresorts.com/maldives) as we went to press.

ℹ Getting There & Away

One of the Maldives' least accessible atolls, Shaviyani has no airport and so the only way to get here is by ferry. Once the resorts are up and running seaplane charters will fly guests directly to their islands, but until then you have to fly to Hanimaadhoo and then take ferry 106 to Kulhuduffushi (Rf 25, seven hours) and connect with ferry 108 to Kanditheemu (Rf 25, seven hours).

Noonu

The southern end of effortlessly pronounceable Miladhunmadulu-Thiladhunmathee Atoll forms the Noonu administrative district, comprising 13 inhabited islands. The capital island, **Manadhoo**, has 1580 people, but **Holhudhoo** (population 2040) and **Velidhoo** (population 2150) are more populous.

On the island of **Landhoo** (population 880) are the remnants of a *hawitta* supposedly left by the fabled Redin, a people who figure in Maldivian folklore. The *hawitta* is a 6m-high mound known locally as *maa badhige* (great cooking place). Thor Heyerdahl writes extensively about the tall, fair-haired Redin in his book *The Maldive Mystery*. He believes them to have been the first inhabitants of the Maldives, as long ago as 2000 BC.

Right now Noonu has just two resorts and one guesthouse, and while another resort is being built, it's still very quiet up here. One recent development that's putting the atoll on the map, though, is the decision to create the Maldives first **National Marine Park** here. This is the first place in the country to be given full national park status, and it's a significant step for marine conservation in the Maldives. The park will cover the Edu Faru Archipelago of nine uninhabited islands on the eastern side of the atoll, with headquarters and a visitor centre on nearby Manadhoo.

🛏 Sleeping

There are now two resorts in Noonu, with a third – the Maison Cheval Blanc Randheli – opening in 2013. This is the first Maldivian property of the LVMH (Louis Vuitton, Moët & Chandon, Hennessey) group, so it should be an impressive luxury product.

TOP CHOICE Palm Villa
GUESTHOUSE **$**

(☑990 0067; www.palmvilla-maldives.com; Velidhoo; s/d incl breakfast US$65/110; ✹@) The only guesthouse in this far-flung part of the country, Palm Villa is a charming place run by a couple of Danish chefs who'll make you feel right at home. Just a short walk from the harbour along the sandy streets of friendly and tidy Velidhoo, Palm Villa is a great place to relax and enjoy island life. The six spacious rooms have tiled floors, nicely painted interiors, semi-outdoor bathrooms and surround a sandy courtyard and lobby area where guests can relax, socialise and sunbathe. There's a communal kitchen, and guests are very welcome to prepare their own meals, or help the owners prepare the evening meal. Full-board options are available, and the food is as excellent as you'd expect from professional cooks. There's also a smoke oven for barbecues available. Diving can be organised by Lazy Gecko, a French-Maldivian diving outfit on the island, while there are plenty of nearby uninhabited islands that can be visited for sunbathing, snorkelling and picnics. The island is a very friendly one, and this is an excellent place to get to know the remote Maldives and its inhabitants.

Hilton Maldives Iru Fushi Resort & Spa
ACTIVITIES RESORT **$$**

(☑656 0591; www.hilton.com; r/wv incl breakfast US$436/801; ✹@🌐🏊) This is the Hilton's largest and most affordable Maldivian resort, an enormous development that is impressive, smart and well run. Its guests are mostly Chinese, followed by Russians, all of whom enjoy the enormous number of activities and excursions on offer. There's no superfluous luxury here, but it's a very solid, smart place that is tastefully designed and rigorously staffed. There is a superb white-sand beach all the way around the long island, making it easy to find a perfect spot in solitude, despite the large number of visitors to the island.

There are 221 rooms, including two enormous sets of water villas, all of which are huge and perhaps slightly characterless in their furnishings, but otherwise excellent. Other villas range from beach villas with charming thatched roofs to the self-contained three-bedroom 'Celebrity Retreat' with its own private pool. Decor throughout is in a minimalist tropical-Asian style, with lots of black wood, rattan furniture and brightly coloured accents.

The list of amenities here is huge: six high-quality restaurants around the island, two pools (one for families, one child-free), free tennis and badminton, a dive centre, a water-sports centre, a golf simulator, a huge spa, a good gym and even a karaoke room (popular with the Chinese guests). The free kids club is superb and has its own pool and infants nursery room.

Arguably the resort lacks individuality or true charm due to its size and functionality, but it ticks so many other boxes that this certainly isn't a big criticism. Come here for a busy, sociable holiday with friends and family and you won't be disappointed.

Zitahli Kuda-Funafaru Maldives
LUXURY HOTEL **$$$**

(☑656 1010; www.zitahlikudafunafaru.com; s/d/wv incl breakfast US$651/1003/1421; ✹@🌐🏊) After three Zitahli resorts opened in the Maldives in 2008, this is the only one left standing a few years later, but it's a worthy winner, a gorgeous island fringed with lovely white-sand beaches and with 50 huge and stylish villas scattered amid the undergrowth as well as over the picture-perfect lagoon.

Rooms stretch from the entry-level 175-sq-metre Deluxe Beach Villas to the two-bedroom 400-sq-metre Zitahli Suite, with its own pool, meaning you won't feel crowded here, no matter which room you're in. The design of the rooms is as fabulous as you'd expect at these prices and features every amenity you can think of – from espresso machines to rain showers and DVD players.

The food is good at the two main restaurants. Zitahli Cuisine serves a mix of buffet and à la carte international cuisine, and the Mosaic contemporary Mediterranean restaurant is open for lunch and dinner and serves up inventive à la carte meals. The resort also offers a full range of additional facilities, including a dive school, a superb spa, a freshwater swimming pool, a full fitness centre and a water-sports centre. This resort has remained below the radar locally, and is perfect for travellers seeking a beautiful, luxurious holiday with plenty of good food and excellent beaches and diving.

ℹ Getting There & Away

Resorts in Noonu are served by seaplane charters from Male. Independent travellers can also use these services by arrangement. Alternatively there's a weekly overnight ferry between Male's Fish Market Harbour and Velidhoo (Rf 200, 10 hours). The ferry leaves Male on

Wednesday night and returns from Velidhoo on Saturday night. This is a very local experience, with no seating and people sleeping on the floor. Ferries 201 and 202 connect the 13 inhabited islands of Noonu daily except Fridays.

Raa

Raa administrative district, with 15 inhabited islands and just one resort, is made up of North Maalhosmadulu Atoll and the island of Alifushi. Development has been slow here, but its isolation has made it popular with diving safari boats, and new dive sites are being discovered and documented all the time.

The sea to the west of Raa has some of the best fishing areas in the country. The capital island **Ugoofaaru** (Map p94; population 1250) has one of the largest fishing fleets in the country.

Tragedy struck Raa in 2004, when the tiny but crowded island of **Kandholhudhoo** was totally destroyed by the tsunami. The almost 4000 people who lived there were dispersed around other islands in the atoll until 2009, when the transfer of the displaced islanders to the previously uninhabited island of **Dhuvaafaru** began. It's now a thoroughly modern place that still looks more like a military base than an inhabited island, but it's a fascinating island to visit to see how a traditional society rebuilds itself from scratch in such situations.

The island of **Alifushi** (Map p94; population 2300), which is actually in a small, separate atoll to the north of Raa proper, is famously home of the finest traditional dhoni builders in the country. **Iguraidhoo** (population 1575) and **Innamaadhoo** (population 715) are also boat-building and carpentry centres that are accessible for excursions from Adaaran Select Meedhupparu.

According to local legend, the now uninhabited island of **Rasgetheemu** (Map p94) is where Koimala Kaloa and his princess wife landed after being exiled from Sri Lanka before moving to Male to found a ruling dynasty. Another important visitor to the atoll was the Arab seafarer Ibn Battuta, who landed at **Kinolhas** in 1343 and then moved on to Male.

The channel between Baa and Raa, locally known as Hani Kandu, is also named Moresby Channel after the Royal Navy officer Robert Moresby, who was responsible for the original marine survey of the Maldives made from 1834 to 1836. There's good diving on both sides of Hani Kandu, as it funnels water between the atolls, bringing pelagic fish and promoting coral growth. Mantas abound in October and November. The channels entering the atoll are studded with interesting thilas, and reefs dot the inside of the atoll.

🛏 Sleeping

Raa Atoll is currently home to just the one resort.

Adaaran Select Meedhupparu ACTIVITY RESORT **$$**
(📞658 7700; www.adaaran.com/selectmeedhupparu; full board r/wv US$381/942; ❄@🛜🏊) Adaaran Select Meedhupparu is the place to go to really get away from it all. You are truly remote here: it's the only island resort in the whole of Raa Atoll, and also has extra resorts within a resort scattered about other parts of the island. Meedhupparu has gorgeous, wide white beaches sloping down to a perfect turquoise lagoon. While once colonised by the Italian market, Meedhupparu today is the biggest Maldivian resort in the Adaaran chain's group of properties and it attracts mostly Indian, Russian and Italian visitors.

The resort is large and features several distinct types of accommodation, including an Ayurvedic Village made up of 24 houses and an area known as the 'Water Villas', which functions as a resort within a resort and includes an exclusive Balinese spa and a charming garden full of Sri Lankan flowers. The rooms elsewhere in the resort are fine, if lacking in character, and the rooms in the Ayurvedic Village are identical but feature thatched roofs. Be aware that on one side of the island there's a seawall preventing sand erosion. It's well worth requesting a room away from the seawall, as it's unsightly and prevents easy sea access.

Water sports and diving are big attractions here. Activities available include two catamarans, while the diving is very diverse due to the remote location of the resort, which means new diving spots are constantly being discovered. Over 30 dive sites are regularly visited and there's a huge variety of fish species to see. Other excellent amenities include a huge pool, a gym, tennis and badminton courts, and two restaurants and bars to keep people fed and entertained.

ℹ Getting There & Away

Resort guests travelling to Raa Atoll use seaplane transfers from Male airport that bring them directly to Meedhupparu. Otherwise the only way to get here is by slow and infrequent ferries from Male. Local ferries 203 and 204 connect the 15 inhabited islands in Raa Atoll daily except Fridays.

Baa

The Baa Atoll is made up of South Maalhosmadulu Atoll and the small Goidhoo Atoll, 10km further south. Its inhabitants are spread over 13 inhabited islands as well as between a variety of resorts. Fishing is the most important local industry, but Baa is also famous for its lacquer work and the fine woven cotton sarong, called a *feyli*. **Eydhafushi**, the atoll capital (population 2800), is also the *feyli* centre. The second-largest island in the atoll and the main centre for the production of lacquered boxes and jars is **Thulhaadhoo** (population 2500). Both of these islands can be visited on excursions from nearby resorts.

Because of its isolation, **Goidhoo** (population 657) has traditionally been a place for castaways and exiles. In 1602 François Pyrard, a French explorer, found himself on the island of **Fulhadhoo** (population 300) after his ship, the *Corbin,* was wrecked. Spending five years here and on Male as an effective prisoner in the Maldives, he learned Divehi and wrote one of the first extensive accounts of Maldivian culture.

🏃 Activities

Baa Atoll includes the Hanifaru Huraa Unesco World Biosphere Reserve, a vital feeding ground for manta rays and whale sharks, meaning that you have an excellent chance to see these incredible sea giants while on diving trips here. There is also a host of superb dive sites to choose from, including the following.

Milaidhoo Reef   DIVING
Strong currents flowing through the Kamadhoo Kandu provide an environment for soft corals, which thrive on Milaidhoo Reef, on the north side of an uninhabited island. The reef top, at 2m, is great for snorkelling, and it drops straight down to about 35m. This cliff has numerous caves and overhangs with sea fans and sponges.

Kakani Thila   DIVING
The north side of Kakani Thila, at 25m to 30m, retains coral formations in excellent condition, and colourful soft corals fill the overhangs. It's also home to lots of fish, including Napoleons, jackfish and Oriental sweetlips.

Dhigali Haa   DIVING
The small Dhigali Haa, though well inside the atoll, commonly attracts pelagic species (barracuda) and grey-tip reef sharks. Other fish include jacks, batfish and trevally. It's also a good place to see nudibranchs, yellow and orange soft corals and anemones (with clown fish).

Madi Finolhu   DIVING
The sandy Madi Finolhu has large coral blocks on which black corals grow. Stingrays can be seen on the sand, and mantas also pass through. This is a good beginners' dive (20m).

Muthafushi Thila   DIVING
Overhangs at Muthafushi Thila are home to soft corals and anemones. Many hard corals are in good condition and also very colourful, soft corals can also be seen. There are large schools of blue-striped snapper.

🛏 Sleeping

Further islands that are earmarked for development include Kihavahuravalhi, which will be the site of another resort from Thailand's Anantara group, as well as Vakkaru and Mudhdhoo.

TOP CHOICE ➤ Four Seasons
Landaa Giraavaru   LUXURY RESORT $$$
(📞660 0888; www.fourseasons.com/maldiveslg; r/ wv incl breakfast from US$1640/1525; ❄@🛜🏊🛶) Four Seasons Landaa Giraavaru is simply extraordinary. It's a palace of a hotel in the grand style, whose combination of brilliantly designed, vast rooms, great beaches and Four Seasons service make it one of the absolute top resorts in the country.

The resort opened in late 2006 on an island that was converted from a coconut plantation (which accounts for the fantastically dense vegetation and high palms). Its style fuses traditional Maldivian village with designer minimalism with stunning effect – bright-blue doors, recycled coral-stone walls and yellow door frames give way to sleek, industrial-style concrete floors, and traditional dark-wood Asian furniture. Rooms in nearly all categories have huge private lap pools, and those on land have big gardens with an outdoor sitting room, day bed and direct access to the beach.

With a choice of three vast pools, four great restaurants, a 1 hectare over-water spa, a kids club, a teenagers club, free water sports and a marine biology lab, it's not a place you can easily be bored. A luxurious diving school runs trips morning and afternoon with a maximum of 12 participants in each group. Twenty dive sites are nearby and whale sharks and mantas are very common in September. The Russians have now overtaken the Brits as the biggest nationality here, but being a Four Seasons it attracts a classy international crowd.

🌿 Soneva Fushi   LUXURY RESORT $$$

(☏660 0374; www.sixsenses.com/soneva-fushi; r incl breakfast from US$1005; ✳@🛜⊠🛖) Rightly one of the most famous resorts in the country, eco-fabulous Soneva Fushi is a place to get back to nature in style. The personal creation of hoteliers Sonu and his wife Eva, it's an incredibly impressive island where rustic private houses are scattered amid the thick vegetation of one of the Maldives' largest resort islands.

Each villa here is like a small (and in many cases not-so-small) house built with natural materials, fitted with designer furnishings and finished in rustic style. All the deluxe and modern features you'd expect of a five-star hotel are included, but most of them are concealed so that no plastic is visible. Villas are well spaced around the edges of the island, affording complete privacy – they're reached by sandy tracks that wind through the lush vegetation, which is kept as natural as possible. Given the island's large size, guests get around by bicycle, and after a couple of days you get to know the initially complex pathways that lead you to the various amenities hidden away in the thick foliage.

There's a big range of villas as well as prices, and even if the 15 'standard' Rehendi Rooms come in comfortably below four figures a night, prices quickly rise as you move up the categories. With the choice of five superb restaurants (including the wonderful treehouse-style Fresh in the Garden, where you cross a rope bridge to get to your table), the food is a real highlight of the resort, with as much of it as possible grown here.

This is a resort that takes its ecocredentials and social responsibility seriously. You can take a tour of the resort's recycling area and see the ingenious ways many things are reused on the island, while across the lagoon on Baa's capital Eydhafushi, the resort has built and continues to fund a school. It's hard not to be impressed.

There is a full range of resort recreations, many of them complimentary. The **Soleni dive school** (www.soleni.com) has years of experience diving the sites around Soneva, while the excellent Six Senses spa is the perfect place to indulge yourself. More unusual (free) activities include watching an outdoor film at the lovely Cinema Paradiso and observing the stars in the only resort observatory in the Maldives.

For back-to-nature meets haute couture, you'll find nowhere better than Soneva Fushi.

🌿 Dusit Thani Maldives   LUXURY RESORT $$$

(☏660 8888; www.dusit.com; r/wv incl breakfast from US$1420/1770; ✳@🛜⊠🛖) Opening in mid-2012, this brand new luxury resort is raising the bar for top-end resorts, boasting, among other things, the largest swimming pool in the country and a tree-top spa for that massage in the sky you've always dreamt of.

With 100 state-of-the-art villas scattered around this breathtaking island ringed by an improbably white beach, you can't really go wrong. Even the lowest room category, the Beach Villa, is an incredible 122 sq metres of gorgeously attired space, complete with fabulous bathroom and direct beach access. All room categories above the Beach Villa have their own private pools, and they're all a very good size. The water villas are particularly stunning, huge and delightfully fitted out with all manner of stylish extras such as espresso machines and iPod docks.

Dusit Thani's environmental credentials include solar panels, no chlorine in its pools, the production of its own drinking water, and LED lighting in all guest areas – all great initiatives that deserve support.

The resort also boasts three restaurants, two bars, tennis courts, a kids club, a water-sports centre, a dive school and perhaps its most impressive feature, the Devarana Spa, which has treatment rooms above in the treetops. This is a gorgeous place, which will inevitably join the ranks of the country's very best and most exclusive resorts.

Anantara Kihavah Villas   LUXURY RESORT $$$

(☏660 1020; www.kihavah-maldives.anantara.com; r/wv incl breakfast from US$2500/2870; ✳@🛜⊠🛖) This latest resort from Thai hotel chain Anantara (it has three further resorts in South Male Atoll) is a spectacular addition to the country's collection of top-end resorts. The island is beautiful, with gorgeous white-sand beaches ringing a thickly vegetated island surrounded by a perfectly circular reef: you couldn't ask for a more perfect-looking island. However, the resort's biggest attraction is its 82 stunning villas, all superbly realised homages to ultimate luxury.

All the accommodation here comes with a private pool, whether on land or in the water villas. This is one place, though, where the beach villas are even better than the more expensive water villas – they enjoy far more seclusion and have huge and stunning bathrooms. The gorgeous Asian furnishings are common to all the rooms, including the enormous pool residences, which are suitable for even the most demanding of royalty (and can host an entire entourage).

The dining options are just as opulent, including the showcase Sea.Fire Salt.Sky (only in the Maldives!) dining complex, made up of four sections, including ones where you can dine on gourmet international cuisine while tropical fish swim around you. You're spoiled for choice, including a top-notch Japanese restaurant (book ahead), an Italian restaurant and various beach dining options.

The resort has every other facility you'd expect at this price – a gorgeous pool, a sumptuous spa, a water-sports centre, a dive school, tennis courts, yoga and cookery lessons and a super kids club. Look no further for a superb and friendly luxury option.

Reethi Beach Resort   ACTIVITIES RESORT **$$$**
(✆660 2626; www.reethibeach.com; r incl breakfast from US$852; ✳@🛜🏊) The Reethi Beach Resort is a smart and beautiful resort with plenty of charm. The island has lots of natural vegetation, fantastic, wide white beaches, an accessible house reef and an expansive lagoon. The buildings, all with thatched roofs, are designed to blend with the environment, and also incorporate some Maldivian design elements such as the deep horizontal mouldings used on the old Friday Mosque in Male. The deluxe villas are more spacious and have better beach frontage, while the water villas are decent but not show-stopping.

There are five restaurants on the island, as well as swimming pool, gym, squash, badminton and tennis courts. Windsurfing, sailing and other water sports are popular because of the wide lagoon. Kitesurfing is also on offer, as are parasailing, wakeboarding and jet skiing. The spa offers a full range of massage and beauty treatments. The **Sea-Explorer dive centre** (www.sea-explorer.net) is professional and reasonably priced, although qualified divers can also make dives off the house reef, and with few resorts in the area you'll probably have good dive sites to yourself. Overall

this is a great option combining comfort, good beaches and quality diving.

Coco Palm Dhuni Kolhu   ACTIVITIES RESORT **$$**
(✆660 0011; www.cococollection.com.mv; r/wv incl breakfast US$644/1042; ✳@🛜🏊) Coco Palm Dhuni Kolhu is a favourite with honeymooners and has an enormous number of repeat visitors. The island is a stunner, with a wide beach on one side, thick vegetation and an architecturally interesting space with a tent-like thatched pavilion for reception, restaurant and bar areas.

The beach villa rooms are circular with high, thatched, conical roofs, quality furnishings and open-air bathrooms, while the deluxe rooms have, in addition, an individual plunge pool, though these are now looking a little tired. These island rooms are value for money as the 14 over-water bungalows now feel somewhat antique, and though nice enough are overpriced. A full refurbishment is planned for the future.

A highlight is the food. All meals are buffet in the main restaurant, but they are very good, while the à la carte Thai restaurant is excellent. Other nice touches include an outdoor cinema, which couples can hire to watch a movie on the beach, a lovely spa and an Ocean-Pro dive centre.

Coco Palm has developed a well-deserved reputation for being an ideal honeymoon and couples' hideaway and will hopefully go from strength to strength after a full revamp brings it up to the standards of sister resort Coco Palm Bodu Hithi (p67).

❶ Getting There & Away

At present guests arrive at Baa resorts via seaplane transfers from Male airport, but a new airport is due to open on the island of Dharavandhoo in late 2012, which will bring daily scheduled flights on **Maldivian** (www.maldivian. aero) to the atoll and greatly open it up to independent travellers. There are seven atoll ferry routes that connect the 13 inhabited islands every day except Friday.

Lhaviyani

Fishing is the main industry of Lhaviyani Atoll, although tourism also employs many people, with four large resorts located here. On the capital island, **Naifaru** (population 4720), the people have a reputation for making attractive handicrafts from coral and mother-of-pearl, and for concocting local medicines. **Hinnavaru** (population 4500) is also densely settled. The island of **Maafilaafushi** today has only around 50 inhabitants, but it had a much greater population in the 17th century and remnants of an old mosque can still be seen. Day trips from the resorts visit all these islands, as well as **Felivaru**, which has a modern tuna-canning plant.

🏃 Activities

Kuredhoo Express   DIVING
Usually done as a long drift dive through the channel next to the Kuredu resort, Kuredhoo Express is a demanding dive in strong currents, but it also offers brilliant snorkelling on the eastern side. Napoleon wrasse, grey-tip reef sharks and trevally frequent the channel entrance, while inside are overhangs dripping with soft corals. Look for morays, turtles and stingrays. It's a Protected Marine Area.

Shipyard   DIVING
Another demanding dive, with two wrecks within 50m of each other. Strong currents around these ships have promoted the rapid growth of soft and hard corals, which now form a habitat for many types of reef fish. Moray eels and sweepers live inside the wrecks, while nurse sharks cruise around the bottom.

Fushifaru Thila   DIVING
When the current is strong, Fushifaru Thila is no place for beginners, but when the currents are slow the top of the thila is superb for snorkelling. The thila, with lovely soft corals, sits in the centre of a broad channel and attracts mantas, eagle rays, sharks, grouper, sweetlips and turtles. Cleaner wrasse abound on the thila, which is a Protected Marine Area.

🛏 Sleeping

Kanuhura   LUXURY RESORT $$$
(☑662 0044; www.kanuhura.com; r/wv incl breakfast from US$1080/1600; ❋@🛜🏊♨) Kanuhura is a sumptuous, impressive place with magnificent beaches, stunning accommodation and top-notch food. This place manages to get it right on so many levels – it's classy and stylish without being too formal, it's romantic without being too quiet and it's welcoming to families without allowing kids to run riot. If you want a laid-back, high-end beach holiday with considerable style, this may be for you.

The rooms combine classical luxury and elegant simplicity. The beach villas have four-poster beds, a separate dressing area, a lovely indoor-outdoor bathroom, lots of polished timber and a frontage onto the perfect beach.

They're equipped with air-con, safe, stereo, satellite TV, DVD, espresso machine, minibar, bathrobes, umbrellas and even slippers, although some are beginning to show their age and some clearly need to be redone. The more expensive suites and water villas are even bigger and feature several rooms, private spas, sun decks and direct sea access.

The resort's public areas, restaurants and spa are focused on the expansive infinity pool near the main jetty. It also has a gym, aerobics studio, karaoke bar, cigar lounge, games room and library with free internet access. Other facilities around the island include the several boutiques, a coffee shop, tennis and squash courts, and an excellent kids club. This is a complete resort.

At the other end of the island is the high-end outdoor dining option of the Veli Café – overlooking the resort's very own desert islet of Jehunuhura. A complimentary boat shuttles guests back and forth between the two. The main attraction of Jehunuhura is its gorgeous restaurant, open for lunch, but it also has beds scattered about the undergrowth for lovers to lounge in while pretending to be in an upmarket version of *Lost*.

Kanahura is a big island, about 1km long, and assiduous landscaping is augmenting the natural vegetation with local species. Lovely, perfect beaches go right around the island, and there's not a sandbag or sea wall in sight. The house reef is not suitable for snorkelling, so take one of the special snorkelling excursions run by the dive school. Over 40 dive sites are accessible. By contrast, the wide lagoon makes for smooth sailing; you can follow the reef for 5km and make your own stops at several tiny uninhabited islands along the way – blissful.

Komandoo Island
Resort   ROMANTIC RESORT $$
(☑662 1010; www.komandoo.com; s/d/wv incl breakfast US$420/570/690; ❋@🛜) Komandoo Island Resort, the smaller and more stylish sibling of Kuredu, shares the same management. The feel at this resort, though, couldn't be more different – instead of crowds of excitable holidaymakers going from activity to activity, at Komandoo the pace is far more relaxed and the resort ethos is one of pampering and relaxation. There are no children allowed here, making this a favourite spot for honeymooners and other couples enjoying a romantic break.

The round island is ringed by a strikingly beautiful beach, although the sea breaks that surround much of the island obscure the desert-island perfection somewhat. The hexagonal rooms, prefabricated in pine from Finland, come with four-poster beds, mini-bars, safes and stereos, and they all front directly onto a pure white beach. Finally there are 15 rustic-style water bungalows that are suitably impressive and equipped with solid teak furniture.

The four reefs accessible through two channels from the island have a wide variety of marine life (256 fish species have been documented) and recovering corals, so are ideal for snorkelling from the beach. The main restaurant and bar buildings have sea views, sand floors and an intimate feel. The food and service get rave reviews, and the Duniye Spa adds another opportunity for indulgence.

The island itself is not lush, but it is impressively landscaped, and if you want a true desert island escape, take the short boat ride across the lagoon to Komandoo's own uninhabited island for sunbathing and a picnic.

Palm Beach Resort ACTIVITIES RESORT $$
(662 0084; www.palmbeachmaldives.com; full board s/d US$550/695; ✳@✆☎) Famous throughout the atoll for being a particularly beautiful island, triangular Palm Beach Resort enjoys some of the best beaches in the atoll along its almost 2km length. The bungalows dotted along both sides of the island are spacious and have all mod cons, though the white walls, tiled floors and bamboo furniture aren't especially stylish. Most of the resort facilities (restaurant, bar, pool, spa, sports centre) are towards one end of the island, quite a way from some of the rooms, but that gives them a sense of real seclusion, and golf buggies and bicycles are available to help guests get around.

The main restaurant serves all meals as buffets with an Italian bias, and they're very good. Several other restaurants, including a seafood and a candlelit à la carte restaurant, and several bars are dotted elsewhere around the island. Tennis, squash and most water sports are free, as are some excursions and snorkelling trips (the lagoon isn't good for snorkelling). The diving school charges very reasonable diving rates and runs the full gamut of courses for beginners. The whole resort has a very casual atmosphere.

**Kuredu Island
Resort & Spa** ACTIVITIES RESORT $
(662 0332; www.kuredu.com; r/wv incl breakfast from US$210/535; ✳@✆☎🛏) Kuredu Island

Resort is about as close as you can get to a resort city in the Maldives – this truly is the resort that has everything, so look no further if you want a fun, sociable and action-packed holiday destination as well as the usual gleaming beaches and great diving. Kuredu has gone upmarket since a refit in 2008, but it has retained its very reasonable prices and is a great place to enjoy a mid-range-style resort at distinctly budget prices.

You can effectively have whatever kind of holiday you're after here – the sheer number of activities and facilities available is mind-boggling. From the only golf course in the Maldives (six holes and a 250m driving range) and kite-boarding to a decompression chamber and a football pitch, Kuredu has it all, as well as all the more normal facilities you'd expect at a resort.

There are nine room categories running from the simple but charming Bonthi Garden Bungalows to the new, all-wood beach villas that face the best beach, have open-air bathrooms, stereos and coffeemakers. The Sangu Resort is an exclusive resort within a resort: the restaurant here does first-class buffet meals and is only for those staying in Sangu.

The main reception, restaurant, bar, swimming pool, shops and dive centre are all near the centre of the island, and cater for the generally younger, livelier crowd in the less expensive rooms. The buffets in the main restaurant are pretty good, with a fair selection of Asian and international dishes. In addition there are three à la carte restaurants. Other facilities include a gym, tennis courts, a well-used beach volleyball court and the golf course. The spa offers Swedish, Thai and Oriental massages as well as lessons. Excellent dive sites are accessible from Kuredu.

All in all, Kuredu is a well-run resort with a lively, sociable atmosphere. If you want high-style luxury or intimate island atmosphere, it may not be for you. But for activities such as diving and snorkelling, plus relaxation, recreation, families and fun, Kuredu is hard to beat.

❶ Getting There & Away

There's no airport in Lhaviyani Atoll, and all resorts use seaplane charters to get guests here. There's a daily ferry connecting the inhabited islands, though, as well as a twice-weekly ferry to and from Male (Rf50, six hours) from Naifaru.

Southern Atolls

Best Places to Stay

» Shangri-La Villingili Resort & Spa (p122)

» Six Senses Laamu (p114)

» Jumeirah Dhevanafushi (p115)

» Ayada Maldives (p117)

» Reveries Diving Village (p114)

Why Go?

The southern atolls have been busy over the past few years providing the Maldives with new resorts on ever more atolls. With better transport infrastructure than the north of the country – there are four regional airports with daily connections to the capital, including an international airport at Gan – there's a lot to be said for the south.

Outside the resorts, the southern atolls have mostly retained a traditional way of life. The exception is Gan, where the British established military facilities in WWII and maintained an air-force base that operated until 1976.

Development is continuing, with each atoll hosting at least one resort and several new guesthouses opening. Safari boats explore dive sites as far south as the Huvadhoo Kandu, and surfing trips visit the remotest breaks of Gaafu Dhaalu. Despite this, the region is almost totally pristine and a wonderful place to visit.

Vaavu

Vaavu is made up of Felidhoo Atoll and the small, uninhabited Vattaru Falhu Atoll. This is the least populous area of the country, with around 2100 inhabitants spread over just five inhabited islands.

The main industry is fishing, and there is some boat building. There are also two budget resort islands and several new guesthouses taking advantage of the atolls' proximity to Male. The capital island is **Felidhoo**, which has only about 500 people, but visitors are more likely to go to its neighbouring island, **Keyodhoo** (population 670), which has a good anchorage for safari boats. At the northern edge of the atoll, **Fulidhoo** (population 390) is an attractive island, regularly visited on day trips from the resorts and known for its boat building. **Rakeedhoo** (population 360), at the southern tip of the atoll, is used as an anchorage by safari boats taking divers to the nearby channel.

🏃 Activities

There are at least 24 recognised dive sites in the atoll, and only two resorts in the area. Some dive sites are not readily accessible, even from the resorts, and are mostly visited by safari boats. The following sites are rated among the best in the whole of the Maldives, and they all offer superb snorkelling.

Devana Kandu DIVING

This is a drift dive that's not too demanding in a channel divided by a narrow thila. Devana Kandu is a great snorkelling area too. There are several entrances to the channel, which has overhangs, caves, reef sharks and eagle rays. The southern side has soft corals and lots of reef fish. Further in, the passages join up and there is a broad area of hard corals, the deeper parts being less affected by bleaching. The whole channel is a Protected Marine Area.

Fotteyo DIVING

Fotteyo is a brilliant diving and snorkelling site in and around a channel entrance – it's worth making several dives here. There are numerous small caves, several large caves and various arches and holes, all decorated with colourful soft corals. Rays, reef sharks, grouper, tuna, jackfish, barracuda, turtles and even hammerhead sharks can be seen. Inside, the channel floor is known as 'triggerfish alley'.

Rakeedhoo Kandu DIVING

Rakeedhoo Kandu is a challenging dive in a deep channel – the east and west sides are usually done as separate drift dives. Broad coral shelves cover overhangs and caves, which have sea fans and black corals. Turtles, Napoleon wrasse, sharks and schools of trevally are often seen, and the snorkelling on the reef top is brilliant.

Vattaru Kandu DIVING

A remote channel dive on the southern edge of Vattaru Falhu, Vattaru Kandu is now a designated Protected Marine Area. It is not too demanding unless the currents are running at full speed. The reef next to Vattaru is a fine snorkelling area. Around the entrance are many caves and overhangs with soft corals, sea fans and abundant fish life – barracuda, fusilier and white-tip reef sharks. Turtles are sometimes seen here, as are manta rays from December to April.

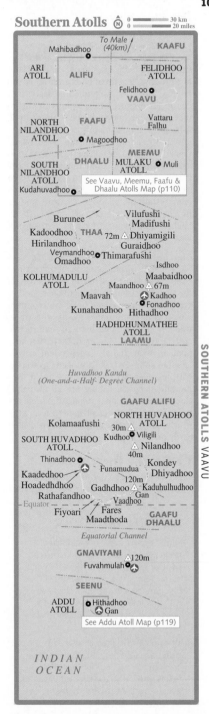

Southern Atolls

🛏 Sleeping

Keyodhoo Guesthouse   GUESTHOUSE $
(☑799 9287; www.islandlifemaldives.net; Keyodhoo; r all inclusive per person US$115; ✸@) This small and friendly guesthouse on the island of Keyodhoo is a great choice for an island holiday. The attentive and enthusiastic staff lay on all manner of excursions to ensure that guests are never bored – snorkelling, fishing, island excursions and barbecues – and they're all included in the price, which makes it a great deal. The accommodation itself is simple, in seven rooms with basic furnishings that range from a family room sleeping four people to doubles. The next-door restaurant provides all meals and is, in fact, the only place to eat on the island! Highly recommended for a relaxed slice of local island life.

Casa Barabaru   GUESTHOUSE $
(☑790 4997; www.barabaru.com; Thinadhoo; r from US$90; ✸@) This Italian-run guesthouse on the charming island of Thinadhoo is another great place for an island holiday. Accommodation is in comfortable rooms with rustic wooden fittings and modern bathrooms, and the sea is just 50m away. It's particularly popular with Italian independent travellers (but some English is spoken), as well as with travellers wishing to fish – night fishing and deep-sea fishing are all available. Good meals and an enthusiastic team are the main highlights of a trip here, as are the nearby great beaches, which can be visited easily on day trips.

ℹ Getting There & Away

Vaavu is easily reached by ferry from Male's Viligili Terminal. Ferries (Rf50, two hours) to the northerly island of Fulidhoo leave Male at 10am on Sunday, Tuesday and Thursday and return from Fulidhoo at 10.30am on Saturday, Monday and Wednesday. From Fulidhoo, it's possible to connect to other inhabited islands in the atoll. The two resorts in Vaavu are reached by **Maldivian Air Taxi** (www.maldivianairtaxi.com) chartered flights from Male airport.

Meemu

Meemu Atoll has eight inhabited islands and opened up to tourism only in the 1990s. The capital island, Muli (population 850) gets a few day visitors from nearby resorts, while next door Mulah and southerly Kolhufushi are more populous with about 1450 and 1225 people, respectively. Both these islands grow yams, which are an important food staple on fertile islands. Elsewhere the main industry in Meemu is fishing.

As well as several superb dive sites, Meemu has some excellent surf breaks on its eastern edge, including Veyvah Point, Boahuraa Point and Mulee Point, which are gradually being explored by more adventurous surfers.

🏃 Activities

Shark's Tongue   DIVING
Shark's Tongue is east of Boli Mulah, in the mouth of the Mulah Kandu. White-tips sleep on the sandy plateau, and grey-tip reef sharks hang around a cleaning station at 20m. In strong currents, black-tip, grey and silver-tip sharks cruise through the coral blocks: this is no place for beginner divers.

Giant Clam   DIVING
Giant Clam is an easy dive around two sheltered giris, where several giant clams are seen between 8m and 15m, even by snorkellers. Numerous caves and overhangs are rich with anemones and home to lobsters, grouper and glassfish. Colourful butterflyfish and clown triggerfish are easily spotted, but look hard for well-camouflaged stonefish and scorpionfish.

🛏 Sleeping

**Chaaya Lagoon
Hakuraa Huraa**   ACTIVITIES RESORT $$
(☑672 0014; www.chaayamaldives.com; r/wv from incl breakfast US$350/420; ✸@🛜) Chaaya Lagoon Hakuraa Huraa, which reopened in 2005 after a post-tsunami refit, is now a well-designed resort combining romance and water sports. With nearly all its unusual villas over water (they have tented white

---

ALSO IN VAAVU ATOLL

Alimatha Aquatic (www.alimatharesort.com) An Italian all-inclusive resort popular with a diving and water-sports enthusiasts. It's a small island, a little bit cramped, but splendidly isolated, with pristine dive sites nearby and a house reef that's accessible for snorkellers.

Dhiggiri (www.dhiggiriresort.com) Sister resort to Alimatha Aquatic, this is another animated club-style Italian resort with Italian food in the buffet and guests on all-inclusive packages.

roofs and are quite unlike the typical water villas you'll see in other places), some stunning beaches and plenty of activities, this is a great place to combine activity and indolence, although you don't get a great sense of privacy in the rooms as they're quite closely packed together.

The lagoon is not good for snorkelling, though snorkelling gear and twice-daily trips are included in the package. The dive school is good value and offers what so few centres in the Maldives can these days – access to truly pristine dive sites. With so many little-visited dive sites in the area, diving might be the best reason to stay at Hakuraa.

Medhufushi   ACTIVITIES RESORT **$$**
(☎672 0026; www.aaaresorts.com.mv/Medhufushi; all inclusive r/wv US$390/455; ✸@☎⬚) Medhufushi re-opened in 2008 after a full refit by its parent group (which also owns Filitheyo in nearby Faafu Atoll) and has established itself as a midrange resort where guests consistently feel they get bang for their buck.

Medhufushi is perfect for romance and tranquillity and attracts many returning guests, most of whom take advantage of the great all-inclusive rates. Rooms are very reasonably priced for what you get – stylish wooden cabins on the beach with thatched roofs, and even better water villas. The main activities are water sports and diving in this pristine atoll, where some fantastic new sites are being logged. It also has an excellent spa, a great selection of beaches and a pretty house reef.

❶ Getting There & Away

The resorts in Meemu Atoll are served by **Maldivian Air Taxi** (www.maldivianairtaxi.com) chartered flights. Locally, three daily ferry routes connect all the inhabited islands in the atoll and there are inter-atoll ferry connections to Male from Muli every other day (Rf150, four hours).

Faafu

Faafu Atoll has about 4000 people living on its five inhabited islands. The capital island, **Magoodhoo** (population 680), is a small fishing village with a very traditional Islamic community, and certainly not a place used to seeing many foreigners, so definitely jump at the chance to go there. There are just two resorts in the atoll, and as one is essentially a private island for multi-millionaires, nearly everyone coming here stays at Filitheyo.

◉ Sights & Activities

Nilandhoo   ISLAND
On the southern edge of the atoll, Nilandhoo (population 1500) has the second-oldest mosque in the country, **Aasaari Miskiiy**, built during the reign of Sultan Mohammed Ibn Abdullah (r 1153–66). It is made of dressed stone and the interior is decorated with carved woodwork. It's possible that the stones were recycled from the ruins of earlier, pre-Islamic structures.

Thor Heyerdahl's book *The Maldive Mystery* has an entire chapter about this island. His expedition unearthed many phallic stone carvings, like the lingam associated with the Hindu god Shiva in his manifestation as the creator. Some of these images can be seen in the National Museum in Male. Heyerdahl's expedition also found ruins apparently from an ancient gate, one of seven surrounding a great pagan temple complex. You can visit Nilandhoo on a full-day excursion from Filitheyo resort, but the ruins are mostly unexcavated. As Heyerdahl wrote:

> Five teams of archaeologists could dig here for five years and still make new discoveries. The magnitude of this prehistoric cult centre seemed quite out of proportion to the size of the island.

Filitheyo Reef   DIVING
Filitheyo Reef, the kandu south of Filitheyo resort, is now a Protected Marine Area and has several diving possibilities. Only accessible by boat, the house reef on the southeast corner of the resort descends in big steps, where great clouds of fish congregate. Swarms of batfish and several Napoleons are resident, while grey-tip reef sharks, rays and trevally are frequent visitors.

Two Brothers   DIVING
The Two Brothers are two thilas located in a narrow channel. The big 'brother' (north) tops out at 3m and is covered with soft corals and sponges, and attracts snorkellers. Many turtles reside here. Big pelagics cruise around both 'brothers' and there are lots of nudibranchs, pipefish, gobies and other small marine species.

🛏 Sleeping

Filitheyo   ROMANTIC RESORT **$$**
(☎674 0025; www.aaaresorts.com.mv; r/wv US$365/510; ✸@☎⬚) Filitheyo is a beautifully designed and finished resort on a large, luscious, triangular island with superb

SOUTHERN ATOLLS FAAFU

Vaavu, Meemu, Faafu & Dhaalu Atoll

South Ari Atoll

67m
Dhangethi

INDIAN OCEAN

Fenfushi

Dhidhdhoo

Dhigurah

Fulidhoo

Kudaboll

Ariadhoo Kandu

See Ari Atoll map (p82)

Kuda Anbaraa

Anbaraa

Kadumoonufushi

2

Protected
Marine Area

Himithi

45m
Viligilivarufinolhu

Minimasgali

19

Diguvarufinolhu

Protected
Marine
Area

FAAFU

16
9

INDIAN OCEAN

North
Nilandhoo
Atoll

Protected
Marine
Area

Maavaruhuraa

Vattarurah
10

Ebulufushi

Bileiydhoo

Magoodhoo

Nilandhoo

Dharaboodhoo

Protected
Marine
Area

20

4

45m
Meedhoo

South
Nilandhoo
Atoll

6

Faandhoo

12

Maagau

Ribudhoo

Kanneiyfaru

Thuvaru

Maadheli

Maalefaru

Hulhudheli

Hulhuvehi

DHAALU

Bulhalafushi

Gemendhoo

Kiraidhoo

Naibukaloabodufushi

Kurali

Minimasgali

Thilabolhufushi

Kuradhigandu

Valla-Ihohi

Olhuveli

Kadimma

Kolhufushi

Bodufushi

Valla

Hiriyafushi

Maafushi

Maaeboodhoo

Kudahuvadhoo

Embudhoofushi

white-sand beaches. The public buildings are spacious, open-sided Balinese-style pavilions with palm-thatch roofs and natural touches, and the whole place feels chic but laid-back and informal.

Most rooms are comfortable timber bungalows facing the beach, nested among the palm trees and equipped with amenities, including open-air bathrooms and personal sun decks. Deluxe villas provide extra space and style, while the water villas have sea views and private balconies. Resort facilities include gym, small spa, infinity pool, reading room and shops. Some low-key evening entertainment is organised, and there's an interesting program of excursions and fishing trips.

Beaches are pretty all around, but the lagoon is shallow on the south side, and not suitable for swimming on the east side. The north side has it all – soft sand, good swimming and an accessible house reef that's great for snorkelling. Qualified divers can do unguided dives off the house reef too.

Rania Experience PRIVATE ISLAND **$$$**
(☑674 0555; www.raniaexperience.com; island all-inclusive per night US$18,000; ☀@🤖) Faafu is home to the faintly ridiculous Rania Experience, perhaps the most exclusive island in the

country, and certainly the most expensive. Here you get the tiny but beautiful island of Maafushi to yourself, a staff of 25, a private yacht and basically anything else you damn well please. There's a minimum three-night stay and, frankly, you probably can't afford it.

ℹ Getting There & Away

Maldivian Air Taxi (www.maldivianairtaxi. com) charter flights connect the two resorts in the atoll to Male. Locally, ferry route 404 connects the five inhabited islands in the atoll daily, while inter-atoll ferry 407 connects Nilandhoo to Meedhoo in Dhaalu, to the south, every day except Friday (Rf20, 30 minutes).

Dhaalu

Dhaalu, or South Nilandhoo Atoll, has about 6500 people living on its seven inhabited islands.

The biggest and most interesting island is the capital, **Kudahuvadhoo** (population 1550), which has an ancient and mysterious mound. The mound is now just sand, but originally this was the foundation of a structure made of fine stonework. The building stones were later removed to build part of the island's mosque. Heyerdahl said the rear wall of this mosque had some of the finest masonry he had ever seen, surpassing even that of the famous Inca wall in Cuzco, Peru. He was amazed to find a masterpiece of stone-shaping art on such an isolated island, although the Maldivians had a reputation in the Islamic world for finely carved tombstones. Kudahuvadhoo is a long way from the resorts on this atoll, so visiting is difficult, but worth enquiring about.

In the north of the atoll are the so-called jewellers' islands. **Ribudhoo** (population 700) has long been known for its silversmiths and goldsmiths, who are believed to have learnt the craft from a royal jeweller banished here by a sultan centuries ago. Another possibility is that they developed their skills on gold taken from a shipwreck in the 1700s. The nearby island of **Hulhudheli** (population 740) is a community of traditional silversmiths. Many of the craftspeople here are now making jewellery, beads and carvings from black corals and mother-of-pearl. Both islands are quite accessible from the nearby resorts.

🏃 Activities

A big attraction of the resorts in this atoll is the access to infrequently explored dive sites.

Fushi Kandu   DIVING
A channel on the northern edge of the atoll, Fushi Kandu is a Protected Marine Area. Steps on the east side have eagle rays and white-tip reef sharks. Thilas inside the channel are covered with hard and soft corals, and are frequented by turtles, Napoleon wrasse and schooling snappers. Look for yellowmouth morays and scorpionfish in the crevices.

Macro Spot   DIVING
Macro Spot, a sheltered, shallow giri, makes a suitable site for snorkellers, novices and macrophotographers. Overhangs and nooks shelter lobsters, cowries, glassfish, blennies and gobies.

🛏 Sleeping

The brand new resort of **Niyama** (www.niyama.peraquum.com) was nearing completion in early 2012, and it set to be a hugely luxurious resort set over the two islands of Embudhufushi and Olhuveli.

TOP CHOICE **Vilu Reef**   ACTIVITIES RESORT **$$**
(📞676 0011; www.vilureef.com; half board s/d/wv US$382/406/585; ❄@🛜☀) Vilu Reef is something of a closely guarded secret for its many repeat visitors. It's small and has huge palms and great beaches (especially good on the lagoon side) almost all the way around the island. The island is thick with trees and bushes and, despite being quite crowded, has been developed with considerable care.

The style is traditional on the outside (white walls, thatched roofs) and modern convenience inside. The rooms range from the attractive but simple beach villas to the far more sumptuous water villas, which mirror the shape of the island forming a huge oval. They are all equipped with mod cons and decent outdoor bathrooms.

On one side, a wide beach faces a lagoon that's perfect for sailing and sheltered swimming, while on the other side a good but narrower beach runs alongside a house reef that offers excellent snorkelling. Divers are well catered for by the reasonably priced diving school, which runs a full range of courses. The resort has a buffet main restaurant and a smarter à la carte place to take care of all your dining needs.

Vilu Reef combines friendly informality with some class and style – and it's suited to people looking for well-priced diving without having to go to a very basic resort.

Angsana Velavaru   LUXURY RESORT $$$

(📞676 0028; www.angsana.com; r/wv US$715/1920; ❄@🛜) This ultra-chic resort is Angsana's second Maldivian property and one that boasts classy accommodation with a strong Asian feel. The deluxe beachfront villas with pools are sumptuous.

Instead of over-water bungalows, the new 'InOcean' villas are stand-alone structures a kilometre out from the main island, connected by boats to the mainland across the lagoon. While they're dazzling, with every possible feature, including vast swimming pools, terraces, day beds and outdoor bathrooms, surely we can't be alone in wondering why you'd want to be so far from the main island?

The island itself is a real stunner – it has wide sandy beaches where turtles once nested (Velavaru means 'turtle island') – and while the wide lagoon is no good for snorkelling, there are free snorkelling trips every day. Dive sites in this atoll are not well documented, but the Velavaru Marine Centre is working on changing that.

Villa Stella   GUESTHOUSE $

(📞778 4769; www.villastellamaldive.it; Ribudhoo; s/d full board $100/200; ❄@) One of the very first guesthouses in the Maldives and to date the only one in Dhaalu, Villa Stella is a great place to enjoy life on an inhabited island and explore several spots around this largely tourist-free atoll. Even though Villa Stella used to catering to Italians, English is spoken, although there's a definite Italian feel to the meals served.

The six rooms here all have private bathrooms and share a living room with satellite TV and a communal kitchen. The staff members keep all visitors busy with daily excursions to a nearby uninhabited island where there's a superb sandy beach and plenty of lush vegetation under which to take shelter from the sun. Snorkelling and fishing trips are also arranged, and Ribudhoo island is a very friendly place to walk around and get to know the locals. If you don't speak Italian, you can book accommodation using www.guesthouses-in-maldives.com.

ℹ Getting There & Away

Trans Maldivian Airways (www.transmaldivian.com) seaplane charters serve the resorts in Dhaalu, while two ferry services connect the atoll's seven inhabited islands. The 405 ferry leaves Meedhoo at 7am on Saturday, Monday and Wednesday, and calls at all the inhabited islands on the western side of the atoll, arriving at Kudahuvadhoo at 10.15am, before making the return journey at 2pm, arriving back in Meedhoo at 5.15pm. The 406 ferry leaves Meedhoo at 7am on Sunday, Tuesday and Thursday and calls at all the islands on the eastern side of the atoll, arriving in Kudahuvadhoo at 10.10am and then makes the return journey at 2pm, arriving back in Meedhoo at 5.10pm. Tickets cost Rf20.

Thaa

Thaa Atoll is a large, slightly flattened circle about 60km across, and one of the major fishing regions of the country. It consists of 13 inhabited islands and is home to about 8500 people and, as yet, no resorts. The capital island is **Veymandhoo** (population 1100). All the islands are on the edges of the atoll, mostly clustered around the kandus, and they're quite densely settled. **Thimarafushi** (population 2400), near the capital, is the most populous island, and with two other islands makes up a sizable community. Ruins of a 25m-wide mound on the island of **Kibidhoo** show this group of islands has been populated for centuries.

On **Guraidhoo** (population 1800), in another island group, is the grave of Sultan Usman I, who ruled the Maldives for only two months before being banished here. On **Dhiyamigili** (population 750) there are ruins of the palace of Mohammed Imaadudeen II, a much more successful sultan who ruled from 1704 to 1721 and founded one of the Maldives' longest-ruling dynasties.

The northern island of **Burunee** (population 560) is a centre for carpenters, many of whom work elsewhere, building boats and tourist resorts. The women make coir rope and reed mats. Around the mosque are an old sundial and tombstones that have been dated to the late 18th century. The island of **Vilufushi** was abandoned by its inhabitants following the 2004 tsunami, but it is slowly being redeveloped as houses and infrastructure are gradually rebuilt.

ℹ Getting There & Away

There is no airport in Thaa Atoll. To get here, fly to nearby Laamu (see p115) and then take inter-atoll ferry route 503 from Kadhoo to Thimarafushi (Rf50, 3½ hours), from where you can connect to the other inhabited islands in the atoll by ferry.

Laamu

Laamu Atoll has about 14,000 people living on its 12 inhabited islands, and it's one of the major fishing centres in the country. Freezer ships anchor near the former capital, **Hithadhoo** (population 970), collecting fresh fish directly from the dhonis.

The island of **Kadhoo** has an airfield that has daily flights from Male. Kadhoo is linked by causeways to the large island of **Fonadhoo** (population 1770) to the south, which is now the atoll capital. The causeway also goes north to the island of **Gan** (population 2500), forming one of the longest stretches of road in the country – all of 12km. Maandhoo has a government-owned STO (State Trading Organisation) refrigeration plant and a fish-canning factory.

There are numerous archaeological sites in Laamu, with evidence of pre-Muslim civilisations on many islands. At the northeastern tip of the atoll, on **Isdhoo**, a giant, black dome rises above the palms. Who built the ancient artificial mound, known as a *hawitta,* and for what reason, is not really known. Buddha images have been found on the island, and HCP Bell (British leader of archaeological expeditions) believed such mounds to be the remains of Buddhist stupas, while Heyerdahl speculated that Buddhists had built on even earlier mounds left by the legendary Redin people. For many years the mound was a landmark for boats navigating between the atolls, but it didn't save the British cargo ship *Lagan Bank,* which was wrecked here on 13 January 1938. The **Friday Mosque** on Isdhoo is around 300 years old. It was probably built on the site of an earlier temple, because it faces directly west, rather than towards Mecca, which is to the northwest.

Bell also found quite a few mounds on Gan, which he also believed to be Buddhist stupas, and he found a fragment of a stone Buddha face, which he estimated was from a statue over 4m high. Almost nothing remains of these structures because the stones have been removed to use in more modern buildings. There are mounds on several other islands in Laamu, including Kadhoo, Maandhoo and Hithadhoo – one is over 5m high.

🛏 Sleeping

TOP CHOICE **Six Senses Laamu** LUXURY RESORT **$$$**
(☏680 0800; www.sixsenses.com; r/wv incl breakfast from US$1450/1570; ❋@🛜) The third resort from the Six Senses group in the Maldives and the first resort of any kind in Laamu Atoll, Six Senses Laamu is an amazing place, combining thoughtful luxury with rustic simplicity and plenty of activities. The island truly feels like it's in the middle of nowhere. Indeed, an hour's flight south of Male followed by a 25-minute speedboat ride to the island may add a significant amount of time to your journey, but it's certainly worth it, with gorgeous white beaches and an amazing cyan-blue lagoon setting the scene.

The 97 villas are all either right on the beach or over water, and they're something truly special, made from ecologically sourced wood and evoking a grand, classic style with plenty of hidden luxuries such as iPod docks and Bose entertainment systems. The water villas are particularly impressive with over-water hammocks, all-glass bathtubs and their own treetop decks, while the beach villas are ringed with trees and feel wonderfully private, but still offer direct beach access with your own loungers and expansive outdoor bathrooms. Each villa has its own GEM (guest experience manager) to look after its guests' needs from the moment they step onto the island.

Elsewhere on the resort, there's every imaginable facility (although no pool – again, for ecological reasons), including several superb restaurants, yoga and meditation centre, gym, gorgeous spa and full diving school and water-sports centre. There's also a fantastically well-trained staff whose efficiency and problem-solving abilities are second to none in an industry where customer service can still be very hit and miss, even at the top end of the market. If you can afford it, this resort is a great choice for intelligent luxury and indulgent ecotourism.

Reveries Diving Village GUESTHOUSE **$**
(☏680 8866; www.reveriesmaldives.com; Gan; r incl breakfast from $100; ❋🛜⊠) The first guesthouse in Laamu is this very smart place, which is about the best compromise between the luxury of a resort and the cost of a guesthouse we have yet found. Gan, the island it's on, is the longest in the country and one of its most interesting too, boasting a large lake (by local standards) and a slew of Buddhist ruins. Moreover, as Gan is connected to Kadhoo and Fonadhoo by causeways, it's possible to explore other nearby islands without hiring a boat, making this a great choice if you'd like to see lots of local life.

As its name suggests, the guesthouse is aimed at divers who take advantage of the incredible diving all over the atoll, much of it still being documented. However, there are plenty of other activities on offer, including surfing, wakeboarding, fishing and kayaking, so it's hard to be bored. The rooms are some of the smartest guesthouse accommodation in the country, with stylish furniture, minibar, good bathrooms and satellite TV. Meals are good and the young staff members are keen to help out and ensure you enjoy your stay on this interesting island.

❶ Getting There & Away

There are four daily flights with **Maldivian** (www.maldivian.aero) from Male to the airstrip on Kadhoo ($268 return, 50 minutes), while two ferry routes connect the inhabited islands in the atoll. Route 504 connects Gan to all islands north to Isdhoo, while route 505 connects Fonadhoo to Maavah, calling at each inhabited island on the way. Inter-atoll ferry route 503 connects Kadhoo with Thimarafushi in Thaa Atoll. It leaves Thimarafushi at 11.15am daily, arriving in Kadhoo at 2.45pm, and then returns to Thimarafushi at 3.15pm. It costs Rf50 each way.

Gaafu Alifu

The giant Huvadhoo Atoll, one of the largest coral atolls in the world, is separated from Laamu by the 90km-wide Huvadhoo Kandu. This stretch of water is also called the One-and-a-Half-Degree Channel, because of its latitude, and it's the safest place for ships to pass between the atolls that make up the Maldives.

Because Huvadhoo is so big, the atoll is divided into two administrative districts. The northern district is called Gaafu Alifu, and it has 11 inhabited islands and about 12,000 people. **Viligili**, the capital island, is also the most populated, with about 3000 people. Just south, the island of **Kudhoo** has an ice plant and fish-packing works. The atoll also has some productive agriculture, much of it on **Kondey** (population 440). This island also has four *hawittas* – evidence of Buddhist settlement. Heyerdahl discovered a limestone carving here, which he believed to be of the Hindu water god Makara. The statue must have been here before the Islamic period and is thought to be over 1000 years old. Its significance, Heyerdahl believed, lay in the fact that it demonstrated that other religions aside from Buddhism permeated the Maldives before Islam took hold in 1153.

In the centre of the atoll, **Dhevvadhoo** (population 1000) is famous for its textile weaving and coir-rope making. There are also mosques from the 16th and 17th centuries.

🛏 Sleeping

A brand new resort, the **Residence Maldives** (www.theresidence.com) was being completed at the time of writing and was due to open in mid-2012.

TOP CHOICE Jumeirah Dhevanafushi   LUXURY RESORT $$$

(📞682 8800; www.reveriesmaldives.com; r incl breakfast from $1500; ✳@🛜🌊) This off-the-scale place, which is already making a name for itself as one of the most indulgent and luxurious resort islands in the country, is the latest venture of Jumeirah in the Maldives. All rooms enjoy their own pools, and even the most basic villa is some 200 sq metres of timber flooring, marble bathrooms, Apple media centres and 24-hour butler service.

Definitely a contender for an incredible honeymoon, Jumeirah Dhevanafushi does it all so well, from personalised service to impeccable rooms and beaches. The style of the resort is thoroughly contemporary, and though there are some traditional touches such as thatched roofs, the rooms would be equally at home in Tokyo or New York, such are their sleek lines, contemporary furnishings and international modernity. The most striking aspect of the resort is the 'Ocean Pearls' water villas, which are not attached to the main island, but are freestanding on the lagoon and only accessible by boat. Everything here is impressive, from the vast 3m-long beds to the enormous bathtubs and the gorgeous over-water spa and gym. Despite the resort being small and exclusive, there are three outstanding dining options to choose from as well as an excellent cocktail bar. Look no further for total luxury and pampering in a contemporary and stylish setting.

ALSO IN GAAFU ALIFU

Robinson Club (www.robinson.com) This popular German-run midrange resort is also booked by agents from non-German-speaking countries and caters very well to them, with a large range of activities, great beaches and comfortable and stylish accommodation.

Laamu, Thaa, Gaafu Alifu & Gnaviyani

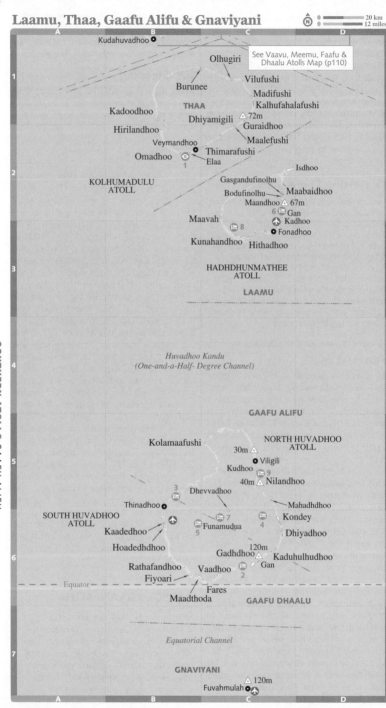

See Vaavu, Meemu, Faafu &
Dhaalu Atolls Map (p110)

0   20 km
0   12 miles

Kudahuvadhoo

Olhugiri

Vilufushi

Burunee

Madifushi

THAA   Kalhufahalafushi

Kadoodhoo   72m

Dhiyamigili

Hirilandhoo   Guraidhoo

Veymandhoo   Maalefushi

Omadhoo   Thimarafushi

Elaa

1

KOLHUMADULU   Isdhoo
ATOLL

Gasgandufinolhu

Bodufinolhu   Maabaidhoo

Maandhoo   67m

6   Gan

Maavah   Kadhoo

8   Fonadhoo

Kunahandhoo   Hithadhoo

HADHDHUNMATHEE
ATOLL

LAAMU

Huvadhoo Kandu
(One-and-a-Half- Degree Channel)

GAAFU ALIFU

NORTH HUVADHOO
Kolamaafushi   ATOLL

30m

Viligili

Kudhoo

9

40m   Nilandhoo

3   Dhevvadhoo

Mahadhdhoo

Thinadhoo   7   Kondey

4

SOUTH HUVADHOO   5   Funamudua
ATOLL   Dhiyadhoo

Kaadedhoo

Hoadedhdhoo

120m

Rathafandhoo   Gadhdhoo   Kaduhulhudhoo

Vaadhoo   2   Gan

Fiyoari

Equator   Fares

Maadthoda   GAAFU DHAALU

Equatorial Channel

GNAVIYANI

120m

Fuvahmulah

SOUTHERN ATOLLS GAAFU ALIFU

Laamu, Thaa, Gaafu Alifu & Gnaviyani

Park Hyatt Maldives Hadahaa   LUXURY RESORT **$$$**
(☏682 1234; www.maldives.hadahaa.park.hyatt.com; r incl breakfast from $1160; ✻@🛜🏊) Park Hyatt's first Maldivian venture offers its own brand of sleek and contemporary comfort in a remote and beautiful island setting.

With 50 villas set on a charmingly beach-ringed island, the look here is more architectural statement of difference than typical beach villa. The water villas are particularly striking: timber structures of very contemporary design open onto private sun decks with day beds and direct water access. The hotel's pool and main restaurant have a similarly modern feel, but it works very well, and guests clearly love the juxtaposition of city-sleek Park Hyatt with the remote Indian Ocean setting. Highly recommended for a glamorous, urban-edged retreat.

❶ Getting There & Away

Nearly all travellers to Gaafu Alifu fly to Kaad-edhoo in nearby Gaafu Dhaalu Atoll (see p118) where they are met by launches from their resort. For independent travellers there are six frequent ferries connecting most of the inhabited islands in the two atolls, including Kaadedhoo. The network is centred on the Gaafu Dhaalu's capital island Thinadhoo, and to a lesser extent on Gaafu Alifu's capital Viligili.

Gaafu Dhaalu

Geographically isolated from Male, but strategically located on the Indian Ocean trade routes, Gaafu Dhaalu – or Huvadhoo Atoll, to use its geographical name – had independent tendencies dating back many years. It had its own direct trade links with Sri Lanka, and the people spoke a distinct dialect almost incomprehensible to other Maldivians. The island of **Thinadhoo** was a focal point of the 'southern rebellion' against the central rule of Male during the early 1960s. So much so that troops from Male invaded in February 1962 and destroyed all the homes. The people fled to neighbouring islands and Thinadhoo was not resettled until four years later. It now has a population of around 6400, while the rest of the atoll's inhabitants are scattered among a further nine inhabited islands.

Although there's now a resort here, Gaafu Dhaalu remains a remote part of the country to visit, though it attracts a consistent number of foreign visitors who make boat trips around the southeastern edge of the atoll to surf the uncrowded waves that break around the channel entrances. On the island of **Kaadedhoo**, near Thinadhoo, a small airport has daily flights to Male, and surfing safari boats meet clients there.

On **Gadhdhoo** (population 2750), women make superb examples of the mats known as *thundu kunaa,* which are woven from special reeds found on an adjacent island. Souvenir shops in Male and on some resorts sell these mats – those from Gadhdhoo are the softest and most finely woven.

Just southwest of Gadhdhoo, the uninhabited island of **Gan** has remnants of one the most impressive *hawittas* in the Maldives, originally a pyramid with stepped ramps on all four sides, like many Mexican pyramids. The ruin was 8.5m high and 23m square. Heyerdahl also found stones here decorated with sun motifs, which he believed were proof of a sun-worshipping society even older than the Buddhist and Hindu settlements.

In the south of the atoll, only about 20km from the equator, the island of **Vaadhoo** has two *hawittas,* and a mosque that dates from the 17th century. The mosque is elaborately decorated inside and has a stone bath outside, as well as ancient tombstones carved with three different kinds of early Maldivian script.

Gaafu Dhaalu now has one functioning resort and the long-anticipated **Raffles Konottaa** (www.raffles.com) is due to open in the near future.

🛏 Sleeping

Ayada Maldives   LUXURY RESORT **$$$**
(☏684 4444; www.ayadamaldives.com; half board r from $1350; ✻@🛜🏊) Opening in late 2011,

SOUTHERN ATOLLS GAAFU DHAALU

the first resort in this pristine corner of the Maldives is a beautifully realised venture, with fantastic accommodation in large and beautifully designed villas on a perfect island surrounded by superb and largely undiscovered reefs for diving.

There are eight different villa types, sized from around 100 sq metres up to 300 sq metres. They're done out in timber and thatch and enjoy their own pools, sleek and contemporary furnishings with an Asian flavour and lots of luxurious extras such as Nespresso machines, iPod docks and full in-room bars. There are three restaurants on the island, as well as the fabulously indulgent overwater Wine and Cheese Island, where you can nibble fine cheeses paired with wines at sundown in a smart, club-like atmosphere. Other facilities include a gorgeous ESPA spa, a *hammam* and steam room, tennis and badminton courts, a full gym, a water-sports centre and a top-of-the-range dive school. This is a great place to escape the crowds and enjoy your own slice of Indian Ocean paradise in sumptuous but laid-back style.

❶ Getting There & Away

There are five daily flights with **Maldivian** (www. maldivian.aero) to and from Male from the airstrip on Kaadedhoo ($305 return, 70 minutes), from which most resorts in Gaafu Alifu also collect travellers. There is also a network of six frequent ferries connecting most of the inhabited islands in the atoll, as well as those in Gaafu Alifu. The network is centred on the capital island Thinadhoo.

Gnaviyani

The interesting island of **Fuvahmulah** (confusingly often called Foammulah or Fuamulaku) makes up the administrative district of Gnaviyani, a solitary place stuck in the middle of the Equatorial Channel with a population of around 11,000. About 5km long and 1km wide, it's the biggest single island in the country and one of the most fertile, producing many fruits and vegetables such as mangoes, papayas, oranges and pineapples. The natural vegetation is lush, and there are two freshwater lakes, making it geographically about the most varied place in the country. In recent years the building of a harbour and an airport here has greatly reduced Fuvahmulah's isolation.

Despite Fuvahmulah's apparent isolation, navigators passing between the Middle East, India and Southeast Asia have long used the Equatorial Channel. Ibn Battuta visited in 1344, stayed for two months and married two women. Two Frenchmen visited in 1529 and admired the old mosque at the west end of the island. In 1922 HCP Bell stopped here briefly, and noted a 7m-high *hawitta*. Heyerdahl found the *hawitta* in poor condition, and discovered remnants of another nearby. He also investigated the nearby mosque, the oldest one on the island, and believed it had been built on the foundations of an earlier structure built by skilled stonemasons. Another old mosque, on the north side of the island, had expertly made stonework in its foundations and in an adjacent stone bath.

There's nothing to stop you visiting Fuvahmulah, but there is no accommodation available on the island yet (though several hotels are in various stages of planning), so you'd have to arrange to stay with locals, or take a ferry to nearby Addu Atoll, where there are several resorts.

❶ Getting There & Away

There is a daily flight with **Maldivian** (www. maldivian.aero) to and from Male from Fuvahmulah's airstrip ($340 return, 70 minutes). There is also a daily ferry to and from Addu Atoll (1½ hours, Rf50), which leaves from the harbour at Maradhoo in Addu at 9.30am each day (2pm on Friday) and returns from Fuvahmulah at 12.30pm daily (4pm on Fridays).

Addu Atoll

Heart-shaped Addu Atoll is the most southern extreme of the country and is home to some of the most colourful corals in the country. There's a splash of late colonial flavour on Gan Island, where there was a British military base until the 1970s, and an independent streak flows through the locals, who even speak a different dialect of Dhivehi to that spoken in Male.

Addu Atoll (often called Addu City these days) is the main economic and administrative centre in the south of the country, and the only place to rival Male in size and importance. Its 18,000 people are spread out over seven islands that are connected to each other by causeways and land reclamation. Tensions with the north came to a head in the 1960s under the leadership of Abdulla Afif Didi, who was elected president

Addu Atoll

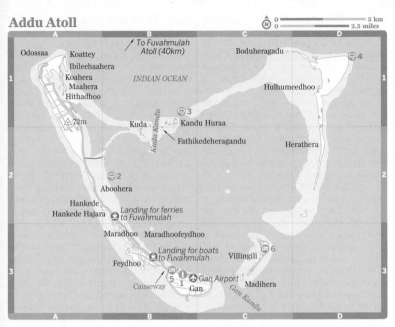

of the 'United Suvadiva Islands', comprising Addu, Fuvahmulah and Huvadhoo. Afif declared independence from the Maldives, but an armed fleet sent south by Prime Minister Ibrahim Nasir quashed the short-lived southern rebellion. Afif fled the country, but is still talked about on his home island of Hithadhoo. He went to live in the Seychelles, where he ultimately rose to the position of foreign minister.

The biggest influence on Addu's modern history has been the British bases, first established on Gan during WWII as part of the Indian Ocean defences. In 1956, when the British could no longer use Sri Lanka, they developed a Royal Air Force base on Addu as a strategic Cold War outpost. The base had around 600 personnel permanently stationed here, with up to 3000 during periods of peak activity. The British built a series of causeways connecting Feydhoo, Maradhoo and Hithadhoo islands and employed most of the population on or around the base. In 1976 the British pulled out, leaving an airport, some large industrial buildings, barracks and a lot of unemployed people who spoke good English and had experience working for Westerners. When the tourism industry took off in the late 1970s, many of the men of Addu went to Male to seek work

in resorts and tourist shops. They have never lost their head start in the tourism business and to this day, in resorts all over the country, there's a better than even chance that the Maldivian staff will be from Addu.

◉ Sights

GAN

Gan is atypical of the Maldives: it has a far more colonial feel and a refreshingly different atmosphere from anywhere else in the country. Inhabited since ancient times, Gan was the site where HCP Bell excavated a large 9m-high mound. He believed it to be the ruins of a Buddhist stupa. His expedition made careful measurements of the site, took photos and made precise drawings that are published in his monograph. This was fortunate, as the archaeological sites and almost everything else on Gan were levelled to create the air-force base in 1956.

The British took over the entire island and constructed airport buildings, barracks, jetties, maintenance sheds, and even a golf course. Many of these structures remain, some picturesquely run-down, others used for various purposes. Most of the island's lush native vegetation was cleared, but the British then landscaped with new plants – avenues of casuarinas, clumps of bougainvillea, swaths of lawn and rose gardens. It's much more spacious than most resort islands and it has a slightly weird and eerie atmosphere, but it's very peaceful and relaxed – like an old, abandoned movie set.

There's a low-key **memorial** to those who served on the base, including Indian regiments based here. Big guns, which were part of the WWII defences, now guard the memorial.

FEYDHOO, MARADHOO & HITHADHOO

Causeways connect Gan to the atoll capital Hithadhoo via Feydhoo and Maradhoo as well as some other tiny islands that are now joined together. There are no spectacular attractions along the way, but the smaller villages are an absolute delight. Local teashops serve tea, cakes and 'short eats', and some will have a more substantial fish curry. Remember that these villages are inevitably very conservative, so dress modestly.

Like most Maldivian villages they are laid out on a rectangular grid with wide, straight, sandy streets and white coral-stone houses. A few vehicles will be seen, but for most of the day the streets are empty. In the early morning, and especially the evening, locals will be out walking or cycling, sitting outside their houses or leaning against the low front walls. Shady trees overhang the streets and you can usually catch a glimpse of the sea at one end of the street or the other.

Most of the houses have corrugated iron roofs, but are otherwise traditional. Older buildings are made of coral-stone while newer ones are made of concrete blocks. There's usually a courtyard or an open space with a shady tree and a *joli* (net seat in a rectangular frame) or *undholi* (swing seat) providing a cool place to sit in the heat of the day. Notice the big, square chimney blocks – there are wooden racks inside them, where fish are hung to be smoked. Another distinctive feature can be seen at street junctions, where walls and buildings all have rounded corners.

You can easily walk from Gan to Feydhoo, which has several mosques – a large white one, a small, pretty blue one, and several old ones on the sandy back roads. On the new lagoon-side road are several new buildings, like the modern petrol station, a big store and a teahouse/cafe offering great 'short eats'. Boats to Fuvahmulah use the small harbour here.

When the British took over, the villagers from Gan were resettled on Feydhoo, and some of the people from Feydhoo were then moved to the next island, Maradhoo, where they formed a new village. Maradhoo now has a population of 3300 in two villages that have run together – the southern one is called Maradhoo-Feydhoo. The first thing you'll see as you approach up the road is the boat-building activity on the lagoon side.

Further north, the road follows an isthmus that was once three narrow, uninhabited islands. One island used to house an ammunition bunker. After a few kilometres of palm tree-lined road you pass a recycling zone and a sports ground with several football pitches and a grandstand. You're on Hithadhoo, the Maldives' largest town outside Male, with a population of 9500.

Near the main road there are several light-industry buildings and a power station, while a grid of streets with traditional houses extends to the western seashore. Beyond the built-up area, the tip of the island bends to the east, and is covered with coconut plantations, swampy lakes and woodland. The coast is mostly too rocky or shallow for bathing, but there are some narrow beaches. Rough roads go right to the tip of the island at Koattey, also called Demon Point. It's said there was once a fort here, and later a British gun emplacement, but there's nothing left to see now. It feels like the end of the earth.

WANT MORE?

Visit Lonely Planet's **Southern Atolls** (http://www.lonelyplanet.com/maldives/southern-atolls) and **Addu Atoll** (http://www.lonelyplanet.com/maldives/southern-atolls/addu-atoll) destination pages for planning advice, author recommendations, traveller reviews and insider tips.

HOW TO SPOT A TRULY LUXURIOUS RESORT

In case you have any doubts about where you're staying, this checklist should help you confirm you're in the very smartest of Maldivian resorts:

» You will not be given a fruit cocktail on arrival, but an iced ginger tea, home-made ice cream or fresh melon juice served in dainty earthenware cups.

» The staff line up on the jetty when you arrive and you have to work the line shaking their hands and feeling like a minor royal.

» Infinity pools all the way, and preferably your own lap pool so you don't have to mix with the hoi polloi in the main one.

» No glass floors in water villas – you should have your own sea garden or at least a staircase into the sea from your veranda.

» You have more towels than you know what to do with in your room, and more brand-name bath products than you can actually be bothered to steal.

» Staff members you have never even seen magically address you by your first name.

» Every time you leave your room a fleet of staff will swarm in to clean it.

HULHUMEEDHOO

At the northeast corner of the lagoon, this island has two adjoining villages, Hulhudoo and Meedhoo, both known as Hulhumeedhoo (total population around 6000). Legend says an Arab shipwrecked here in about 872 converted the islanders to Islam 280 years before the people of Male. The cemetery is known for its ancient headstones, many of which are beautifully carved with the archaic Dhives Akuru script. The southern half of Hulhumeedhoo is now the enormous J Resort Handhufushi, which is the second-largest resort in the country, and unusual for being on the same island as Maldivian settlements.

 ### Activities

A highlight of Addu is the magnificent coral, much of which escaped the widespread bleaching of 1998, which still affects much of the coral elsewhere in the country, despite impressive regrowth. If you've been diving elsewhere in the Maldives and then come here you'll be amazed. On the northern edge of the atoll you can see huge table corals that might be hundreds of years old, and fields of staghorns that have all but disappeared in most parts of the country. It's not all good, though – corals inside the lagoon suffered as badly as anywhere else from coral bleaching.

British Loyalty Wreck   DIVING

The British Loyalty Wreck has a good covering of soft corals, and turtles, trevally and many reef fish inhabit the encrusted decks. This oil tanker was torpedoed in 1944 by the German submarine U-183, which fired through an opening in the antisubmarine nets at the entrance to Gan Kandu. The disabled ship stayed in the atoll until 1946 when it was towed to its present location and used for target practice by another British ship. The 140m wreck lies in 33m of water with its port side about 16m below the surface.

Maa Kandu   DIVING

The northeastern edge of Maa Kandu has a wide reef top covered with live acrophora corals, big brain corals, long branching staghorns and table corals. White-tip reef sharks, eagle rays and sometimes mantas can be spotted, along with turtles and numerous reef fish. It's also excellent for snorkelling.

Kuda Kandu   DIVING

Near Maa Kandu, Kuda Kandu is a superb site where a huge array of coral thrives between 5m and 15m. Currents can be strong here, so it's not for novices.

Shark Point   DIVING

Off the northeast corner of the atoll, Shark Point, sometimes called the Shark Hotel, is a plateau at about 30m. Grey-tip reef sharks cruise around here, white-tip reef sharks lie on the sand and other sharks can be seen in deeper water further out.

Sleeping

Be aware that if you plan to stay in the country's far south, you'll need to take a 70-minute flight from Male, which can be exhausting after a long-haul flight. However, the magnificent diving and snorkelling are well worth the extra effort to get here.

SOUTHERN ATOLLS ADDU ATOLL

Shangri-La Villingili Resort & Spa
LUXURY HOTEL $$$

(☎689 7888; www.shangri-la.com/male/villingili resort; r/wv incl breakfast from US$1582/1930; ❄@ 🛜❄🛥) The Shangri-La group's first venture in the Maldives finally opened in 2009 after several years delay. However, it's truly been worth the wait, as the result is stunning and joins the ranks of the absolute top resorts in the country. With seven types of villa, each with its own private pool, Middle Eastern- and Indian-influenced decor and every little luxury you could wish for, from Nespresso machines to iPod docks, even the most discerning and demanding travellers will be hard pushed to find fault. Particularly great are the treehouse-style villas, which are raised off the ground and look and feel like a luxury version of *Swiss Family Robinson*, complete with a raised infinity pool. At the very top end, you'll find the amazing Villa Laalu, a two-bedroom villa over almost 1 sq km that features its own spa pavilion and is stuffed full of original artwork from all over Asia.

There are three restaurants here, but with a head chef who cut his teeth at Barcelona's El Bulli, this is no normal resort buffet fare. The main restaurant, Dr Ali's, is effectively three restaurants in one, with separate chefs specialising in Indian, Chinese and Arabic flavours.

The rest of the resort is just as impressive, including the incredibly lavish CHI spa, stunning white powder sand beaches, a nine-hole golf course, a full gym that includes a sauna and steam room, a superb kids club called the Cool Zone, tennis courts, a state-of-the-art dive centre, a water-sports centre and a great reef for snorkelling. You may have to travel a little further to get here, but Shangri-La Maldives really is worth it – a truly amazing slice of the Maldives paired with utter luxury and sophistication.

Equator Village
DIVING RESORT $

(☎689 8721; www.equatorvillage.com; s/d/tr all-inclusive US$146/208/281; ❄@❄) Equator Village is, for our money, one of the best-value diving resorts in the country. The additional expense of flying to Gan from Male is quickly offset by the low, low room rates and the all-inclusive packages they come with. More than anywhere else, though, staying here gives you the unique opportunity to see something of 'normal life' in the Maldives – this is no picture-perfect Maldivian desert island resort, and all the better for it.

It's clear this was formerly a British RAF base; neat lines of rooms (former barracks!) fan out from the main building, and are surrounded by well-tended gardens that overflow with exotic flowers and plants. The rooms are functional and thoroughly unromantic – this is not a honeymooners' destination.

The reception, bar and dining areas have been created from the old mess, completely redecorated in very unmilitary pink, white and grey. These open-sided spaces with their cane furniture and ceiling fans look out onto a sizable swimming pool and through palm trees to the blue sea beyond. The full-sized billiard table is a handsome inheritance from the Brits, as are the first-class tennis courts. The meals are all buffet with a limited selection. However, most guests are on an all-inclusive package, and can wash it down with beer and house wine. The all inclusive packages include free bike use, an island-hopping excursion with a barbecue, and a twice-daily boat to Villingili for snorkelling and beach time, which is important as the beach here on Gan itself isn't great. However, divers take note: the coral here is flabbergasting – and this should definitely be high on your list of top diving resorts. The dive centre is a small but friendly operation run by Diverland (www.diverland.com) and includes the great dive sites in the area at very reasonable prices.

❶ Getting There & Away

Maldivian (www.maldivian.aero) flies from Male to Gan and back four to five times a day. The fare for foreigners is US$350 return. There is also a daily ferry to and from Fuvahmulah (1½ hours, Rf50), which leaves from the harbour at Maradhoo at 9.30am each day (2pm on Friday) and returns at 12.30pm daily (4pm on Fridays).

Private yachts should report by radio to the National Security Service (NSS) in Gan or Hithadhoo to arrange security and customs clearance, but may have to continue to Male for health and immigration checks to complete the 'clear-in' process.

❶ Getting Around

The best way to get around Gan and over the causeway to neighbouring villages is by bicycle. Equator Village includes bike hire in its rates, but they aren't too comfortable for tall people. Taxis shuttle between the islands and around the villages; from Gan to Hithadhoo should cost about Rf100. Taxis wait at the airport and you can order one from Equator Village. The buses you see on the main road are only for workers in the Gan garment factories.

Understand the Maldives

≈ 250 people

Maldives Today

» Population: 328,536

» Percentage of population living in Male: 31%

» Area: 90,000 sq km (above water 298 sq km)

» Percentage of the country that is water: 99.9%

» Number of atolls: 26

» Number of shark attacks since 1976: none

The Maldives today is a country undergoing faster change than at any other time in its long history. After decades of extremely tight control and one-party rule, the country emerged blinking into a new dawn in 2008 with the election of its first democratically elected president, Mohammed Nasheed. The four years that followed saw momentous changes including the introduction of a tax system, a health-care system, a state pension, the creation of a national ferry network, the lifting of travel restrictions for foreigners and the building of guesthouses on inhabited islands for the first time. However, this culminated in Nasheed's sudden resignation in February 2012, which he later claimed was forced upon him at gunpoint. Nasheed's removal plunged the infant Maldivian democracy into a deep crisis.

The direction of the country following the February 2012 upheaval remains anyone's guess. While Nasheed's successor, his one-time deputy, Dr Mohammed Waheed Hassan, has stated his commitment to the constitutionally mandated presidential elections in 2013, he has rejected calls from the international community to call an earlier vote due to the controversial nature of his rise to the presidency.

In many ways it was an incredible feat for the conservative, poorly educated Maldives to move so boldly to full democracy in 2008, becoming one of the first true Islamic democracies in the world, and it's sadly unsurprising that President Nasheed fell so dramatically from grace, as his modernising, reformist agenda was at odds with the country's rich elite.

Politics is therefore never far from conversations you'll have with locals, and you'll hear all kind of opinions about recent events, from claims that Nasheed was conspiring with Jews and Christians and had overreached his constitutional powers by arresting the chief justice to

Dos & Don'ts

» On inhabited islands you must conform to local dress codes. This means shoulders and midriffs need to be covered and, for women, the knees too.

» During Ramazan it's not acceptable to eat in public during daylight hours, except in resorts.

» In the atolls men don't normally shake hands with women, but it's quite acceptable for women to shake hands with other women. Likewise, foreign women shaking hands with local men isn't seen as unusual.

Dhivehi Greetings

Hello *A-salam alekum*
How are you? *Haalu kihine?*
Thank you *Shukria*
See you later *Fahung bada-luvang*

belief systems
(% of population)

Sunni Muslim

if Maldives were
100 people

65 would work in services
24 would work in secondary industries
11 would work in agriculture

counterclaims by Nasheed's allies that his removal was engineered by his predecessor, Maumoon Abdul Gayoom, and rich resort owners.

Beyond politics, religion and the changing nature of tourism are other subjects you'll hear a lot about. In recent years the practice of Islam has changed due to the lifting of media controls, which previously sought to contain religious programming. This is best illustrated by the number of women who now cover their heads in the country – just five years ago this was a rare sight in almost-secular Male, whereas today it's rare to see a woman without a covered head, and totally unheard of in the atolls.

While tourism has long been the main industry in the Maldives, its very nature is changing as the long-established model of keeping visitors separate from locals has been abandoned and new guesthouses are opening each month on inhabited islands that until recently had barely had any foreign visitors. This cultural shift has created a range of reactions in the country; in broad terms younger people seem to view it positively, while religious conservatives worry that the influence of Westerners on the devout Muslim population is more likely overall to be corrupting than beneficial.

Now is a fascinating time to visit the Maldives, especially if you're lucky enough to visit the capital or any other inhabited islands. The fast pace of change here, whether it be embracing modernity or reinvigorating traditional values, is all part of the charm of discovering this proud and fiercely independent island nation.

» GDP per capita: US$8,400

» Percentage of GDP spent on defence: 5.5%

» Minimum number of Maldivians legally required to be employed at a resort: 50%

» Inflation: 6%

Jinnis

Belief in traditional folklore is widespread. Particularly strong is the belief in jinnis, spirits that can be benevolent or malevolent. They're believed to influence humans, causing everything from illness to successful careers.

Films & Books

The Island President (Jon Shenk, 2011) Depressing and revealing documentary about former President Nasheed and his quest to make the world care about climate change and do something about it.

Beach Babylon (Imogen Edwards-Jones, 2004) An amusing behind the scenes exposé set in a luxurious Maldivian resort.
Dive the Maldives (Sam Harwood & Rob Bryning, 2009) The best guidebook to dive sites, fish and other marine life for the Maldives.

History

The history of the Maldives is that of a small, isolated and peaceful nation constantly trying to contain the desires of its powerful neighbours and would-be colonisers. It's also an incredibly hazy history for the most part – of which little before the conversion to Islam in 1153 is known. Indeed, the pre-Muslim period is full of heroic myths, mixed with conjecture based on inconclusive archaeological discoveries.

The Maldivian character has clearly been shaped by this tumultuous past: hospitable and friendly but fiercely proud and independent at the same time. It's safe to say that conquering armies haven't got very far trying to persuade the Maldivian people of their benevolence.

Early Days

Some archaeologists, including the now discredited Thor Heyerdahl, believe that the Maldives was well-known from around 2000 BC, and was a trading junction for several ancient maritime civilisations, including Egyptians, Romans, Mesopotamians and Indus Valley traders. The legendary sun-worshipping people called the Redin may have descended from one of these groups.

Around 500 BC the Redin either left or were absorbed by Buddhists, probably from Sri Lanka, and by Hindus from northwest India. HCP Bell, a British commissioner of the Ceylon Civil Service, led archaeological expeditions to the Maldives in 1920 and 1922. Among other things, he investigated the ruined, dome-shaped structures *(hawittas),* mostly in the southern atolls, which he believed were Buddhist stupas similar to the *dagobas* found in Sri Lanka.

The Portuguese

Early in the 16th century the Portuguese, who were already well established in Goa in western India, decided they wanted a greater share of the profitable trade routes of the Indian Ocean. They were given permission

TIMELINE	1117	1194	1333
	The first king of the Theemuge dynasty, and the first king of the whole Maldives, Sri Mahabarana, is crowned, bringing together under one ruler the many fiefdoms that made up the country at the time	The Isdhoo Loamaafaanu, a copperplate now believed to show the earliest recorded example of Maldivian script, is made. Among other things it details the execution of Buddhist monks in the south of the Maldives.	Ibn Battuta arrives in the Maldives for a nine-month stay, during which time he marries twice and leaves disappointed by the moral laxity of the locals.

by the sultan to build a fort and a factory in Male, but it wasn't long before they wanted more from the Maldives.

In 1558, after a few unsuccessful attempts, Captain Andreas Andre led an invasion army and killed Sultan Ali VI. The Maldivians called the Portuguese captain 'Andiri Andirin' and he ruled Male and much of the country for the next 15 years. According to some Maldivian beliefs, Andre was born in the Maldives and went to Goa as a young man, where he came to serve the Portuguese. (Apart from a few months of Malabar domination in Male during the 18th century, this was the only time that another country has occupied the Maldives; some argue that the Portuguese never actually ruled the Maldives at all, but had merely established a trading post.)

According to popular belief, the Portuguese were cruel rulers, and ultimately decreed that Maldivians must convert to Christianity or be killed. There was ongoing resistance, especially from Mohammed Thakurufaanu, son of an influential family on Utheemu Island in the northern atoll of Haa Alifu. Thakurufaanu, with the help of his two brothers and some friends, started a series of guerrilla raids, culminating in an attack on Male in which all the Portuguese were slaughtered.

This victory is commemorated annually as National Day on the first day of the third month of the lunar year. There is a memorial centre on the island of Utheemu to Thakurufaanu, the Maldives' greatest hero, who went on to found the next sultanic dynasty, the Utheemu, which ruled for 120 years. Many reforms were introduced, including a new judicial system, a defence force and a coinage to replace the cowry currency.

The Story of Mohamed Thakurufaanu, by Hussain Salahuddeen, tells the story of the Maldives' greatest hero, who liberated the people from the Portuguese.

CONVERSION TO ISLAM

For many years Arab traders stopped at the Maldives en route to the Far East – their first record of the Maldive islands, which they called Dibajat, is from the 2nd century AD. Known as the 'Money Isles', the Maldives provided enormous quantities of cowry shells, an international currency of the early ages. It must have seemed a magical land to discover at the time – forget money growing on trees, in the Maldives it was washed up on the shore!

Abul Barakat Yoosuf Al Barbary, a North African, is credited with converting the Maldivians to Islam in 1153. Though little is really known about what happened, Barakat was a Hafiz, a scholar who knew the entire Quran by heart, and who proselytised in Male for some time before meeting with success. One of the converts was the sultan, followed by the royal family. After conversion the sultan sent missionaries to the atolls to convert them too, and Buddhist temples around the country were destroyed or neglected.

A series of six sultanic dynasties followed, 84 sultans and sultanas in all, although some did not belong to the line of succession. At one stage, when the Portuguese first arrived on the scene, there were actually two ruling dynasties, the Theemuge (or Malei) dynasty and the Hilali.

1337

The Friday Mosque in Male is rebuilt by order of Sultan Ahmed Shihabuddin. The previous Friday Mosque, dating from 1153, had become run down.

1573

The Portuguese are driven out of the Maldives following an attack on the Portuguese garrison led by Mohammed Thakurufaanu. To this day, the event is celebrated as the country's National Day.

1796

The British expel the Dutch from Ceylon and stake their claim to the Maldives, declaring it a 'British Protected Area'.

» Maldivian carving

DOMINIC SANSONI/ALAMY ©

128

Protected Independence

The Portuguese attacked several more times, and the rajahs of Cannanore, South India (who had helped Thakurufaanu), also attempted to
gain control. In the 17th century, the Maldives accepted the protection
of the Dutch, who ruled Ceylon at the time. They also had a short-lived
defence treaty with the French, and maintained good relations with the
British, especially after the British took possession of Ceylon in 1796.
These relations enabled the Maldives to be free of external threats while

THE LEGEND OF THAKURUFAANU

As the man who led a successful revolution against foreign domination, and then as the
leader of the newly liberated nation, Mohammed Thakurufaanu (sultan from 1573 to 1585)
is the Maldives' national hero. Respectfully referred to as Bodu Thakurufaanu (*bodu* meaning 'big' or 'great'), he is to the Maldives what George Washington is to the USA. The story
of his raid on the Portuguese headquarters in Male is part of Maldivian folklore and incorporates many compelling details.

In his home atoll of Thiladhunmathee, Thakurufaanu's family was known and respected
as sailors, traders and *kateebs* (island chiefs). The family gained the trust of Viyazoaru,
the Portuguese ruler of the four northern atolls, and was given the responsibility of dis-
seminating orders, collecting taxes and carrying tribute to the Portuguese base in Ceylon.
Unbeknown to Viyazoaru, Thakurufaanu and his brothers used their position to foster
anti-Portuguese sentiment, recruit sympathisers and gain intelligence. It also afforded the
opportunity to visit southern India, where Thakurufaanu obtained a pledge from the rajah
of Cannanore to assist in overthrowing the Portuguese rulers of the Maldives.

Back in Thiladhunmathee Atoll, Thakurufaanu and his brothers built a boat in which to
conduct an attack on Male. This sailing vessel, named *Kalhuoffummi*, has its own legendary
status – it was said to be not only fast and beautiful, but to have almost magical qualities
that enabled it to elude the Portuguese on guerrilla raids and reconnaissance missions.

For the final assault, they sailed south through the atolls by night, stopping by day to
gather provisions and supporters. Approaching Male, they concealed themselves on a
nearby island. They stole into the capital at night to make contact with supporters there and
to assess the Portuguese defences. They were assisted in this by the local imam, who subtly
changed the times of the morning prayer calls, tricking the Portuguese into sleeping late
and giving Thakurufaanu extra time to escape after his night-time reconnaissance visits.

In the ensuing battle the Maldivians, with help from a detachment of Cannanore soldiers, defeated and killed some 300 Portuguese. The Thakurufaanu brothers then set
about re-establishing a Maldivian administration under Islamic principles. Soon after, Bodu
Thakurufaanu became the new sultan, with the title of Al Sultan-ul Ghazi Mohammed
Thakurufaanu Al Auzam Siree Savahitha Maharadhun, first Sultan of the third dynasty of
the Kingdom of the Maldives.

1834	1887	1932	1953
Captain Robert Moresby, the British maritime surveyor, begins his celebrated charting of the Maldives' waters, the first time the complex atolls, islands and reefs are mapped.	The Maldives becomes a self-governing British Protectorate after Borah merchants, British citizens from India, become embroiled in local disagreements. The British step in, but Maldivian sultans continue to rule.	The country writes its first constitution, curbing the sultan's powers.	The Maldives declares itself a republic within the British Commonwealth and dissolves the sultanate.

maintaining internal autonomy. Nevertheless, it was the remoteness of the islands, the prevalence of malaria and the lack of good ports, naval stores or productive land that were probably the main reasons neither the Dutch nor the British established a colonial administration.

In the 1860s Borah merchants from Bombay were invited to Male to establish warehouses and shops, but it wasn't long before they acquired an almost exclusive monopoly on foreign trade. The Maldivians feared the Borahs would soon gain complete control of the islands, so Sultan Mohammed Mueenuddin II signed an agreement with the British in 1887 recognising the Maldives' statehood and formalising its status as a protectorate.

The Early 20th Century

In 1932 the Maldives' first constitution was drawn up under Sultan Shamsuddin, marking the dawn of true Maldivian statehood. The sultan was to be elected by a 'council of advisers' made up of the Maldivian elite, rather than being a hereditary position. In 1934 Shamsuddin was deposed and Hasan Nurudin became sultan.

WWII brought great hardship to the Maldives. Maritime trade with Ceylon was severely reduced, leading to shortages of rice and other necessities – many died of illness or malnutrition. A new constitution was introduced in 1942, and Nurudin was persuaded to abdicate the following year. His replacement, the elderly Abdul Majeed Didi, retired to Ceylon leaving the control of the government in the hands of his prime minister, Mohammed Amin Didi, who nationalised the fish export industry, instituted a broad modernisation program and introduced an unpopular ban on tobacco smoking.

When Ceylon gained independence in 1948, the Maldivians signed a defence pact with the British, which gave the latter control over foreign affairs but not the right to interfere internally. In return, the Maldivians agreed to provide facilities for British defence forces, giving the waning British Empire a vital foothold in the Indian Ocean after the loss of India.

In 1953 the sultanate was abolished and a republic was proclaimed with Amin Didi as its first president, but he was overthrown within a year. The sultanate was returned, with Mohammed Farid Didi elected as the 94th sultan of the Maldives.

British Bases & Southern Secession

While Britain did not overtly interfere in the running of the country, it did secure permission to re-establish its wartime airfield on Gan in the southernmost atoll of the country, Addu. In 1956 the Royal Air Force began developing the base, employing hundreds of Maldivians and resettling local people on neighbouring islands. The British were informally granted a 100-year lease of Gan that required them to pay £2000 a year.

The Maldive Islands: Monograph on the History, Archaeology & Epigraphy is HCP Bell's main work. The Ceylon Government Press published it in 1940, three years after his death. Original copies of the book are rare, reprints are available from bookshops in Male.

1954	**1959**	**1962**	**1965**
The sultanate is restored as debate rages about how best to replace the institution.	The three southernmost atolls of the Maldives – Addu, Gnaviyani and Huvadhoo – declare their independence from the rest of the country founding the United Suvadive Republic.	The United Suvadive Republic is forced to give up its independence bid, fostering wide resentment against the British, who many in the southern atolls believe betrayed them.	The Maldives finally gains full independence from the UK. The country does not opt to join the British Commonwealth, however, and remains outside the organisation until 1982.

When Ibrahim Nasir was elected prime minister in 1957, he immediately called for a review of the agreement with the British on Gan, demanding that the lease be shortened and the annual payment increased. This was followed by an insurrection against the Maldivian government by the inhabitants of the southern atolls of Addu, Huvadhoo and Gnaviyani, who objected to Nasir's demand that the British cease employing local labour. They decided to cut ties altogether and form an independent state in 1959, electing Abdulla Afif Didi president and believing that the so-called United Suvadive Republic would be recognised by the British.

In 1960 the Maldivian government officially granted the British the use of Gan and other facilities in Addu Atoll for 30 years (effective from December 1956) in return for the payment of £100,000 a year and a grant of £750,000 to finance specific development projects. Brokering a deal with the British on Gan effectively ruled out the UK recognising the breakaway south, and indeed Nasir eventually sent gunboats from Male to quash the rebellion. Afif fled to the Seychelles, then a British colony, while other leaders were banished to various islands in the Maldives.

In 1965 Britain recognised the islands as a sovereign and independent state, and ceased to be responsible for their defence (though it retained the use of Gan and continued to pay rent until 1976). The Maldives was granted independence on 26 July 1965 and later became a member of the UN.

Travels in Asia & Africa 1325–54, by Ibn Battuta, is the account of a great Moorish globetrotter's travels and includes early testimony of life in the Maldives shortly after the arrival of Islam.

The Republic

Following a referendum in 1968, the sultanate was again abolished, Sultan Majeed Didi retired to Sri Lanka and a new republic was inaugurated. Nasir was elected president, although as political parties remained illegal, he didn't face much opposition. In 1972 the Sri Lankan market for dried fish, the Maldives' biggest export, collapsed. The first tourist resorts opened that year, but the money generated didn't benefit many ordinary inhabitants of the country. Prices kept going up and there were revolts, plots and banishments as Nasir clung to power. In 1978, fearing for his life, Nasir stepped down and skipped across to Singapore, reputedly with US$4 million from the Maldivian national coffers.

The Maldive Mystery, by Thor Heyerdahl, the Norwegian explorer of *Kon-Tiki* fame, describes a short expedition in 1982–83 looking for remains of pre-Muslim societies.

A former university lecturer and Maldivian ambassador to the UN, Maumoon Abdul Gayoom, became president in Nasir's place. Hailed as a reformer, Gayoom's style of governing was initially much more open, and he immediately denounced Nasir's regime and banished several of the former president's associates. A 1980 attempted coup against Gayoom, involving mercenaries, was discovered and more banishment occurred. Despite Gayoom's reputation as a reformer, he made no move to institute democracy in the Maldives.

Gayoom was re-elected in 1983 and continued to promote education, health and industry, particularly tourism. He gave the tiny country a

1968	1972	1976	1978
The Maldives abolish the sultanate and declare themselves a republic again. Ibrahim Nasir becomes the first president of the country.	Kurumba Island, the Maldives' first holiday resort, just a short distance from Male, opens and a small trickle of intrepid travellers begin to arrive in search of the best beaches in the world.	The British Royal Air Force base at Gan in the southern Maldives closes and economic recession in the Maldives follows.	President Gayoom comes to power, ushering in three decades of massive development and growth in the tourism industry, but simultaneously seeing the stifling of dissent and the banning of political parties.

higher international profile with full membership in the Commonwealth and the South Asian Association for Regional Co-operation (SAARC). The focus of the country's economy remained the development of tourism, which continued throughout the 1980s.

The 1988 Coup

In September 1988, 51-year-old Gayoom began a third term as president, having again won an election where he was the only candidate. Only a month later a group of disaffected Maldivian businessmen attempted a coup, employing about 90 Sri Lankan Tamil mercenaries. Half of these soldiers infiltrated Male as visitors, while the rest landed by boat. The mercenaries took several key installations, but failed to capture the National Security Service (NSS) headquarters.

More than 1600 Indian paratroopers, immediately dispatched by the Indian prime minister, Rajiv Gandhi, ended further gains by the invaders who then fled by boat towards Sri Lanka. They took 27 hostages and left 14 people dead and 40 wounded. No tourists were affected – many didn't even know that a coup had been attempted. The mercenaries were caught by an Indian frigate 100km from the Sri Lankan coast. Most were returned to the Maldives for trial: several were sentenced to death, but reprieved and returned to Sri Lanka.

The coup attempt saw the standards of police and NSS behaviour decline. Many people in police captivity reportedly faced an increased use of torture and the NSS became a widely feared entity.

Norwegian explorer and ethnographer Thor Heyerdahl was fascinated by the Maldives and its pre-Islamic culture. Although he spent many years trying to uncover the secrets of the past, many of his conclusions were later rejected.

Growth & Development

In 1993 Gayoom was nominated for a fourth five-year term, and confirmed with an overwhelming referendum vote (there were no free elections again). While on paper the country continued to grow economically, through the now massive tourism industry and the stable fishing industry, much of this wealth was concentrated in the hands of a small group of people, and almost none of it trickled down to the people of the atolls.

At the same time, the Maldives experienced many of the problems of developing countries, notably rapid growth in the main city, the environmental effects of growth, regional disparities, youth unemployment and income inequality.

The 1998 El Niño event, which caused coral bleaching throughout the atolls, was detrimental for tourism and it signalled that global warming might threaten the existence of the Maldives. When Gayoom began a fifth term as president in 1998, the environment and sea-level rises were priorities for him.

The 1990s saw the Maldives develop hugely – the whole country became linked up with a modern telecommunications system, and mobile

HEYERDAHL

1988

A coup d'état attempt by Sri Lankan mercenaries in Male is quickly foiled with Indian assistance.

1998

The El Niño weather system causes water temperatures to rise above 32°C for two weeks, this kills off vital algae and brings about coral bleaching still in evidence over a decade later.

2003

The beating to death of 19-year old Evan Naseem at Maafushi prison causes public protests in Male and across the country, and the first cracks in the Gayoom regime begin to show.

» Coral bleaching

phones and the internet became widely available. By the end of the century 90% of Maldivians had electricity and basic hospitals, and secondary school centres had been established in outer atolls. With Japanese assistance, Male was surrounded by an ingenious sea wall (which was to prove very useful just a few years later when the tsunami struck). In 1997, to accommodate a growing population, work began on a new island near the capital, which is an extra metre or so above sea level.

The Evan Naseem Killing

When a 19-year-old inmate at Maafushi Prison in South Male Atoll was beaten to death by guards in September 2003, a public outcry quickly followed. When Evan Naseem's family put their son's brutally tortured corpse on display Male spontaneously erupted in rioting. The People's Majlis (parliament), also known as the Citizens' Council, was stoned and police stations were burned by the mob. The NSS arrested and beat many rioters. In the same month President Gayoom was renominated as the sole presidential candidate for the referendum by the Majlis, a body made up in no small part of Gayoom family members and people appointed by the president.

Realising that something was up, Gayoom did make an example of the torturers who killed Evan Naseem, but stopped short of punishing or removing any senior ministers or Adam Zahir, the NSS chief of staff. Meanwhile, the Maldivian Democratic Party (MDP) was founded in Colombo in nearby Sri Lanka by young democracy activist and former political prisoner Mohammed Nasheed.

Under pressure from colleagues, and in a move to outflank the growing reform movement, Gayoom launched his own reform program in 2004. His proposals included having multiple candidates in the presidential election, a two-term limit for the president and the legalisation of political parties.

Democracy Arrives

Gayoom surprised many observers by following through with his reform package and a new constitution was ratified in August 2008, which led to the country's first freely contested elections later that year. As no party got an overall majority in the first round, a run-off was held on 29 October in which the Maldivian Democratic Party's Mohammed Nasheed, with the other candidates throwing their weight behind him, took 53.65% of the vote, becoming the country's first democratically elected leader.

One of Nasheed's first pronouncements as president was that his administration would not seek to prosecute any member of the former government, and in particular former president Gayoom. The government then embarked on a radical reform and liberalisation agenda with pledges to make the Maldives a carbon-neutral country within a decade,

The emblem of the Maldives Monetary Authority is the cowry shell, which is very common locally. These shells were used as currency in the ancient world, explaining the Arab sailors' delight when they discovered 'the Money Isles'.

For a detailed overview of Maldivian history see www.maldives story.com.mv.

2004	2005	2007	2008
The Indian Ocean tsunami wreaks havoc on the island chain, wiping out many towns and villages, leading to the abandonment of several islands and creating thousands of internally displaced people.	The People's Majlis, the Maldivian Parliament, votes to allow multiparty elections after a campaign for democracy that saw many activists beaten, imprisoned and harassed by the authorities.	A bomb in Sultan's Park in Male explodes, injuring 12 tourists. Later the same year three men are sentenced to 15 years in jail for terrorism, admitting they were targeting non-Muslims as part of a jihad.	The first democratic election in the Maldives sees Mohammed Nasheed elected to the presidency, beating Maumoon Abdul Gayoom and beginning a new era in Maldivian politics.

the creation of a fund to buy land for the future of the Maldives in the event that the country would eventually be lost to rising sea levels, a total ban on shark hunting, the privatisation of over 20 cumbersome state-run enterprises, the introduction of a national transportation network, the diversification of the tourism industry by the ending of the long-term policy of separating locals and travellers, and the creation of tax, pension and health-care systems. In just four years the Nasheed government dragged the country into the 21st century and made a name for the Maldives as a progressive Muslim state.

February 2012

All that changed on 7 February 2012, when President Nasheed resigned following a mutiny against his rule by first the police and then the army. As mandated in the constitution, the then vice president, Dr Mohammed Waheed Hassan, assumed the mantle of the presidency, and the country's new government was quickly recognised by all major powers as legitimate.

Over the next few days, however, it transpired that things weren't as cut and dry as they appeared. The former president claimed that he had been pressured at gunpoint to resign, with various businessmen known to be close to his predecessor, Maumoon Abdul Gayoom, being named as ringleaders in what was soon being called a coup d'état by the world's press.

The catalyst for the tide turning against the president was his arrest of the chief justice of the criminal court, Abdulla Mohamed, who President Nasheed claimed was blocking investigation of former Gayoom loyalists and who had ordered the release of Mohamed Jaleel Ahmed. Jaleel, an opposition politician, had been inciting demonstrations against the president by distributing leaflets accusing him of conspiring with Christians and Jews against Islam. Before finally deciding to arrest Abdulla Mohamed, Nasheed had tried to investigate his allegedly corrupt behaviour only to have the civil court ban the Judicial Services Commission from proceeding with its inquiries, effectively making Abdulla Mohamed untouchable. Eventually, Nasheed sent the Maldivian military to make the arrest, which immediately brought criticism both domestically and internationally, saying that the president had over-reached his power.

The arrest triggered protests in Male in late January and early February 2012, culminating in the resignation of the president on 8 February. While the Maldives quickly returned to business as usual under the new government of Dr Mohammed Waheed Hassan, it's still too early to say how this abrupt change of leadership will affect the Maldives fragile infant democracy.

President Mohammed Waheed Hassan was coincidentally the first person ever shown on the first broadcast of Maldivian TV back in 1978.

2009	2010	2012	2012
President Nasheed holds the world's first ever underwater cabinet meeting to highlight the effects of global warming and rising sea levels on the world's lowest-lying country.	A couple having a wedding at the Vilu Reef resort are filmed being insulted by the Maldivian staff in Dhivehi during their ceremony, causing a huge embarrassment for the country's tourist industry.	Mohammed Nasheed resigns from the presidency in what is quickly called a coup worldwide following a military mutiny against the government and weeks of protests in Male.	Mohammed Waheed Hassan takes over as president of the Maldives.

Maldivian Way of Life

National Psyche

Maldivians are devout Muslims. In some countries this might be considered incidental, but the national faith is the cornerstone of Maldivian identity and it is defended passionately at all levels of society. Officially 100% of the population are practising Sunni Muslims, and indeed, under the 2008 constitution, it's impossible to be a citizen of the Maldives if you are a non-Muslim. There's no scope for religious dissent, but frankly, there's also almost no desire *to* dissent.

This deep religious faith breeds a generally high level of conservatism, but that does not preclude the arrival of hundreds of thousands of non-Muslim tourists to the islands every year, coming to bathe semi-naked, drink alcohol and enjoy pork. It's definitely an incongruous situation, and one that is likely to come under some strain now that the tourist industry is no longer so separate from the local population following the recent government decision to permit the building of guesthouses on inhabited islands. While the fledgling guesthouses enforce local standards of dress and behaviour, just the regular presence of foreigners on islands that have historically been isolated from the outside world will inevitably bring change.

A deep island mentality permeates the country, so much so that people's first loyalty is to their own small island before their atoll or even the country as a whole. Not quite Asia, not quite Africa and not the Middle East, despite the cultural similarities, the Maldives has been slow to join the international community (it joined the Commonwealth and the South Asian Association for Regional Co-operation only in the 1980s).

The hardship implicit in survival on these remote and relatively barren islands has created a nation of hard workers. The work ethic runs throughout the country; historically a lazy Maldivian was a Maldivian who didn't eat.

Another feature of the Maldivian people is their earthy humour and cheerfulness. Joking and laughter is a way of life and you'll notice this without even leaving your resort – take a few minutes to speak to the local staff and you'll soon witness this for yourself.

Lifestyle

The most obvious dichotomy in lifestyle in the Maldives is between people in the capital Male and those 'in the atolls' – the term used by everyone to denote 'islanders' or anyone who lives outside the immediate area of bustling modernity that is Male.

In Male life is considerably easier and more comfortable than in the rest of the country on most fronts, with the obvious exception of space.

The Maldivian caste system has effectively disappeared today. Traditionally the very lowest caste was that of the palm-toddy tappers *(raa-veri)*.

Learn more about the amazing development of Hulhumale island, the artificial island next to Male that will provide the future base for the government and much of the city's population in the face of rising sea levels, at www.hdc.com.mv.

Life in Male, one of the most densely populated places on earth, is very crowded and can feel intensely claustrophobic. The past two decades of extraordinary growth have created a massive economy in Male, although many residents of the city complain that while there are plenty of opportunities to earn and live well in the commercial and tourism sectors, there's a great lack of challenging, creative jobs if exporting fish and importing tourists are not your idea of fun. With limited education beyond high school and few careers for those who are ambitious but lack good connections, it's no surprise that many young people in Male dream of going abroad, at least to complete their education and training.

On the islands things are far more simple and laid-back, but people's lives aren't always as easy as those in Male. In the atolls most people live on the extended family homestead (it's unusual to live alone or just as a couple in a way that it wouldn't be in Male), and both men and women assume fairly traditional roles. While men go out to work (in general either as fishermen or on jobs that keep them away from home for long stretches at a time in the tourist or shipping industries), women are the homemakers, looking after the children, cooking and maintaining the household. Fish are traded for other necessities at the nearest big island. Attending the mosque is the main religious activity, and on smaller islands it's probably the main social and cultural activity as well.

> Life expectancy for a Maldivian is about 63 years for men and 65 years for women.

The most important ritual in a male's life comes when he is circumcised at the age of six or seven. These are big celebrations that last for a week and are far more significant than marriages and birthdays (not celebrated). Marriage is of course important, but it's not the massive celebration it is in most of the rest of Asia.

Rural life for the young can be fairly dull, although despite appearances even tiny fishing villages are surprisingly modern; most now have telephones, radio and TV. Nevertheless, many teenagers effectively go to boarding school, as provision for education outside population centres is

ALL-PURPOSE, ALL-MALDIVIAN DHONI

The truck and bus of the Maldives is the sturdy dhoni, a vessel so ubiquitous that the word will become part of your vocabulary just hours after landing. Built in numerous shapes and sizes, the dhoni has been adapted for use in many different ways. The traditional dhoni is thought to derive from the Arab dhow, but the design has been used and refined for so long in the Maldives that it is truly a local product.

Traditionally, dhonis have a tall, curved prow that stands up like a scimitar cutting through the sea breezes. Most Maldivians say this distinctive prow is purely decorative, but in shallow water a man will stand at the front, spotting the reefs and channels, signalling to the skipper and holding the prow for balance.

The flat stern is purely functional – it's where the skipper stands and steers, casually holding the tiller with his foot or between his legs. The stern platform is also used for fishing, and for one other thing – when a small dhoni makes a long trip, the 'head' is at the back. If nature calls, go right to the stern of the boat, face forward or backwards as your needs and gender dictate, and rely on the skipper, passengers and crew to keep facing the front.

The details on a dhoni are a mix of modern and traditional. The rudder is attached with neat rope lashing, but nowadays the rope is always plastic, not coir (coconut fibre). The propeller is protected so it won't snag on mooring lines or get damaged on a shallow reef.

The best dhoni builders are said to come from Raa Atoll, and teams of them can be contracted to come to an island to make a new boat. Twelve workers, six on each side of the boat, can make a 14m hull in about 45 days if their hosts keep them well fed. The keel is made from imported hardwood, while the hull planks are traditionally from coconut trees. A lot of the work is now done with power tools, but no plans are used.

scant. There are a few preschools or kindergartens, where children start learning the Quran from about the age of three. There are government primary schools (madrasa) on every inhabited island, but some are very small and do not go past fifth grade. For grades six and seven, children may have to go to a middle school on a larger island. Atoll capitals have an Atoll Education Centre (AEC) with adult education and secondary schooling to grade 10 (16 years old).

Officially, 90% of students finish primary school, and the adult literacy rate is 98%. English is taught as a second language from grade one and is the usual language of instruction at higher secondary school – most Maldivians with a secondary education will speak decent English.

The best students can continue to a free-of-charge higher secondary school, which teaches children to the age of 18 – there's one in Male, one in Hithadhoo, in the country's far south, and one in Kulhuduffushi, in the far north. Students coming to Male to study generally take live-in domestic jobs, affecting their study time. Girls are often expected to do a lot of housework.

The Maldives College of Higher Education, also in Male, has faculties of health, education, tourism-hospitality and engineering as well as one for Sharia'a law. For university studies, many young Maldivians go abroad, usually to Sri Lanka, India, Britain, Australia or Fiji, and while there have been plans to found the country's first university for some time, the project has yet to materialise.

There is a system of bonded labour under which people must work for the government at a meagre wage for a period that depends on the length of their education in government schools. For many this means a stint in the National Security Service or in a government office. They may pursue another occupation part-time to establish their career or to make ends meet. Many people in Male have a second job or a business interest on the side.

Politics

A multiparty system was created by a unanimous vote of the People's Majlis (parliament; also known as the Citizens' Council) in 2005, followed by the promulgation of a new constitution in 2008. Under the 2008 constitution, which enacts the separation of powers and provides for a bill of rights, the Maldives is a presidential republic, with the president both head of state and head of government.

The Maldivian president is directly elected by the people and is limited to two five-year terms in office. The People's Majlis is in Male, the

The Maldives' biggest international ally is India, which has supported the new government and donated US$100m to the tiny island nation. Cynics point out that this generosity might have been because China is also wooing the Maldives as a friend, with an eye to building a submarine base in the country.

MEDIA IN THE MALDIVES

Until the election of a democratic government in 2008, the media in the Maldives was exceptionally tame and did very little but repeat the government line on the issues of the day. Debate was stifled, religious programming was almost nonexistent and the only possible means of dissent was online, which saw the rise of internet news sites such as the excellent *Minivan News* (www.minivannews.com), still your best first port of call for an overview of Maldivian news and opinion.

Things are rather different today, with a vibrant national debate being carried out in all media. Daily newspapers include *Miadhu* (www.miadhu.com) and *Haveeru* (www.haveeru.com.mv), both of which have excellent online English editions. You'll also see *Jazeera* and *Aufathis* on sale, but neither of these has an English edition online.

TV and radio stations are now crowded with debate and political programming too – the state-owned TV channel TVM often hosting talk shows and discussion panels about the political situation in the country.

capital island, and each of the 20 administrative atolls plus the island of Male have two representatives each, elected for five-year terms. The president chooses the remaining eight parliamentary representatives, has the power to appoint or dismiss cabinet ministers, and appoints all judges. All citizens over 21 years of age can vote.

The main political parties operating in the Maldives are the ruling Gaumee Itthihaad (National Unity Party), former President Nasheed's Maldivian Democratic Party (MDP), former President Maumoon Gayoom's Dhivehi Rayyithunge Party (DRP) and the Republican Party (Jumhooree Party).

Politics is likely to be a subject you'll hear many people talking about due to the abrupt resignation of the country's first democratically elected president, Mohammed Nasheed, in February 2012. The current president, Dr Mohamed Waheed Hassan, was previously Nasheed's vice president, and assumed the presidency on Nasheed's resignation following weeks of protests and a police and military mutiny that many people see as a coup d'état.

Economy

Fish and ships just about sum up the Maldivian economy beyond the tourist industry. Tourism accounts for 28% of GDP and up to 90% of government tax revenue. Each traveller pays a US$8 'bed tax' per night in the Maldives, and with almost one million visitors usually spending at least a week in the country per year, that's a considerable amount!

As with luxury destinations around the world, the Maldives felt the pinch of the global economic turndown quite severely, particularly in the budget and midrange categories, with many travellers cancelling their holidays in the wake of economic uncertainty. The Russian millionaires kept coming, however. They're just, in the words of one five-star-resort general manager, 'buying a little less vintage champagne'. The sky-rocketing Chinese market has helped too, with hundreds of thousands of Chinese middle-class visitors now swelling resort numbers, bringing a totally new demographic to the country's tourism industry. Finally, the sudden change of government in 2012 did lead to some cancellations, but in general doesn't seem to have affected the tourism industry too much.

The other major field of industry is fishing. Previous policies helped to mechanise the fishing fleet, introduce new packing techniques and develop new markets, which has seen the Maldives remain a major fish supplier to markets in Asia and the Middle East.

Nevertheless, the fishing industry is vulnerable to international market fluctuations. Most adult males have some experience in fishing, and casual employment on fishing boats is something of an economic backstop. Men are unlikely to take on menial work for low pay when there is a prospect that they can get a few days or weeks of relatively well-paid work on a fishing boat or dhoni. The 2009 ban on all shark fishing has earned the Maldives valuable environmental credibility, but has unsurprisingly been unpopular with fishermen, many of whom hunted sharks in Maldivian waters for sale to China.

Trade and shipping (nearly all based in Male) is the third-biggest earner; nearly all food is imported and what little domestic agriculture there is accounts for less than 6% of GDP. Manufacturing and construction make up 17% of GDP: small boat yards, fish packing, clothing and a plastic-pipe plant are modern enterprises, but mostly it's cottage industries producing coconut oil, coir (coconut-husk fibre) and coir products such as rope and matting. Some of the new industrial activities are on islands near Male while others, such as fish-packing plants, are being established in the outer atolls.

Income tax was introduced to the Maldives in 2012, along with a sales tax of 6% – the first time most Maldivians had ever had to pay tax in their life. As well as generating important income for the government, it was also aimed at getting the population to have more of a stake in their society.

Religion

Islam is the religion of the Maldives, and officially there are no other religious groups present. All Maldivians are Sunni Muslims. No other religions or sects are permitted and it is impossible to become a citizen of the country unless you are a Sunni Muslim.

Officially only Muslims may become citizens of the Maldives. It is possible for foreigners to convert and later become Maldivian nationals, although this is extremely rare.

The Maldives observes a liberal form of Islam, like that practised in India and Indonesia. Maldivian women do not observe purdah, although the large majority wear a headscarf. Ironically this has been driven by religious freedom and fashion more than anything else. Until the election of President Nasheed in 2008, the media was strictly controlled and religious broadcasts were not common. Since the onset of free speech, religious programming has become extremely popular, and young women throughout the country (though not in resorts) have reverted to covering their heads in huge numbers, making it fashionable and not always just a sign of particular religious devotion.

Prayer Times

The initial prayer session is in the first hour before sunrise, the second around noon, the third in the mid-afternoon around 3.30pm, the fourth at sunset and the final session in the early evening.

The call to prayer is delivered by the *mudhim* (muezzin). In former days, he climbed to the top of the minaret and shouted it out. Now the call is relayed by loudspeakers on the minaret and the *mudhim* even appears

---

WOMEN IN SOCIETY *AISHATH VELEZINEE*

In the 14th century, long before the call for equality gained momentum, the Maldives was ruled by women. Three queens reigned; one, Sultana Khadija, held the throne for 33 years from 1347 to 1379. The shift from monarchy to a constitutional republic barred women from the post of president, and this clause was only removed by the new 2008 constitution.

Traditional lifestyle, especially on the islands away from the capital, dictated gender-specific roles for women and men. Women tended to their children and household duties during the day, and cooked fish in the evenings. Men spent the day fishing and then rested in the evenings. Modernisation and development changed the traditional way of life and conferred a double burden on many women – income generation plus domestic responsibilities. More opportunities and better education mean that more women are ready to join the workforce or take up income-generating activities at home. This has become a necessity rather than a choice for most women living in Male, as rising expenses and changing lifestyles demand a dual income to meet basic family expenses.

Traditionally, a woman could choose a suitor and name a bride-price *(rhan)*. The bride-price is paid by the husband to the wife, at the time of marriage or in instalments as mutually agreed, but must be repaid in full if there's a divorce. Young women today quote higher bride-prices, reflecting higher expectations, and perhaps a scepticism about the fairytale happy-ever-after marriage. The wedding itself is a low-key affair, but is often followed by a large banquet for all family and friends, who can easily number in the hundreds.

Women in the Maldives can, and do, own land and property but in general women have a fraction of the property that men do. While inheritance generally follows Islamic Sharia'a law in the Maldives, land is divided according to civil law, whereby a daughter and son inherit equal shares of land.

There is little overt discrimination between the sexes. Although it's a fully Muslim society, women and men mingle freely and women enjoy personal liberty not experienced by women in most Muslim societies. However, Islam is used as a tool by some patriarchs to counter gender equality, even as they proclaim that Islam grants equality to women and men.

Aishath Velezinee is a Maldivian writer, researcher and women's rights advocate

IDOLATRY

Most countries prohibit the importation of things like narcotics and firearms, and most travellers understand such restrictions, but when you're forbidden to bring 'idols of worship' into the Maldives, what exactly does that mean? The Maldives is an Islamic nation, and it is sensitive about objects that may offend Muslim sensibilities. A small crucifix, worn as jewellery, is unlikely to be a problem, and many tourists arrive wearing one. A large crucifix with an obvious Christ figure nailed to it may well be prohibited. The same is true of images of Buddha – a small decorative one is probably OK, but a large and ostentatious one may not be.

Maldivian authorities are concerned about evangelists and the objects they might use to spread their beliefs. Inspectors would not really be looking for a Bible in someone's baggage, but if they found two or more Bibles they would almost certainly not allow them to be imported. It would be unwise to test the limits of idolatrous imports – like customs people everywhere, the Maldivian authorities take themselves very seriously.

on TV. All TV stations cut out at prayer time, although only TVM (the national channel) cuts out for the entire duration – satellite channels just have their broadcasts interrupted to remind Muslims to go to the mosque.

Shops and offices close for 15 minutes after each call. Some people go to the mosque, some kneel where they are and others do not visibly participate. Mosques are busiest for the sunset prayers and at noon on Fridays.

Ramazan

This month of fasting, which begins at the time of a particular new moon and ends with the sighting of the next new moon, is called Ramazan in the Maldives. The Ramazan month gets a little earlier every year because it is based on a lunar calendar of 12 months, each with 28 days. Ramazan begins on 10 July in 2013, 29 June in 2014 and 18 June in 2015.

During Ramazan Muslims do not eat, drink, smoke or have sex between sunrise and sunset. Exceptions to the eating and drinking rule are granted to young children, pregnant or menstruating women, and those who are travelling. It can be a difficult time for travel outside the resorts, as teashops and cafes are closed during the day, offices have shorter hours and people may be preoccupied with religious observances or the rigours of fasting. Visitors should avoid eating, drinking or smoking in public, or in the presence of those who are fasting. After a week or so, most Muslims adjust to the Ramazan routine and many say they enjoy it. There are feasts and parties long into the night, big breakfasts before dawn and long rests in the afternoon.

Kuda Eid, the end of Ramazan, is a major celebration that is marked by three days of public holidays. The celebrations begin when the new moon is sighted in Male and a ceremonial cannon is fired to mark the end of Ramazan. There are large feasts in every home for friends and family, and in the atolls men participate in frenzied *bodu beru* (big drum) ceremonies and other dancing, often all night. At this time, it's polite to wish locals 'Eid Mubarak'.

Local Beliefs

On the islands people still fear jinnis, the evil spirits that come from the sea, land and sky. They are blamed for everything that can't be explained by religion or education.

To combat jinnis there are *fandhita*, which are the spells and potions provided by a local hakim (medicine man), who is often called upon when illness strikes, if a woman fails to conceive or if the fishing catch is poor.

The hakim might cast a curing spell by writing phrases from the Quran on strips of paper and sticking or tying them to the patient or

You can address Maldivians by their first or last name. Since so many men are called Mohammed, Hassan or Ali, the surname is more appropriate. In some cases an honorary title like Maniku or Didi is used to show respect.

writing the sayings in ink on a plate, filling the plate with water to dissolve the ink, and making the patient drink the potion. Other concoctions include *isitri,* a love potion used in matchmaking, and its antidote *varitoli,* which is used to break up marriages.

Sport

Soccer is the most popular sport and is played all year round. On most islands, the late-afternoon match among the young men is a daily ritual, although volleyball and cricket are also common. There's a football league in Male, played between club teams with names such as Valencia and Victory, and annual tournaments against teams from neighbouring countries. Matches are also held at the National Stadium (p55) in Male.

Cricket is played in Male for a few months, beginning in March. Volleyball is played indoors, on the beach and in the waterfront parks. The two venues for indoor sport are the Centre for Social Education, on the west side of Male, and a newer facility just east of the New Harbour, used for basketball (men and women), netball, volleyball and badminton.

The Maldives has participated in the Olympics since 1988, but have yet to win any medals. Unsurprisingly, the team has never taken part in the winter Olympics.

Traditional games include *bai bala,* where one team attempts to tag members of the other team inside a circle, and a tug-of-war, known as *wadhemun. Bashi* is a women's game, played on something like a tennis court, where a woman stands facing away from the net and serves a tennis ball backwards, over her head. There is a team of women on the other side who then try to catch it.

Thin mugoali (meaning 'three circles') is a game similar to baseball and has been played in the atolls for more than 400 years. The *mugoali* (bases) are made by rotating on one foot in the sand through 360 degrees, leaving a circle behind. You'll sometimes see *bashi* in Male parks or on village islands in the late afternoon, but traditional games are becoming less popular as young people are opting for international sports.

Marine Life in the Maldives

The world beneath the water is one of the most compelling reasons to visit the Maldives, and whether you're diving on a reef thriving with life or walking across your resort's lagoon on a wooden walkway, you'll find yourself seeing many of the spectacular and unusual creatures for which the Maldives is famous.

Indeed, divers and snorkellers come back here again and again. The Maldives' combination of amazingly clear and warm water, rich and non-harmful marine life, and good environmental protection ensures that anyone with an interest in the marine life won't go home disappointed.

However, to really enjoy what you see, it's well worth reading about some of the more common creatures on the reef, as by doing so you'll be more able to understand their behaviour, recognise their habits and describe them to other divers and snorkellers.

Life on the Reef

Reefs are often referred to as the rainforests of the sea, and rightly so – even though they take up just 0.1% of the ocean's surface, they are home to around a quarter of all underwater species. Reefs are created by the calcium carbonate secreted by corals, and are most commonly found in shallow, warm waters, making the Maldives a perfect environment for these complex and very delicate ecosystems.

As well as the many types of coral, there are various shells, starfish, crustaceans and worms living directly on the reef. Then there are the 700 species of fish that directly or indirectly live off the reef, which can be divided into two types: reef fish, which live inside the atoll lagoons, on and around coral-reef structures; and pelagics, which live in the open sea, but come close to the reefs for food. These include some large animals, such as turtles, whales and dolphins, which are very popular with divers.

Despite its total size of 90,000 sq km, the Maldives is 99% water, and has just 298 sq km of land, effectively making it smaller than Andorra.

Coral

These are coelenterates, a class of animal that also includes sea anemones and jellyfish. A coral growth is made up of individual polyps – tiny tube-like fleshy cylinders. The top of the cylinder is open and ringed by waving tentacles (nematocysts), which sting and draw any passing prey inside. Coral polyps secrete a calcium-carbonate deposit around their base, and this cup-shaped skeletal structure is what forms a coral reef – new coral grows on old dead coral and the reef gradually builds up.

Most reef building is done by hermatypic corals, whose outer tissues are infused with zooxanthellae algae, which photosynthesises to make food from carbon dioxide and sunlight. The zooxanthellae is the main food source for the coral, while the coral surface provides a safe home for the zooxanthellae – they live in a symbiotic relationship, each dependent

The whale shark is the largest fish in the world – they regularly reach up to 12m in length and are one of the biggest diving attractions when they cruise the kandus in May.

on the other. The zooxanthellae give coral its colour, so when a piece of coral is removed from the water, the zooxanthellae soon die and the coral becomes white. If the water temperature rises, the coral expels the algae, and the coral loses its colour in a process called 'coral bleaching', something that happened in the Maldives during the El Niño weather incident in 1997–98, and the legacy of which can still be seen very clearly today.

Polyps reproduce by splitting to form a colony of genetically identical polyps – each colony starts life as just a single polyp. Although each polyp catches and digests its own food, the nutrition then passes between the polyps to the whole colony. Most coral polyps only feed at night; during the day they withdraw into their hard limestone skeleton, so it is only after dark that a coral reef can be seen in its full, colourful glory, which is the reason so many divers like to do night dives.

Hard Corals

These *Acropora* species take many forms. One of the most common and easiest to recognise is the staghorn coral, which grows by budding off new branches from the tips. Brain corals are huge and round with a surface looking very much like a human brain. They grow by adding new base levels of skeletal matter then expanding outwards. Flat or sheet corals, like plate coral or table coral, expand at their outer edges. Some corals take different shapes, depending on their immediate environment.

Soft Corals

These are made up of individual polyps, but do not form a hard limestone skeleton. Lacking the skeleton that protects hard coral, it would seem likely that soft coral would fall prey to fish, but they seem to remain relatively immune either due to toxic substances in their tissues or to the presence of sharp limestone needles. Soft corals can move around and will sometimes engulf and kill off a hard coral. Attractive varieties include fan corals and whips. Soft corals thrive on reef edges washed by strong currents.

CORAL BLEACHING – DEATH ON THE REEF

In March 1998, the waters of the Maldives experienced a temporary rise in temperature associated with the El Niño effect. For a period of about two weeks, surface-water temperatures were above 32°C, resulting in the loss of the symbiotic algae that lives within the coral polyps. The loss of the zooxanthellae algae causes the coral to lose its colour ('coral bleaching'), and if this algae does not return, the coral polyps die. Coral bleaching has occurred, with varying degrees of severity, in shallow waters throughout the Maldives archipelago. When the coral dies the underlying calcium carbonate is exposed and becomes more brittle, so many of the more delicate branch and table structures have been broken up by wave action. Mainly hard corals were damaged – soft corals and sea fans are less dependent on zooxanthellae algae and are thus less affected by sea temperature changes, allowing them to recover more quickly.

Some corals, particularly in deeper water, recovered almost immediately as the symbiotic algae returned. In a few places the coral was not damaged at all. In most areas, however, virtually all the old hard corals died, and it will take years, perhaps decades, for them to recover. Some of the biggest table corals may have been hundreds of years old. Marine biologists are watching this recolonisation process with interest .

The Maldives' dive industry has adapted to the changed environment, seeking places where the regrowth is fastest and where there are lots of attractive soft corals. There's still a vast number and variety of reef fish to see, and spotting pelagic species, especially mantas and whale sharks, is a major attraction. Some long-time divers have become more interested in the very small marine life and in macrophotography.

Reef Fish

Hundreds of fish species can be spotted by anyone with a mask and snorkel. They're easy to see and enjoy, but people with a naturalist bent should buy one of the field guides to reef fish, or check the posters that are often displayed in dive schools. On almost any dive or snorkelling trip in the Maldives you're pretty certain to see several types of butterfly-fish, angelfish, parrotfish, rock cod, unicornfish, trumpetfish, bluestripe snapper, Moorish idol and Oriental sweetlips, but as well as these common fish, you'll inevitably see far less common ones. For more on fish, see p146.

Sharks

It's not a feat to see a shark in the Maldives, even if you don't get in the water; juvenile reef sharks love to swim about in the warm water of the shallow lagoon right next to the beach and eat fish all day long. They're tiny – most never grow beyond 50cm long – but are fully formed sharks, and so can scare some people! They don't bite, although feeding or provoking them still isn't a good idea.

Get out into the deeper water and sharks are visible, but you'll have to go looking for them. The most commonly seen shark in the Maldives are white-tip and grey-tip reef sharks. The white-tip reef shark is a small, nonaggressive, territorial shark, rarely more than 1.5m long and often seen over areas of coral or off reef edges. Grey-tip reef sharks are also timid, shallow-water dwellers and often grow to over 2m in length.

Other species are more open-sea dwellers, but do come into atolls and especially to channel entrances where food is plentiful. These include the strange-looking hammerhead shark and the whale shark, the world's largest fish species, which is a harmless plankton eater. Sharks do not pose any danger to divers in the Maldives – there's simply too much else for them to eat.

In 2009 the Maldivian government outlawed the hunting of sharks, making the Maldives the world's first shark sanctuary. Seeing one of these graceful creatures up close on a reef is undoubtedly a highlight of any visit.

Whales & Dolphins

Whales dwell in the open sea, and so are not found in the atolls. Species seen in the Maldives include beaked, blue, Bryde's dwarf, false killer, melon-headed, sperm and pilot whales. You'll need to go on a specialised whale-watching tour to see them, however.

Dolphins are extremely common throughout the Maldives, and you're very likely to see them, albeit fleetingly. These fun-loving, curious creatures often swim alongside speedboats and dhonis, and also swim off the side of reefs looking for food. Most resorts offer dolphin cruises, which allow you to see large schools up close. Species known to swim in Maldivian waters include bottlenose, Fraser's, Risso's, spotted, striped and spinner dolphins.

Stingrays & Manta Rays

Among the most dramatic creatures in the ocean, rays are cartilaginous fish – like flattened sharks. Ray feeding is a popular activity at many resorts and it's quite something to see these muscular, alienesque creatures jump out of the water and chow down on raw steak. Stingrays are sea-bottom feeders, and are equipped with crushing teeth to grind the molluscs and crustaceans they sift out of the sand. They are occasionally found in the shallows, often lying motionless on the sandy bottom of lagoons. A barbed and poisonous spine on top of the tail can swing up and

Male sharks show their interest in females by biting them on the sides, often causing wounds, even though the female shark skin has evolved to be thicker than the male equivalent!

Hammerhead sharks are among the most spectacular underwater creatures in the Maldives. Your best chance of seeing them is early in the morning in Northern Ari and Rasdhoo Atolls.

The sea snake is an air-breathing reptile with venom 20 times stronger than any snake on land. Basically, don't touch them if you're lucky enough to see any!

Big Creatures of the Deep

Marine life on the reef is fabulous, colourful and fascinating, but what divers and snorkellers really want to see are the big creatures of the deep. Indeed, an encounter with an enormous whale shark can be the experience of a lifetime.

Sharks

1 If you're lucky, you'll see a wide range of sharks in the Maldives. Reef sharks are commonly seen, but one of the most impressive sights in the country is a school of hammerheads at Rasdhoo Madivaru (aka Hammerhead Point; p83) in Rasdhoo Atoll.

Moray Eels

2 The moray eel and its slightly manic expression as it leans out of its protective hole are standard sights on almost any Maldivian reef, and some can be playful with divers. Be careful of its bite, though – once it closes its teeth, it never lets go.

Turtles

3 Turtles often swim around the reefs and can be curious around snorkellers and divers. Five different types of turtles swim in Maldivian waters. The most common are green and hawksbill turtles.

Rays

4 These creatures are a favourite with divers. Smaller stingrays and eagle rays often rest in the sand, while enormous manta rays can have a 'wingspan' of around 4m, and seeing one swoop over you is an extraordinary experience.

Whale Sharks

5 These gentle giants eat nothing but plankton and the odd small fish, but somehow have evolved to be the biggest fish in the world, measuring up to 12m long. They can often be spotted cruising Dhidhdhoo Beyru (p86) on the edge of Ari Atoll.

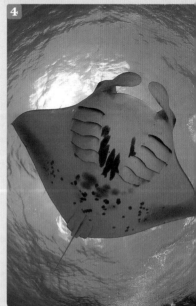

Clockwise from top left
1 Grey reef shark 2 Two spotted morays 3 Turtle
4 Manta ray

forward, and will deliver a very painful injury to anyone who stands on one, but you're unlikely to get close to it as the sound of you approaching will probably frighten it away first.

Manta rays are among the largest fish found in the Maldives and a firm favourite of divers. They tend to swim along near the surface and pass overhead as a large shadow. They are quite harmless and, in some places, seem quite relaxed about divers approaching them closely. Manta rays are sometimes seen to leap completely out of the water, landing back with a tremendous splash. The eagle ray is closely related to the manta, and is often spotted by divers.

Fish-Spotters' Guide

You don't have to be a hardcore diver to enjoy the rich marine life of the Maldives. You'll see an amazing variety just snorkelling, walking in the shallows, or peering off the end of a jetty. This guide will help you identify a few of the most colourful and conspicuous varieties. A point to remember is that even within the same species, colour and patterning can vary greatly over a fish's life cycle and according to gender.

For a comprehensive online guide to the fish of the Maldives, visit www.popweb.com/maldive. For more information, try *Photo Guide to Fishes of the Maldives* by Rudie H Kuiter (Atoll Editions), the classic guide to the fish of the Maldives.

Anemonefish

Maldives anemonefish (also known as black-footed anemonefish) are indigenous to the Maldives. They are around 11cm long, orange, dusky orange or yellow, with differences in face colour and the shape and thickness of the head bar marking. Their mucous coating protects them from the venomous tips of sea anemone tentacles, allowing them to hide from predators among the anemones' tentacles. In return for this protection, they warn the anemones of the approach of fish such as butterflyfish, which feed on the tentacle tips. Juveniles are lighter in colour than adults, and have greyish or blackish pelvic fins.

Young male anemonefish living within the anemone are under the control of a single dominant female. When she dies, the largest male fish changes sex and replaces her as the dominant female.

Angelfish

Of the many species, 14 are found in the Maldives, mostly found in shallow water, though some inhabit reef slopes down to 20m. They can be seen individually or in small groups. Small species are around 10cm, the largest around 35cm. They feed on sponges and algae. Regal (or empress) angelfish have bright yellow bodies with vertical dark blue and white stripes. The emperor, or imperial, angelfish are larger (to 35cm) and live in deeper water, with almost horizontal blue-and-yellow lines and a dark blue mask and gill markings; juveniles are quite different in shape and markings. The shy blue-faced angelfish also change colour dramatically as they age.

Sea urchins are rare in the sandy shallows of the lagoons, but numerous deeper on the reefs – wearing fins or other protective footwear is always a good idea to avoid their nasty needles.

Boxfish

These unusual looking and highly poisonous fish are sometimes encountered by divers in the Maldives. They usually grow up to half a metre in length and feed on worms and other invertebrates on the reef and ocean floor. Boxfish are literally boxed in by a thick external skin, with holes for moving parts such as the eyes, gills and fins. That, coupled with their poisonous flesh, makes them formidable creatures. It's a joy to see them swimming, their tiny fins moving their large bodies effortlessly across the reef.

Butterflyfish

There are over 30 species in the Maldives; they are common in shallow waters and along reef slopes, singly, in pairs or in small schools. Species vary in size from 12cm to 30cm when mature, with a flattened body shape and elaborate markings. Various species of this carnivorous fish have specialised food sources, including anemones, coral polyps, algae and assorted invertebrate prey. Bennett's butterflyfish, bright yellow and 18cm long, is one of several species with a 'false eye' near the tail to make predators think it's a larger fish facing the other way. Spotted butterflyfish, which grow to 10cm long, are camouflaged with dark polka dots and a dark band across its real eye.

Flutemouth

The smooth flutemouth is very common in shallow waters in the Maldives, often occurring in small schools. They are very slender, elongated fish, usually around 60cm in length, but deep-sea specimens grow up to 1.5m. Flutemouths (cornetfish) eat small fish, often stalking prey by swimming behind a harmless herbivore. The silver colouring seems almost transparent in the water, and it can be hard to spot flutemouths even in shallow sandy lagoons.

Flying Gurnard

These beautiful fish feature wing-like fins that make them look like smalls rays from afar, something it uses to its advantage when trying to catch prey, as well as to defend itself by frightening off would be attackers. Juveniles even have a pattern on their fins that looks like an eye, a good defence tactic. Flying Gurnards usually don't grow to more than 30cm and feed on bottom fish.

Groupers

This large reef fish is commonly seen on the reef, normally alone, and it can be very skittish when approached by divers. Most commonly spotted are black groupers with blue spots or red groupers with green or blue spots; they tend to be around 40cm to 60cm in length. Groupers feed on mobile invertebrates and small fish, generally hunting in the evening when other species on the reef are looking for a place to sleep for the night. Groupers are cunning hunters and juveniles often mimic wrasses to get close to prey.

Jacks & Trevallies

These fast silver fish are formidable hunters. While they spend much of their time in the open ocean, they feed on reefs, preying on confused fish that stray too far from safety. With 20 different kinds of jacks and trevallies in the Maldives, it's common to see them hunting on the reef. The giant trevally truly lives up to its name and can measure up to 1.7m.

Lionfish

These attractive fish are firm favourites with divers and are easily recognised by their long and thin fanlike fins, which deliver a very painful sting and are used to trap prey. Raised fins can be a sign of alarm – in such a case stay clear and don't corner the fish, as it may attack. Usually reddish brown in colour and growing only to 20cm, lionfish are commonly seen on the reef, although they are experts at camouflage, and so are often missed even by experienced divers.

The whale shark is an evolutionary oddity, skipping almost the whole food chain to ensure its survival: despite being the biggest fish in the water, it feeds solely on plankton.

Pilot fish can often be seen swimming alongside sharks or other large pelagic fish, with whom they swim to eat scraps of whatever the larger fish kills. In return the pilot fish eats parasites on the larger fish.

CASEY MAHANEY/LONELY PLANET IMAGES ©

MICHAEL AW/LONELY PLANET IMAGES ©

Light and colour
Schooling pennant butterflyfish (p147)
around a diver on Felidhoo Atoll

Blue lips
Three-spot angelfish (p146) with its
remarkable blue lips hides among the coral

Joker of the pack
Clown anemonefish (p146) amidst
anemone tentacles; a mucous coating
protects them from the poisonous tips of
the anemones

A hidden sting
The remarkable red lionfish (p147); its
spike-like fins can deliver a nasty sting

JURGEN FREUND/NATURE PICTURE LIBRARY ©

Moray Eel

A common sight on the reefs of the Maldives, these large, usually spot-ted eels are routinely seen with their heads poking out of holes on the reef edge. Those on reefs visited by divers tend to be extremely easy to approach, but will withdraw entirely into their holes (or swim away al-together) if humans come too close. They can also deliver an extremely strong bite, so do not feed or provoke them. Growing up to 2m long, they are one of the most easily spotted large creatures on the reef.

Moray eels' bodies are almost entirely made up of muscle, which they employ when hunting to twist and crush their prey, much like a constrictor.

Moorish Idol

The Moorish idol is commonly seen on reef flats and reef slopes in the Maldives, often in pairs. Usually 15cm to 20cm long, it is herbivorous, feeding primarily on algae. They are attractive, with broad vertical yel-low-and-black bands, pointed snouts, and long, streamer-like extensions to the upper dorsal fin.

Parrotfish

More than 20 of the many parrotfish species are found in the Maldives – they include some of the most conspicuous and commonly seen reef fish. The largest species grow to more than a metre, but those around 50cm long are more typical. Most parrotfish feed on algae and other organ-isms growing on and around a hard-coral structure. With strong, beak-like mouths they scrape and bite the coral surface, then grind up the coral chunks, swallowing and filtering to extract nutrients. Snorkellers often hear the scraping, grinding sound of parrotfish eating coral, and notice the clouds of coral-sand faeces that parrotfish regularly discharge. Colour, pattern and even sex can change as parrotfish mature – juveniles and females are often drab, while mature males can have brilliant blue-green designs. Bicolour parrotfish start life white with a broad orange stripe, but the mature males (up to 90cm) are a beautiful blue, with hot-pink highlights on the scale edges, head, fins and tail. Green-face parrot-fish grow to 60cm, with the adult male identified by its blue-green body, bright green 'face' and white marks on fins and tail. Heavybeak (or steep-head) parrotfish can be 70cm long, and have a distinctive rounded head

Pufferfish

There are 18 species of the aptly named pufferfish in the Maldives. These incredible creatures have poisonous flesh (which can kill a human if eaten without the correct preparation) and the amazing power to inflate themselves like a balloon when attacked or feeling threatened. Pufferfish vary enormously in colour and size, though Bennett's pufferfish, with its green, orange and blue pattern is the most beautiful. The scribbled pufferfish, one of the largest seen in Maldivian waters, is the most com-monly seen.

Reef Shark

Several smaller shark species frequent reef flats and reef edges inside Maldivian atolls, often in schools, while larger pelagic species congregate around channels in the atoll rim at certain times of the year. Most reef species are small, typically 1m to 2m. Reef sharks hunt small fish (at-tacks on swimmers and divers are totally unknown). White-tips grow from 1m to 2m long and have white tips on dorsal fins. They are often seen in schools of 10 or more in the sandy shallows of a lagoon. Black-tips, distinguished by black tips on dorsal fins and tail, grow to 2m. Grey reef sharks are thicker in the midsection and have a white trailing edge on the dorsal fin.

Male and female shark populations live in same-sex groups and rarely meet, save for mating.

Rock Cod

Hundreds of species are currently classified as *Serranidae*, including rock cod and grouper, which are common around reefs. Smaller species reach 20cm; many larger species grow to 50cm and some to over a metre. Rock cod are carnivorous, feeding on smaller fish and invertebrates. Vermillion rock cod (or coral grouper) are often seen in shallow waters and near the coral formations in which they hide; they are a brilliant crimson colour covered with blue spots and are up to 40cm long.

Snapper

There are 28 species of snapper that have been documented in the Maldives, mostly in deep water. Small species are around 20cm and the largest grow to 1m (snapper, themselves carnivorous, are popular with anglers as a fighting fish and are excellent to eat). Blue-striped snapper, commonly seen in schools near inshore reefs, are an attractive yellow with blue-white horizontal stripes. Red snapper (or red bass) are often seen in lagoons.

Stingray

Several species of stingray, such as the black-spotted stingray, are often seen in very shallow water on the sandy bed of a lagoon, where they are often well camouflaged. Most rays seen inshore are juveniles, up to about 50cm across; mature rays can be over a metre across and 2m long if you include the whiplike tail. A barbed and venomous spine on top of the tail can swing up and forward, and will deliver a painful injury to anyone who stands on it.

Surgeonfish

The surgeonfish are so named for the tiny scalpel-sharp blades that are found on the sides of their bodies, near their tails. When they are threatened they will swim beside the intruder swinging their tails to inflict cuts, and can cause nasty injuries. Over 20 species of surgeon, including the powder-blue surgeonfish, are found in the Maldives, often in large schools. The adults range from 20cm to 60cm. All species graze for algae on the sea bottom or on coral surfaces.

Sweetlips

Only a few of the many species are found in the Maldives, where they inhabit outer-reef slopes. Some species grow up to 1m, but most are between 50cm and 75cm; juveniles are largely herbivorous, feeding on algae, plankton and other small organisms; older fish hunt and eat smaller fish. Oriental sweetlips, which grow to 50cm, are superb-looking, with horizontal dark and light stripes, dark spots on fins and tail, and large, lugubrious lips. Brown sweetlips are generally bigger, duller and more active at night.

Triggerfish

There are over a dozen species in the Maldives, on outer-reef slopes and also in shallower reef environments. Small species grow to around 25cm and the largest species to over 75cm. Triggerfish are carnivorous. Orange-striped triggerfish (30cm) are common in shallow reef waters. Titan triggerfish have yellow and dark-brown crisscross patterning and grow up to 75cm; they can be aggressive, especially when defending eggs, and will charge at divers. The clown triggerfish (up to 40cm) is easily recognised by its conspicuous colour pattern, with large, round, white blotches on the lower half of its body.

MARINE LIFE IN THE MALDIVES

Pipefish have a very unusual mating system. The female deposits the egg into the sperm on the underside of the male's body, where fertilisation occurs and the pregnant male then incubates the eggs for a month before hatching.

Anemonefish are so-called as they cover themselves in a special mucous from the anemone, which protects them from its sting.

Unicornfish

From the same family as the surgeonfish, unicornfish grow from 40cm to 75cm long (only males of some species have the horn for which the species is named), and are herbivores. Spotted unicornfish are very common blue-grey or olive-brown fish with narrow dotted vertical markings (males can change their colours for display, and exhibit a broad white vertical band); their prominent horns get longer with age. Bignose unicornfish (or Vlaming's unicorn) have only a nose bump for a horn.

Wrasse

Some 60 species of this large and very diverse family can be found, some on reefs, others on sandy lagoon floors, others in open water. The smallest wrasse species are only 10cm; the largest over 2m. Most wrasse are carnivores; larger wrasse will hunt and eat small fish. Napoleonfish (also called Napoleon wrasse and humphead wrasse) are the largest wrasse species, often seen around wrecks and outer-reef slopes; they are generally green with fine vertical patterning. Large males have a humped head.

The hump on the head of a Napoleon wrasse becomes larger and more pronounced as the fish ages.

Moon wrasse, about 25cm, live in shallow waters and reef slopes, where adult males are beautifully coloured in green with pink patterning and a yellow marking on the tail. Cleaner wrasse have a symbiotic relationship with larger fish, which allow the wrasse to eat the small parasites and food scraps from their mouths, gills and skin surface. At certain times, large numbers of pelagic species congregate at 'cleaning stations' where cleaner wrasse abound – a great sight for divers.

Environmental Issues & Responsible Travel

Adrift in the middle of the Indian Ocean and almost totally reliant on the marine environment for its food, the Maldives is a country where environmental issues play a larger than normal role in everyday life. Moreover, lying at such a low level above the sea makes the Maldives one of the most vulnerable places on earth to rising sea levels, and its fragile and unusual ecology means that responsible and thoughtful travel is important for anyone who cares about the impact of their holiday on locals.

However you spend your time in the country, environmental issues are never far removed from you. Resorts use enormous amounts of electricity and water, their imported food (not to mention guests) have significant environmental consequences, and in some cases resorts are not particularly responsible about their sewage disposal or energy use. In research for this book we've always taken into account a resort's environmental policy and have highlighted resorts that have implemented particularly sustainable and ecologically sound practices.

Environmental Issues

As a small island nation in a big ocean, the Maldives had a way of life that was ecologically sustainable for centuries, but certainly not self-sufficient. The comparatively small population survived by harvesting the vast resources of the sea and obtaining the other necessities of life through trade with the Middle East and Asia.

In the modern age the Maldives' interrelationship with the rest of the world is greater than ever, and it has a high rate of growth supported by two main industries: fishing and tourism. Both industries depend on the preservation of the environment, and there are strict regulations to ensure sustainability. To a great extent, the Maldives avoids environmental problems by importing so many of its needs. This is, of course, less a case of being environmentally friendly than just moving the environmental problems elsewhere.

Bluepeace (www.bluepeacemaldives.org) is an organisation campaigning to protect the Maldives' unique environment. Its comprehensive website and blog is a great place to start for anyone interested in the ecology of the Maldives and the most pressing environmental issues of the day.

The Maldives has a very small proportion of arable land – just 13% – meaning that fish and imported foods make up the bulk of most people's diets.

Global Warming

Along with Tuvalu, Bangladesh and parts of the Netherlands, the Maldives has the misfortune to be one of the lowest-lying countries in the world at a time in history when sea levels are rising. Indeed, its highest

BIG WAVE

Bodu raalhu
(big wave) is a
relatively regular
event in the
Maldives, when
the sea sweeps
over the islands,
causing damage
and sometimes
even loss of life.

natural point – 2.4m – is the lowest in any country in the world. Thanks in part to its crusading former president, the Maldives has become a byword around the world for the human consequences of global warming and rising sea levels, as an entire nation seems set to lose its way of life and may even be forced to leave for good the islands it calls home. While the political will to get an international agreement on how best to combat climate change may finally be within sight, the Maldives has long been making contingency plans in the likely event that whatever the international community does will be too little, too late.

These contingency plans range from an already well-established project to reclaim land on a reef near Male to create a new island 2m above sea level, to a plan to set aside a portion of the country's annual billion-dollar tourism revenue for a sovereign wealth fund to purchase a new homeland for the Maldivians if rising sea levels engulf the country in decades to come. Both options are fairly bleak ones – the prospect of moving to the new residential island of Hulhumale is not one relished by most Maldivians, who are attached to their home islands and traditional way of life, but the prospect of the entire country moving to India, Sri Lanka or even Australia (as has been suggested) is an even more sobering one.

Perhaps because of its perilous situation, the Maldives has become one of the most environmentally progressive countries in the world. Before its dramatic collapse in 2012, the Nasheed government pledged to make the country carbon neutral within a decade, managed to impose the first total ban on shark hunting anywhere in the world and made ecotourism a cornerstone of its tourism strategy. Quite how the new government will proceed is still unclear, but it's certain that environmental issues will continue to play a prominent role in Maldivian politics.

In the long term it's simply not an option to protect low-lying islands with breakwaters, and if the sea continues to rise as predicted then there is no long-term future for much of the country. There have been bold efforts made to ensure the survival of the human population of the Maldives in the future in the worst case scenario when waters wash over many of the lower-lying islands. Most obviously this includes the land reclamation project that has created 2m-high Hulhumale island (see p58) next to the airport, which one day will house around half the country's population and all of the government.

If the day does indeed come when waters engulf the entire country, then in theory the government's sovereign wealth fund may be used to buy land elsewhere in the world for at least some, if not all, of the Maldivian population. India and Sri Lanka are the most likely destinations due to proximity and similarities in culture, climate and cuisine, but Australia is also frequently mooted given its large amount of free space.

The 2011 film *The Island President* is a fascinating documentary that followed the progress (or frankly, lack of progress) of former president Nasheed as he lobbied internationally for an agreement to curtail global warming and prevent the Maldives from being one of the first victims of the world's rising sea levels. It's well worth watching to see just what an enormous challenge it is for such a tiny country to be heard on the international stage, regardless of the urgency of its message.

An excellent
organisation to
look out for is
the nonprofit
environmental
protection NGO
Ecocare (www.
ecocare.mv),
whose compre-
hensive website
gives interesting
accounts of
environmental
problems and
current cam-
paigns.

Fisheries

Net fishing and trawling is prohibited in Maldivian waters, which include an 'exclusive economic zone' extending 320km beyond the atolls. All fishing is by pole and line, with over 75% of the catch being skipjack or yellowfin tuna. The no-nets policy helps to prevent over-fishing and protects other marine species, such as dolphins and sharks, from being inadvertently caught in nets – something that has catastrophic implications for marine biodiversity elsewhere around the world.

AN ALTERNATIVE GEOGRAPHY

While the Maldives has appeared in the *Guinness Book of Records* as the world's flattest country, with no natural land higher than 2.4m above sea level, it's also one of the most mountainous countries in the world. Its people live on peaks above a plateau that extends 2000km from the Lakshadweep Islands near India to the Chagos Islands, well south of the equator. The plateau is over 5000m high and rises steeply between the Arabian Basin in the northwest and the Cocos-Keeling Basin in the southeast. Mountain ranges rise above the plateau, and the upper slopes and valleys are incredibly fertile, beautiful and rich with plant and animal life. The entire plateau is submerged beneath the Indian Ocean and only scattered, flat-topped peaks are visible at the surface. These peaks are capped not with snow, but with coconut palms.

The local tuna population appears to be holding up despite increased catches, and Maldivian fisheries are patrolled to prevent poaching. But the tuna are migratory, and can be caught without limit in international waters using drift nets and long-line techniques.

The Nasheed government banned the hunting of reef sharks in 2009, extending the ban to all sharks a year later. The ban was intended to arrest the plummeting number of sharks, whose fins were sold by local fishermen to Asian markets. This move has been widely celebrated by environmentalists, although there's a long way still to go before shark populations rebuild.

The small but active shark-meat trade was still claiming thousands of sharks a year until a nationwide ban was introduced in 2009. Hopefully shark numbers will now recover.

Tourism

Tourism development is strictly regulated and resorts are established only on uninhabited islands that the government makes available. Overwhelmingly, the regulations have been effective in minimising the impact on the environment – the World Tourism Organization has cited the Maldives as a model for sustainable tourism development.

Construction and operation of the resorts does use resources, but the vast majority of these are imported. Large amounts of diesel fuel are used to generate electricity and desalinate water, and the demand for hot running water and air-conditioning has raised the overall energy cost per guest.

Extraordinarily, most resorts simply pump sewage directly out into the sea. While an increasing number of resorts do treat their own sewage and dispose of it responsibly, the majority still do not. New resorts are now required to do so by law, but the older resorts can still get away with this negligent behaviour.

Beach erosion is a constant problem facing most islands in the Maldives. Changing currents and rising sea levels mean that beaches shrink and grow, often unpredictably.

Efficient incinerators must be installed to get rid of garbage that can't be composted, but many resorts request that visitors take home plastic bottles, used batteries and other items that may present a disposal problem.

When the first resorts were developed, jetties and breakwaters were built and boat channels cut through reefs without much understanding of the immediate environmental consequences. In some cases natural erosion and deposition patterns were disrupted, with unexpected results. More structures were built to limit damage and sand pumped up to restore beaches. This was expensive and it marred the natural appearance of islands. Developers are now more careful about altering coasts and reefs. Environmental studies are required before major works can be undertaken.

Responsible Travel

Given the strictures of travelling to the Maldives in most cases your chances to be a truly responsible tourist are limited. First, you're likely to arrive in the country by a long-haul flight, with all the emissions that entails. Second, you'll be using electricity-thirsty air-conditioning wherever you go, eating imported food and drinking expensively desalinated water (or even more costly imported water). Nevertheless, there are a few things you can do to lessen your carbon footprint and care for the local environment.

First of all, choose your resort carefully. We have given resorts with excellent sustainability credentials a sustainable icon in the reviews – these are resorts with the best environmental records in the country. This can mean anything from having a comprehensive recycling program, using home-grown food, not using plastic bottles, using ecologically sound wood for their buildings and serving only sustainably sourced food in their restaurants, to running environmental education programs for the local community, stimulating coral growth on the reef and donating money to

WATER, WATER, EVERYWHERE

Ensuring a supply of fresh water has always been imperative for small island communities. Rainwater quickly soaks into the sandy island soil and usually forms an underground reservoir of fresh water, held in place by a circle of salt water from the surrounding sea. Wells can be dug to extract the fresh ground water, but if water is pumped out faster than rainfall replenishes the supply, then salty water infiltrates from around the island and the well water becomes brackish.

One way to increase the freshwater supply is to catch and store rainwater from rooftops. This wasn't feasible on islands that had only small buildings with roofs of palm thatch, but economic development and the use of corrugated iron has changed all that. Nearly every inhabited island now has a government-supported primary school, which is often the biggest, newest building on the island. The other sizable building is likely to be the mosque, which is a focus of community pride. Along with education and spiritual sustenance, many Maldivians now also get their drinking water from the local school or the mosque.

Expanding tourist resorts required more water than was available from wells or rooftops, and as resorts grew larger, tourists' showers became saltier. Also, the ground water became too salty to irrigate the exotic gardens that every tourist expects on a tropical island. The solution was the desalination of sea water using 'reverse osmosis' – a combination of membrane technology and brute force.

Now every resort has a desalination plant, with racks of metal cylinders, each containing an inner cylinder made of a polymer membrane. Sea water is pumped into the inner cylinder at high pressure and the membrane allows pure water to pass through into the outer cylinder from which it is piped away. Normally, when a membrane separates fresh water from salt water, both salt and water will pass through the membrane in opposite directions to equalise the saltiness on either side – this process is called osmosis. Under pressure, the special polymer membrane allows the natural process of osmosis to be reversed.

Small, reliable desalination plants have been a boon for the resorts, providing abundant fresh water for bathrooms, kitchens, gardens and, increasingly, for swimming pools. Of course, it's expensive, as the plants use lots of diesel fuel for their powerful pumps and the polymer membranes need to be replaced regularly. Many resorts ask their guests to be moderate in their water use, while a few are finding ways to recycle bath and laundry water onto garden beds. Most have dual water supplies, so that brackish ground water is used to flush the toilet while desalinated sea water is provided in the shower and the hand basin.

Is desalinated water good enough to drink? If a desalination plant is working properly, it should produce, in effect, 100% pure distilled water. The island of Thulusdhoo, in North Male Atoll, has the only factory in the world where Coca-Cola is made out of sea water. In most resorts, the water from the bathroom tap tastes just fine, but management advises guests not to drink it.

off-set the carbon footprint of its guests. If in doubt, contact your resort directly before you book with them and ask them for some information on their environmental record – any good resort will very happily provide this, and if they don't, then don't book with them.

Other things you can do to be a responsible visitor to the Maldives include taking home any plastic bottles or batteries you brought with you, respecting rules about not touching coral when diving or snorkelling, picking up any litter you may see on the beach, using water and air-conditioning judiciously, avoiding imported mineral water and drinking desalinated water instead, not replacing your towels daily and not buying souvenirs made from turtle-shell or coral.

The approximately 1200 islands that make up the Maldives account for less than 1% of the country's area – the other 99% is water.

Wildlife

Stand still on a Maldivian beach for a minute or two and you'll see a surprising amount of wildlife: hermit crabs scurrying across the warm sands; cawing crows in the palm trees, their call instantly recognisable; juvenile sharks chasing schools of little fish through the shallows; majestic flying foxes swooping over the islands during the late afternoon; you will rapidly realise that the Maldives is a fun place for nature lovers. And that's before you get to the amazing variety of life down on the reef. The best thing about wildlife in the Maldives is that it's universally safe. Who said this wasn't paradise?

Animals

One of the most unforgettable sights in the Maldives is giant fruit bats flying over the islands to roost in trees at dusk. Their size and numbers can make it quite a spectacle. Colourful lizards and geckos are very common and there is the occasional rat, usually euphemistically dismissed as a 'palm squirrel' or a 'Maldivian hamster' by resort staff.

The mosquito population varies from island to island, but it's generally not a big problem. Nearly all the resorts spray pesticides daily to get rid of those that are about. There are ants, centipedes, scorpions and cockroaches, but they're no threat to anyone.

Local land birds include crows (many of which are shot by resorts on regular culls), the white-breasted water hen and the Indian mynah. There are migratory birds, such as harriers and falcons, but waders like plover, snipe, curlew and sandpiper are more common. Thirteen species of heron can be seen in the shallows (nearly every resort has one or two in residence) and there are terns, seagulls and two species of noddy.

In 2009 the Maldivian government set aside large areas of Baa and Ari Atolls as Marine Protected Areas for the breeding of endangered whale sharks, manta rays and reef sharks.

Endangered Species

Most turtle species are endangered worldwide. Four species nest in the Maldives: green, olive ridley, hawksbill and loggerhead. Leatherback turtles visit Maldivian waters, but are not known to nest. Turtle numbers have declined in the Maldives, as elsewhere, but they can still be seen by divers at many sites. The catching of turtles and the sale or export of turtle-shell products is now totally prohibited.

Turtles are migratory and the population can be depleted by events many miles from their home beach, such as accidental capture in fishing nets, depletion of sea-grass areas and toxic pollutants. Widespread collection of eggs and the loss of nesting sites are both problems in the Maldives today, although both the government and various environmental foundations have done a lot to educate locals about the importance of turtle protection. Nevertheless, turtle eggs are a traditional food and are used in *velaa folhi,* a special Maldivian dish, which is still legally made today.

Maldivian turtles are protected, but they are still caught illegally. The charity Ecocare Maldives has campaigned to raise awareness of the turtles' plight. See www.ecocare.mv.

THE MALDIVES' VOLCANIC PAST

The geological formation of the Maldives is fascinating and unique. The country is perched on the top of the enormous Laccadives-Chagos ridge, which cuts a swath across the Indian Ocean from India to Madagascar. The ridge, a meeting point of two giant tectonic plates, is where basalt magma spews up through the earth's crust, creating new rock. These magma eruptions created the Deccan Plateau, on which the Maldives sits. Originally the magma production created huge volcanoes that towered above the sea. While these have subsequently sunk back into the water as the ocean floor settled, the coral formations that grew up around these vast volcanoes became the Maldives, and this explains their idiosyncratic formation into vast round atolls.

Resort development has reduced the availability of nesting sites, while artificial lights confuse hatchling turtles, which are instinctively guided into the water by the position of the moon. Beach chairs and boats can also interfere with egg laying and with hatchlings. Some attempts are being made to artificially improve the survival chances of hatchlings by protecting them in hatching ponds.

National Parks

The depletion of freshwater aquifers is one of the Maldives' biggest environmental problems. As all fresh water comes from rainwater collected below ground and from desalination, water conservation is extremely important.

There are 25 Protected Marine Areas in the Maldives, usually popular diving sites where fishing of any kind is banned. These are excellent as they have created enclaves of marine life that's guaranteed a safe future. At the time of writing the Maldives first Marine National Park was in the process of being formed. The as-yet-unnamed park covers nine uninhabited islands in Noonu Atoll (p98) and will be by far the biggest reserve in the country, enjoying full national park status.

Aside from the new Marine National Park, there are no specially designated island reserves in the Maldives. However, the vast majority of the islands in the Maldives are uninhabited and permission from the government is needed to develop or live there. With some of the tightest development restrictions in the world, the Maldives' future as pristine wilderness in many parts is assured.

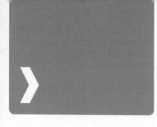

Arts, Crafts & Architecture

Despite the Maldives being a small country with a widely dispersed population, Dhivehi culture has thrived in isolation from the rest of the world, finding expression in Maldivian arts and crafts, and retaining a strong national identity even in the modern age.

Islamic fundamentalism, Western and Indian fashions, pop music and videos have all shaped local culture, but on public occasions and festivals the celebrations always have a Maldivian style. *Bodu beru* remains vibrant, rock bands sing Dhivehi lyrics, and traditional crafts are surviving in the face of modernity. It's actually remarkable that such a tiny population maintains such a distinctive culture.

Arts

Song & Dance

Bodu beru means 'big drum' and gives its name to the best-known form of traditional music and dance. It is what tourist resorts put on for a local culture night, and it can be quite sophisticated and compelling. Dancers begin with a slow, nonchalant swaying and swinging of the arms, and become more animated as the tempo increases, finishing in a rhythmic frenzy. In some versions the dancers even enter a trance-like state. There are four to six drummers in an ensemble and the sound has strong African influences.

However, these performances are not just to be found in resorts. If you're staying on an inhabited island, you'll often hear the *bodu beru* being played as groups of young men hang out and dance together after sundown. Witnessing it can be an fantastic experience, as the dancing becomes more and more frenetic as the night goes on.

Apart from *bodu beru*, the music most visitors will experience at resorts will rarely be a highlight. Local rock bands often perform in the bars in the evening, where they usually do fairly naff covers of old favourites as well as performing their own material. They may incorporate elements of *bodu beru* in their music, with lots of percussion and extended drum solos when they're in front of a local audience. Some popular contemporary bands are Seventh Floor, Mezzo and Zero Degree Atoll – CDs from these, and quite a few other bands, are sold in Male's music shops.

Literature

Despite the unique Maldivian script that dates from the 1600s, most Maldivian myths and stories are from an oral tradition and have only recently appeared in print. Many are stories of witchcraft and sorcery, while others are cautionary tales about the evils of vanity, lust and greed, and the sticky fates of those who transgressed. Some are decidedly weird and depressing, and don't make good bedtime reading for young children. Male bookshops sell quite a range of local stories in English. Again, most of these are legends of the past, many overlaid with Islamic meaning. Novelty Press published a small book called *Mysticism in the Maldives,* which is still available in some shops.

Alternatively, if you're looking for thematic beach reading, you could always try the Hammond Innes thriller *The Strode Venturer,* which is set in the Maldives, or for some real escapist fun and a great behind-the-scenes look at one of the country's top resorts, Imogen Edwards-Jones' *Beach Babylon* is a good pick.

Visual Arts

There is no historical tradition of painting in the Maldives, but demand for local art (however fabricated) from the tourist industry has created a supply in the ultra-savvy Maldivian market, with more than a few locals selling paintings to visitors or creating beach scenes for hotel rooms.

The National Art Gallery in Male (p47) puts on an exhibition of Maldivian art every few years. It combines photography, painting and some conceptual art, and is well worth a visit if it happens to coincide with your time in Male. Some local names to look out for are Eagan Badeeu, Ahmed Naseer and Hassan Shameem.

Some islands were once famous for wood and stone carving – elaborate calligraphy and intricate intertwining patterns are a feature of many old mosques and gravestones. A little of this woodcarving is still done, mainly to decorate mosques. The facade of the Majlis building in Male is decorated with intertwined carvings.

Crafts

Mats

Natural-fibre mats are woven on many islands, but the most famous are the ones known as *thundu kunaa,* made on the island of Gadhdhoo in Gaaf Dhaal Atoll. This may have been an endangered art form, but renewed interest thanks to the increase in tourism has arguably saved it from disappearing. A Danish researcher in the 1970s documented the weaving techniques and the plants used for fibre and dyes, and noted that a number of traditional designs had not been woven for 20 years. Collecting the materials and weaving a mat can take weeks, and the money that can be made selling the work is not much by modern Maldivian standards. Some fine examples now decorate the reception areas of tourist resorts, and there's a growing appreciation of the work among local people and foreign collectors.

Lacquer Work

Traditionally, lacquer work *(laajehun)* was for containers, bowls and trays used for gifts to the sultan – some fine examples can be seen in the National Museum in Male (p45). Different wood is used to make boxes,

---

SITTING IN THE MALDIVES

The Maldives has two unique pieces of furniture. One is the *undholi,* a wooden platform or netting seat that's hung from a tree or triangular frame. Sometimes called a bed-boat, the *undholi* is a sofa, hammock and fan combination – swinging gently creates a cooling movement of air across the indolent occupant.

The *joli* is a static version – net seats on a rectangular frame, usually made in sociable sets of three or four. Once made of coir rope and wooden sticks, these days steel pipes and plastic mesh are now almost universal – it's like sitting in a string shopping bag, but cool.

LOCAL VOICE: EAGAN MOHAMED BADEEU

Eagan talks about living and working as an artist in Male.

What can visitors expect from the Maldivian art scene? Souvenirs, such as the traditional Maldivian lacquered vases, jewellery and other craftwork, do still tend to dominate the art scene, but in fact most of this is imported and little is locally made. Beyond the touristy stuff there is an emerging art scene, which was boosted by the founding of the National Art Gallery in Male in 2005 (p47), currently the only space where Maldivian artists can show their work. Most painted themes portray the natural beauty of the islands, though more contemporary and conceptual art styles are also becoming popular.

Is there a big artistic tradition in the Maldives? The Maldives has a rich culture and tradition of craftsmanship, especially for stone carving and lacquer work – the Old Friday Mosque in Male, for example, is a masterpiece of both, with the complicated floral and symmetrical patterns showing us how creative these craftsmen were. Our ancestors used organic dyes to colour the traditional *feyli* (Maldivian sarong) and *tundu kunaa* (reed mats), but there is no evidence of paintings in our tradition before the early 20th century.

You paint a lot of traditional Maldivian scenes. Are you worried that some of these traditions will be lost in the future? Yes, for me it is sad to see the dredged concrete harbours taking over from the timber jetties of our islands. Thirty years ago I remember young people sailing small dhonis for fun, learning how to use the ocean currents and the monsoon winds to navigate. However, today a young Maldivian is more likely to circle the island on a motorcycle than in a dhoni! Most of our traditions will be lost in the future, so it's up to us to keep traditions passed on by our forefathers alive for the next generation.

You must have travelled a lot in your country; do you have a favourite part of the Maldives? My favourite part of the country is Haa Dhaalu Atoll in the north Maldives. I particularly love the island of Hanimaadhoo, which has a charming old village and a thick palm and banyan tree forest. Most of all, the lovely people there are very friendly. The island of Kulhuduffushi, the capital of Haa Dhaalu, is another favourite of mine. The islanders are famous for celebrating Eid by performing lots of traditional dances, and people travel there to see them.

What is your favourite thing about Maldivian village life? I like to sit in a *holhuashi* (small beach hut) and chat with the island folk. On any island the *holhuashi* is where the village men gather to talk politics and play cards and chess. For me the most interesting time of the day is when the fishermen return with the day's catch. People gather on the beach to clean and buy the fish before the village women prepare a delicious *garudia* (fish broth) with rice, lime and chillies.

Does life vary strongly between the rural areas in Maldives and the bigger towns? Which do you prefer? Of course – Male is now the world's most densely populated island, with all the problems of any big city, while rural islands are quiet, spacious and clean. Despite this, many families blindly migrate from their islands to Male. If it were possible, I would do the opposite as I'd love to live in the atolls – this is actually the dream of many people living in the capital!

bowls, vases and other turned objects. Traditionally the lathe is hand-powered by a cord pulled round a spindle. Several layers of lacquer are applied in different colours. They then harden, and the design is incised with sharp tools, exposing the bright colours of the underlying layers. Designs are usually floral motifs in yellow with red trim on a black background (most likely based on designs of Chinese ceramics). Production of lacquer work is a viable cottage industry in Baa Atoll, particularly on the islands of Eydhafushi and Thulhaadhoo.

Jewellery

Ribudhoo Island in Dhaalu (South Nilandhoo Atoll) is famous for making gold jewellery, and Hulhudheli, in the same atoll, for silver jewellery. According to local belief, a royal jeweller brought the goldsmithing skills to the island centuries ago, having been banished to Ribudhoo by a sultan. It's also said that the islanders plundered a shipwreck in the 1700s, and reworked the gold jewellery they found to disguise its origins.

Architecture

A traditional Maldivian village is notable for its neat and orderly layout, with wide sandy streets in a regular, rectangular grid. Houses are made of concrete blocks or coral stone joined with mortar, and the walls line the sides of the streets. Many houses will have a shaded courtyard in front, enclosed by a chest-high wall fronting the street. This courtyard is an outdoor room, with *joli* and *undholi* seats (see the boxed text, p160), where families sit in the heat of the day or the cool of the evening. A more private courtyard behind, the *gifili,* has a well and serves as an open-air bathroom.

Mosques tend to be the most interesting and attractive buildings you'll see on inhabited islands. Some date back to the 16th century and are extremely impressive examples of craftsmanship both for their coral-carved exteriors and their teak and lacquer-work interiors, although in most cases you'll have to view the insides from the doorway, as non-Muslims are not normally allowed to enter mosques in the Maldives.

Male has several very beautiful 16th and 17th century mosques, as well as its impressive, modern Grand Friday Mosque, the city's most striking and, arguably, iconic building – its large golden dome visible for miles around.

One island that is particularly worth visiting to see traditional Maldivian architecture is Utheemu (see p93), in the very far northern atoll of Haa Alifu. Here you'll find the best example of a 16th-century Maldivian nobleman's house. Although rather hyperbolically called Utheemu Palace, the building is nevertheless fascinating to tour for its interiors and interesting outer design.

The government plans to properly excavate the country's large number of pre-Islamic Buddhist sites in a bid to attract travellers interested in more than just beaches and diving.

Taste of the Maldives

Your culinary experience in the Maldives could be, depending on your resort, anything from *haute cuisine* ordered from a menu you've discussed with the chef in advance to bangers and mash at the all-you-can-eat buffet in the communal dining room. What it's unlikely to be in either case is particularly Maldivian, given the dislocation from local life experienced in resorts. However, anyone staying in Male or on an inhabited island should take advantage of this opportunity to try real Maldivian food, and this is easily done by visiting the so called 'teashops' or 'hotels', where delicious 'short eats' are served up to an all-male crowd of locals, but where foreigners, including accompanied women, will normally be very welcome. Maldivian cuisine is unsurprisingly simple due to the lack of variety provided by local agriculture. However, it is nevertheless testament to a nation's historical survival on a relatively small, but bountiful, amount of locally occurring ingredients.

Staples & Specialities

Essentially all that grows in the Maldives are coconuts, mangoes, papayas and pineapples; the only other locally occurring product is fish and seafood, which explains the historical simplicity of Maldivian cuisine. However, as trade with the Indian subcontinent, Africa, Arabia and the Far East have always brought other, more exciting influences, the result is far less bland than it could be.

The Indian influence is clear in local cuisine above all; Maldivian food is often hot and spicy. If you're going to eat local food, prepare your palate for spicy fish curry, fish soup, fish patties and variations thereof. A favourite Maldivian breakfast is *mas huni,* a healthy mixture of tuna, onion, coconut and chilli, eaten cold with *roshi* (unleavened bread, like an Indian chapati) and tea.

For snacks and light meals, Maldivians like *hedhikaa,* a selection of finger foods. In homes the *hedhikaa* are placed on the table and everyone helps themselves. In teashops this is called 'short eats' – a choice of things like *fihunu mas* (fish pieces with chilli coating), *gulha* (fried dough balls filled with fish and spices), *keemia* (fried fish rolls in batter) and *kuli boakiba* (spicy fish cakes). Sweets include little bowls of *bondi bai* (rice pudding), tiny bananas and *zileybee* (coloured coils of sugared, fried batter). Generally, anything small and brown will be savoury and contain fish, and anything light or brightly coloured will be sweet.

A main meal will include rice or *roshi* or both, plus soups, curries, vegetables, pickles and spicy sauces. In a teashop, a substantial meal with rice and *roshi* is called 'long eats'. The most typical dish is *garudia,* a soup made from dried and smoked fish, often eaten with rice, lime and chilli. The soup is poured over rice, mixed up by hand and eaten with the

Bis hulavuu is a popular snack – a pastry made from eggs, sugar and ghee and served cold. You may well be invited to try some if you visit an inhabited island.

fingers. Another common meal is *mas riha*, a fish curry eaten with rice or *roshi* – the *roshi* is torn into strips, mixed on the plate with the curry and condiments, and eaten with the fingers. A cup of tea accompanies the meal, and is usually drunk black and sweet.

The Maldivian equivalent of the after-dinner mint is the areca nut, chewed after a meal or snack. The little oval nuts are sliced into thin sections, some cloves and lime paste are added, the whole lot is wrapped in an areca leaf, and the wad is chewed whole. It's definitely an acquired taste.

Drinks

The only naturally occurring fresh water in the Maldives is rainwater, which is stored in natural underground aquifers beneath each island. This makes getting water quite a feat, and water conservation has always been extremely important in Maldivian culture, to the extent that the Maldives Tourism Law states that no water resources may be diverted from an inhabited island to supply a resort. All resorts have their own desalination plants to keep visitors supplied with enough water for their (by local standards incredibly wasteful) water needs.

The main drinks other than rainwater are imported tea and toddy tapped from the crown of the palm trunk at the point where the coconuts grow. Every village has its toddy man *(raa veri)*. The *raa* is sweet and delicious if you can get over the pungent smell. It can be drunk immediately after it is tapped from the tree, or left to become a little alcoholic as the sugar ferments.

Fermented *raa* is of course the closest most Maldivians ever get to alcohol; the Maldives is strictly dry apart from the resorts (and Maldivian staff cannot drink alcohol even there). This may be a consideration if you're planning to travel independently in the country and stay in guesthouses on inhabited islands – your holiday will have to be totally dry. On the other hand, alcohol is allowed on live-aboard dive boats.

Despite the ban on alcohol, nonalcoholic beer is very popular in Male. Soft drinks, including the only Coca-Cola made from salt water anywhere in the world, are available all over the country at prices much lower than in resorts. Outside resorts the range of drinks is very limited. Teashops will always serve *bor feng* (drinking water) and, of course, *sai* (tea). Unless you ask otherwise, tea comes black, with *hakuru* (sugar). *Kiru* (milk) isn't a common drink, and is usually made up from powder, as there are no cows in the Maldives.

Where to Eat & Drink

In budget resorts you won't usually have any choice – most cheaper resorts have just one restaurant – while midrange places typically have two or more to afford some variety, and top-end resorts often boast three or more. Buffets (always for breakfast, often for lunch and dinner too) allow for lots of different cuisines and plenty of choice. In Male, where there's a much broader choice, the most obvious place for authentic Maldivian 'short eats' is in a teashop. In recent years traditional teashops (confusingly sometimes also called 'hotels') have modernised so that they look

---

Wine is available in the better resorts. Expect to pay extraordinary mark-ups; you'll do well to find anything under US$50. It's illegal to bring wine into the country (luggage is X-rayed on arrival to check for bottles).

Don't be fooled by beer in Male – it's all nonalcoholic, even if it doesn't look it. For those gasping for the real thing, you'll need to cross the lagoon to the airport island where alcoholic beer is widely available.

TRAVEL YOUR TASTEBUDS

If you feel like trying something both exotic and dear to the Maldivian people, go for *miruhulee boava* (octopus tentacles). This is not commonly found in resorts or in Male, but is often prepared in the atolls as a speciality should you be lucky enough to visit an inhabited island. The tentacles are stripped and cleaned, then braised in a sauce of curry leaves, cloves, garlic, chilli, onion, pepper and coconut oil – delicious.

less forbidding and are now more pleasant places at which to eat. Small towns and villages elsewhere will also have teashops and are a great way to sample real Maldivian food. If you're staying on an inhabited island, most guesthouses will provide all your meals as part of the room price because so few islands have sufficient or decent-enough restaurants for you to eat comfortably elsewhere.

Vegetarians & Vegans

Vegetarians will have no problem in resorts (although at cheaper resorts where there may be a set meal rather than a buffet spread, veggies will often be stuck with an unimaginative pasta dish or a ratatouille). In general, resorts are well prepared for all types of diet, and in better resorts the chef may cook you a dish by request if what's on offer isn't appealing. Vegans will find the Maldives quite a challenge, though soya milk is on offer in most resorts and the buffet allows each diner to pick and mix. On inhabited islands things won't be so easy – fish and seafood dominate menus in the islands, so those who don't eat fish will have trouble.

Eating with Kids

In resorts menus sometimes have kids' sections, giving youngsters a choice of slightly less sophisticated foods, ranging from spaghetti to fish fingers and chicken nuggets. Even if there's nothing dedicated to the kids' tastes, resort buffets are usually diverse enough to cater to even the fussiest eaters. However, it's always best to check what resorts offer before booking a holiday with young kids. We've heard complaints from travellers about the poor availability of child-suitable foods even at the very best resorts. Note that baby-food products are not on sale in resorts, so bring whatever you will need for the trip.

Habits & Customs

There's not a huge amount of etiquette to worry about if you eat in Male or resorts. If you're lucky enough to be entertained in a local house you should obey some basic rules. That said, Maldivians are very relaxed and as long as you show respect and enjoyment, they'll be glad to have you eating with them.

When going to eat, wait to be shown where to sit and wait for the *kateeb* (island chief) or the male head of the household to sit down before you do. Take a little of everything offered and do so only with your right hand, as the left hand is considered unclean by Muslims. Do ask for cutlery if you find it hard to roll your food into little balls like the Maldivians do; this is quite normal for foreigners.

COFFEE

Maldivians love their coffee. You can get very good espresso, latte or cappuccino anywhere in Male, as well as at most resorts and guesthouses.

Kavaabu are small deep-fried dough balls with tuna, mashed potato, pepper and lime – a very popular 'short eat'.

Independent Travel

A mini-revolution has occurred in Maldivian travel in the past few years, stemming from the decisions of the Nasheed government to lift all travel restrictions on foreigners, allow the building of hotels on inhabited islands and create a national ferry network. These three factors combined now mean that the Maldives is open for business as an independent travel destination for the first time. Despite the change of government, the genie is out of the bottle now, and there seems to be no going back.

A Total Rethink

Maldivian tourism developed in a very unusual way. From the inception of the first resorts in the 1970s the government ensured that the devout and conservative local population was kept entirely separate from the alcohol-drinking, bikini-wearing Westerners frolicking on the beaches. Amazingly, until 2009, a permit was needed for foreigners to stay overnight anywhere outside a resort island or the capital, meaning that the only contact that most island populations had with the outside world were the occasional tour group from a nearby resort visiting for an hour or two to buy souvenirs before disappearing back to the infinity pool. Now tourists are free to travel and overnight wherever they please – so options beyond the 100 or so resorts are now almost limitless.

While this is exciting, it's not totally problem free. The Maldives isn't overflowing with great sights or cultural events to attend – indeed, save the incredible underwater world and various sports there's very little to do here except enjoy the beauty and tranquillity of the islands, and even this has to be done in accordance with fairly strict local customs (see box, p167). Yet for those who itch to enjoy the magnificent snorkelling, beaches, diving, surfing and fishing of the Maldives, but can't imagine anything worse than being confined to a resort, your hour to visit the country has finally come.

> Travelling by ferry is remarkably cheap in the Maldives. Short journeys within an atoll cost only Rf20, rising to Rf50 for longer journeys between atolls, while even huge inter-atoll trips will set you back only Rf100 (around US$7).

The National Ferry Network

Another persistent problem facing independent travellers was always the lack of transport infrastructure in a country where even the shortest journey must be done by boat. While there have always been public dhoni ferries connecting the islands, their timetables were guesswork and journeys achingly slow, so it was totally unrealistic for most people to journey around the country this way. Now there is a national ferry network based on Male and in the individual atoll capitals that regularly (and cheaply) connects all the inhabited islands in the country. Timetables can still be infuriatingly difficult to obtain, but as in most cases you'll be travelling from one guesthouse to another, staff will be able to tell you what time the ferries go and from where.

THOSE ISLAND RESTRICTIONS...

Travelling independently among the inhabited islands of the Maldives means that you'll need to be prepared to adapt to local standards of dress and behaviour, many aspects of which don't exactly gel with most people's idea of a holiday. Perhaps the most restrictive of all is the total lack of alcohol anywhere in the country outside the resorts. You can't even bring alcohol with you, as its import is banned and all luggage is X-rayed on arrival. You'll be limited to widely available non-alcoholic beer for the duration of your stay.

Just as limiting for many are the dress requirements (mainly for women, though men need to be aware of them too). On inhabited islands it's not currently possible for women to wear normal swimsuits (and certainly not bikinis). Local women bathe fully clothed, and often men keep their T-shirts on too, which means that all guesthouses organise daily trips to nearby uninhabited islands where visitors can swim and sunbathe as they would anywhere else in the world. However, this means that you can't usually enjoy a quick swim at the beach but must spend several hours there on a day trip, which can take the spontaneity away somewhat. Some larger inhabited islands are developing 'Western beaches', where tourists can swim in their normal swimsuits, a safe distance away from local eyes, but in most cases the islands are simply too small to allow for this.

The ferries themselves remain as slow as ever, but they're a fascinating cultural experience, and you'll often find yourself the only non-Maldivian on the creaking old dhonis and *vedhis* that make the journeys between islands and atolls – a great way to meet people and get a feel for local life.

The Growing Guesthouses

There's now an ever-growing number of independently run guesthouses in the villages and towns that make up the Maldives beyond the resorts. These are most prevalent in the atolls near to the capital, making a ferry ride from Male a maximum of three or four hours, although they can be found as far away as Noonu Atoll (a 10-hour overnight ferry away from Male) or even in Haa Dhaalu Atoll, on the island of Hanimaadhoo (an hour's flight north of the capital).

In general the guesthouses are similar. They tend to be modest and fairly small (normally six rooms or so), but comfortable, aiming at budget and midrange travellers. They generally offer full-board accommodation (usually as there are few or no other eating options on the island) and a full list of excursions and activities to ensure that boredom doesn't encroach. The latter is important, as there is often relatively little to do on a small, conservative island.

Activities are pretty similar across the country: desert-island visits, beach barbecues, snorkelling, diving and fishing expeditions. Staff members at guesthouses tend to be a highlight. Young, enthusiastic and entrepreneurial, they are pioneers of local tourism and, for the most part, speak great English and have a real passion for showing foreigners the very best of their country.

Many guesthouses are still strangers to the internet, and websites are not common. For easy booking, try either www.guesthouses-in-maldives.com or www.islandlifemaldives.net, both of which are helpful and offer great package deals, including help with your transfers.

Survival Guide

Directory A–Z

Accommodation

Ouch. That's most people's reaction to Maldivian resort prices, and it's fair to say this is not and will never be a cheap place to stay. Even budget hotels cost more than a top-end place in India or Sri Lanka.

In this book we list accommodation for each chapter, divided into three groups: budget, midrange and top end. For each option a room rate is quoted for the height of the season (mid-Jan to April) unless otherwise stated, with the normal meal plan with which rooms are sold. There are almost no single rooms in resorts, so singles are nearly always doubles for single occupation, with a similar price tag to a double room. Where there is a separate price for singles (s), we list this; otherwise we just list the standard room price (r) in the cheapest accommodation category. As many travellers specifically want a water villa (a room on stilts over the water), we also list the cheapest water villa price for two people in the height of the season. All the prices in the book include a service charge (normally 10%), GST (6%) and the government bed tax (US$8 per person per night).

Resorts

The vast majority of accommodation for travellers consists of the roughly 110 self-contained island resorts throughout the country. We list most, but not all of the operating resorts in this book, including those we think are worthwhile considering.

Each resort is totally self-contained and provides accommodation, meals and activities for its guests, ranging from the most basic beach huts, with a buffet three times a day and a simple diving school, to vast water villas with every conceivable luxury, à la carte dining and all kinds of activities, from kiteboarding to big-game fishing.

Most resorts have a range of room categories, so for the sake of ease we give the rate for the cheapest room and for the cheapest water villa (if available). However, be warned, these prices are nothing more than a guideline. They are rack rates, and so booking through a travel agent will get you access to far better deals and lower rates.

Budget resorts (up to US$350 per double room per night) tend to be busier and more basic in their facilities and level of sophistication than more expensive resorts. Few budget resorts are being built these days, so those that do exist tend to date from the 1980s or '90s and often need a lick of paint.

Midrange resorts (from US$350 to US$750 per night) are noticeably slicker, better run and have a better standard of facilities and accommodation, all carried off with some style, and can be rather luxurious at the top end of the bracket.

Top-end resorts (more than US$750 per night) are currently what the Maldives is all about. The standards in this category range from the very good to the mind-bogglingly luxurious.

Booking resorts through travel agents is nearly always cheaper than doing so directly, with some amazing deals to be had compared with the eye-watering rack rates. However, increasingly some resorts offer great deals via their websites.

Hotels & Guesthouses

Previous laws prohibited the construction of hotels

BOOK YOUR STAY ONLINE

For more accommodation reviews by Lonely Planet authors, check out http://hotels.lonelyplanet.com. You'll find independent reviews, as well as recommendations on the best places to stay. Best of all, you can book online.

and guesthouses on most of the islands inhabited by locals. This law was changed in 2009 and guesthouses have now sprung up on in-habited islands throughout the Maldives. As hotels in Male are far cheaper than the island resorts, we've used a separate price breakdown for the capital's hotels: budget (under US$80), midrange (US$80 to US$150) and top end (over US$150).

We've listed the best of the growing number of guesthouses in this guide as well. They offer a totally dif-ferent experience to staying in a resort, far more contact with local life and far cheaper accommodation, but staying in one also entails certain restrictions, particularly with regards to alcohol and attire (see p166).

Safari Boats

Live-aboard safari boats al-low you to travel extensively throughout the country, visit-ing great dive sites, desert islands and small local settle-ments usually too remote to see travellers. Live-aboards also range from simple to luxury, and you get what you pay for. The advantage is that you can visit many places off-limits to resort travellers, dive in pristine waters and enjoy a very sociable atmosphere. Prices range from bargain basement to exorbitant, depending on the facilities available (see p20).

Business Hours

Male is really the only place you have to worry about business hours in the Mal-dives. The resorts are far more flexible, as they have to cater round the clock to visitors.

Typical business hours outside resorts are as fol-lows:

Banks 8am-1.30pm Sun-Thu
Businesses 8am-6pm Sun-Thu

PRICE RANGES

The following price ranges refer to a double room per night in high season (mid-Jan to April), with the normal meal plan with which rooms are sold. All the prices in this book include a service charge (normally 10%), GST (6%) and the government bed tax (US$8 per person per night).

CATEGORY	RESORTS	HOTELS IN MALE
$ budget	<US$350	<US$80
$$ midrange	US$350-750	US$80-150
$$$ top end	>US$750	>US$150

Government offices
7.30am-2pm Sun-Thu
Restaurants noon-10pm Sat-Thu, 4-11pm Fri

Nearly all Male businesses stop several times a day for prayers, which can be frus-trating for shoppers, as busi-nesses suddenly close for 15 minutes to half an hour. Teashops can open very early or close very late. During Ramazan the places where locals eat will probably be closed during daylight hours, but will bustle after dark.

Children

Younger children will enjoy a couple of weeks on a Maldivian resort island, par-ticularly if they like playing in the water and on the beach. Although exotic cuisine is sometimes on the menu, there are always some pretty standard Western-style dish-es that kids will find edible.

Older children and teenag-ers could find a resort a little confining after a few days, and they may get bored. Canoeing and fishing trips might provide some diver-sion, while a course in sailing or windsurfing could be a great way to spend a holiday. The minimum age for scuba diving is 10 years, but most resorts offer a 'bubble blow-ers' introduction for younger kids, which is very popular.

Kids clubs for 12s and un-der and teen clubs are very common in bigger, smarter resorts. These are free and the kids clubs run activities all day long to keep the little ones busy, while teenagers are able to do what they want – even if it means play-ing computer games in a darkened air-conditioned room. Where resorts have good kids clubs or a gener-ally welcoming child-friendly policy, we've included the child-friendly icon [image].

Be aware that young chil-dren are more susceptible to sunburn than adults, so bring sun hats and sunblock. Lycra swim shirts are an excellent idea – they can be worn on the beach and in the water and block out most UV radiation.

Practicalities

Note that some resorts do not encourage young children – check with the resort – and that children under five are often banned from honey-moon resorts. Where kids are welcome, it's no problem booking cots and organising high chairs in restaurants, and there's often a babysitting service and kids club in big-ger, family-oriented resorts. Nappies are available in Male, but usually not in resorts, so bring all the nappies and formula you'll need for the du-ration of the holiday. Outside resorts, breast-feeding should only be done in private.

Customs Regulations

The immigration cards issued to you on your flight to Male include a great list of items that are banned from the republic. Alcohol, pornography, pork, narcotics, dogs, firearms, spear guns and 'idols of worship' cannot be brought into the country and you're advised to comply. Baggage is always X-rayed and may be searched carefully, and if you have any liquor it will be taken and held for you till you're about to leave the country. This service will not extend to other prohibited items, and the importation of multiple bibles (one for personal use is fine), pornography and, in particular, drugs, will be treated very seriously. The export of turtle shell, or any turtle-shell products, is forbidden.

Electricity

230V/50Hz

Embassies & Consulates

The foreign representatives in Male are mostly honorary consuls with limited powers; some countries have

Climate
Male

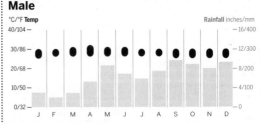

no representatives in the Maldives at all. In an emergency contact your country's embassy or high commission in Colombo, Sri Lanka.

Germany & Austria (☑332 2971; Universal Enterprises, 38 Orchid Magu)
India (☑332 3016; Athireege Aage, Ameeru Ahmed Magu)
Italy (☑332 2451; Cyprea, 25 Boduthakurufaanu Magu)

Food
See p163.

Gay & Lesbian Travellers

This is a grey area legally in the Maldives, where gay awareness isn't high. By Maldivian law all extramarital sex is illegal, although such mores are not applied to the resorts, where in practice anything goes as long as it is low key or behind closed doors. Same-sex couples will be able to book a double room with no questions asked (from budget to luxury, Maldivian hotel staff are the model of discretion), and it's common to see same sex-couples enjoying Maldivian holidays, although only Island Hideaway and W Resort & Spa actively market themselves to the gay community. Public displays of affection may embarrass Maldivian resort staff, but won't result in anything but blushes on their part. In Male and on inhabited islands discretion is key and public displays

of affection should not be indulged in by anyone, gay or straight – the Maldives remains an extremely conservative place.

Insurance

A travel-insurance policy to cover theft, loss and medical problems is highly recommended. Some policies offer lower and higher medical-expense options; the higher ones are chiefly for countries that have high medical costs, and this would be a good idea for a Maldives trip.

Some policies specifically exclude 'dangerous activities', which can include diving, so check your policy carefully if you plan to dive.

Worldwide travel insurance is available at www. lonelyplanet.com/travel _services. You can buy, extend and claim online anytime – even if you're already on the road.

Internet Access

All but the most basic resorts have internet access for guests. There is usually some wi-fi in communal areas for free, and either wi-fi or cable internet access in the rooms (depending on the resort size), which can be free or charged depending on the resort. Most resorts offer at least some free access, but extraordinarily some still charge for any kind of connection.

Nearly all resorts have terminals connected to the

internet (again, either for free or charged) for the use of guests without their own laptops or smartphones.

In Male and the atolls internet cafes are pretty obsolete, while wi-fi hotspots (usually paid) and access via mobile-phone networks are increasingly common.

Legal Matters

» Alcohol is illegal outside resorts – you're theoretically not even allowed to take a can of beer out on a boat trip. Some foreign residents in the capital have a liquor permit, which entitles them to a limited amount per month, strictly for personal consumption at home.

» Illicit drugs are around, but are not widespread. Penalties are heavy. 'Brown sugar', a semirefined form of heroin, has become a problem among some young people in the capital and even in some outer islands.

» Apart from the police and the military, there is a chief on every atoll and island who must keep an eye on what is happening, report to the central government and be responsible for the actions of local people.

» Resorts are responsible for their guests and for what happens on their island. If a guest sunbathes or goes swimming in the nude, the resort can be fined, as well as the visitor.

Maps

Put simply, the Maldives is a nightmare to map. The islands are so small and scattered that you're forever trying to distinguish between the tiny islands and the reefs that surround them. Another problem is scale – the country is over 800km from north to south, but the largest island is only about 8km long.

For anyone doing a serious amount of travel, especially diving, *Maps of the Maldives*

(Water Solutions, 2008) is indispensable and in a very practical book form, alleviating the need to fold out a vast map. It includes everything from shipwreck sites to Protected Marine Area plans. It's on sale at bookshops in Male.

Money

The currency of the Maldives is the rufiyaa (Rf), which is divided into 100 larees. Notes come in denominations of 500, 100, 50, 20, 10, five and two rufiyaa, but the last two are uncommon. Coins are in denominations of two and one rufiyaa, and 50, 25 and 10 larees. Most resort and travel expenses will be billed in dollars, and most visitors never even see rufiyaa. If you're staying in a resort, all extras (including diving costs) will be billed to your room, and you pay the day before departure. Resorts accept cash, credit cards or travellers cheques in all major currencies, although unless specified (some European resorts now use the euro as their default currency) US dollars are preferred.

ATMs

There are a large number of ATMs in Male – most (but not all) allow you to withdraw funds from international accounts. Those that definitely do are the ones outside the major banks on Boduthakurufaanu Magu. Note that while you can do cash advances on credit cards over the counter at Male airport and at most resorts, there are no internationally compatible ATMs outside Male.

Cash

It's perfectly possible to have a holiday in the Maldives without ever touching cash of any sort, as in resorts everything will be chalked up to your room number and paid by credit card or travellers cheques on departure. However, it's a good idea to have some cash with

you – small-denomination US dollars are most handy for tipping staff and buying sundries in transit. You won't need Maldivian rufiyaa unless you're using local shops and services. Even these will usually take dollars, but you'll be given change in rufiyaa.

Be aware that there are restrictions on changing rufiyaa into foreign currency. If you take out cash in rufiyaa from an ATM, you won't be able to change the remainder back into US dollars or any other foreign currency. Therefore if you need lots of local currency, exchange foreign cash for rufiyaa at a bank and keep the receipt to be allowed to change the remainder back at the airport.

Credit Cards

Every resort takes major credit cards including Visa, Amex and MasterCard. A week of diving and drinking could easily run up a tab over US$2000, so ensure your credit limit can stand it. The cashier may want 24 hours' notice to check your credit. Many resorts apply a surcharge of 5% to credit-card payments, so it may be best to have enough travellers cheques to cover the bulk of your extras bill.

Tipping

Tipping is something of a grey area in the Maldives, where a 10% service tax is added to nearly everything from minibar drinks to room prices. In many places this would mean that you don't need to tip in addition, but it's still the case that people serving you personally will often expect something. It's good form to leave a tip for your room staff and in smarter resorts your *thakuru* (butler). Give any tips to the staff personally, not to the hotel cashier – US dollars, euros and local currency are equally acceptable. A few dollars a day is fine for room staff, while anyone carrying your bags might expect US$1 or so per bag. There's no need to tip bar staff.

In Male the fancier restaurants usually add a 10% service charge, so you don't need to tip. Tipping is not customary in local teashops. Taxi drivers are not tipped, but porters at the airport expect Rf10 or US$1.

Travellers Cheques

Banks in Male will change travellers cheques and cash in US dollars, and possibly UK pounds, euros, Japanese yen and Swiss francs. Most will change US-dollar travellers cheques into US dollars cash with a commission of US$5. Changing travellers cheques to Maldivian rufiyaa should not attract a commission.

Some of the authorised moneychangers around town will exchange US-dollar or euro travellers cheques at times when the banks are closed. You can always try some of the hardware shops, souvenir shops and guesthouses. Most tourist businesses will accept US dollars in cash at the standard rate, and euros at reasonable rates.

Photography

» There are no restrictions on photography in the resorts or much of the rest of the country, so snap away – photography is very popular among visitors.

» Do be aware that photographing the National Security Services Headquarters in Male is not allowed and that you could be quickly arrested for breaking this rule.

» On inhabited islands in the atolls, exercise caution about photographing locals. Always ask for permission before you take a picture, and remember that the islands are conservative places, so be polite and not too intrusive.

Post

Postal services are quite efficient, with mail to overseas destinations delivered promptly; mail from overseas, especially packets and parcels, is subject to customs screening and can take considerably longer. The **main post office** (Boduthakurufaanu Magu; ☉8.15am-9pm Sun-Thu, 3-9pm Fri, 9.15am-9pm Sat) in Male has a poste restante service.

A high-speed Express Mail Service (EMS) is available to many countries. Parcel rates can be quite expensive and will have to clear customs at the main post office, where a bored-looking customs official will be stationed to inspect any packages you're sending home.

At the resorts you can buy stamps and postcards at the shop or the reception desk. Generally there is a mailbox near reception.

Public Holidays

If you're in a resort, Maldivian holidays will not affect you – service will be as normal. If you visit Male or an inhabited island on a holiday, you might see some parade or public celebration, shops may not open or may open late in the day,

---

PRACTICALITIES

Newspapers & Magazines

Of the main Dhivehi daily papers, *Miadhu* (www.miadhu.com) and *Haveeru* (www.haveeru.com.mv) both have excellent English editions online. Far better for current affairs is *Minivan News* (www.minivannews.com), an English language web-based paper with sharp and well-researched local reporting. A smattering of international papers and magazines are available from bookshops in Male.

TV

Television Maldives, the national TV station, is broadcast from Male during the day, with regular breaks for prayer. The rest of the schedule is made up of political programs, variety shows and Al Jazeera rebroadcasts in English. There's news in English at 9pm. Other local TV channels include DhiTV and VillaTV.

Nearly all resorts and most Male hotels have satellite TV, including BBC World News, CNN, Al Jazeera, Star Movies and HBO alongside Sri Lankan, Indian and European channels.

Electricity

Electricity supply is 220V to 240V, 50Hz AC. The standard socket is the UK-style three-pin, although there are some variations, so an international adaptor can be useful (and is essential for non-UK travellers).

Weights & Measures

Although the Maldives now officially uses the metric system, imperial measures are still sometimes used and are widely understood. Metric measurements are used in this book.

and government offices and most businesses will be closed. Christmas, New Year, Easter and European school holidays will affect you more – they're the busiest times for tourists and bring the highest resort prices.

If a holiday falls on a Friday or Saturday, the next working day will be declared a holiday 'on the occasion of' whatever it was. Most Maldivian holidays are based on the Islamic lunar calendar and the dates vary from year to year.

Ramazan Known as Ramazan or *roarda mas* in the Maldives rather than Ramadan, the Islamic month of fasting is an important religious occasion that starts on a new moon and continues for 28 days. Expected starting dates for the next few years are: 10 July 2013, 29 June 2014, and 18 June 2015. The exact date depends on the sighting of the new moon in Mecca and can vary by a day or so either way.

Kuda Eid Also called Id-ul-Fitr or Fith'r Eid, this occurs at the end of Ramazan, with the sighting of the new moon, and is celebrated with a feast.

Bodu Eid Also called Eid-ul Al'h'aa (Festival of the Sacrifice), 66 days after the end of Ramazan, this is the time when many Muslims begin the pilgrimage (haj) to Mecca.

National Day A commemoration of the day Mohammed Thakurufaanu and his men overthrew the Portuguese on Male in 1578. It's on the first day of the third month of the lunar calendar.

Prophet's Birthday The birthday of the Prophet Mohammed is celebrated with three days of eating and merriment. The approximate start dates for the next few years are 24 January 2013, 14 January 2014 and 3 January 2015.

Huravee Day The day the Malabars of India were kicked out by Sultan Hassan Izzuddeen after their brief occupation in 1752.

Martyr's Day Commemorates the death of Sultan Ali VI at the hands of the Portuguese in 1558.

The following are fixed holiday dates:

New Year's Day 1 January

Independence Day Celebrates the ending of the British protectorate (in 1965) on 26 and 27 July.

Victory Day Celebrates the victory over the Sri Lankan mercenaries who tried to overthrow the Maldivian government in 1988. A military march is followed by lots of schoolchildren doing drills and traditional dances, and more entertaining floats and costumed processions on 3 November.

Republic Day Commemorates the second (current) republic, founded in 1968 on 11 November. Celebrated in Male with lots of pomp, brass bands and parades. Sometimes the following day is also a holiday.

Telephone

» There are two telephone providers operating in the Maldives: Dhiraagu and Wataniya.

» Both providers offer good coverage, although given the unique geography of the country there are still lots of areas without coverage in the atolls.

» You can buy a local SIM card for around US$10 and use it in your own phone if it's been unlocked at home (check with your provider) – this becomes worth the price almost immediately if you're using your phone locally.

» All resorts have telephones, either in the rooms or available at reception. Charges vary from high to astronomical, starting around US$15 for three minutes; our advice is to avoid using them and stick to Skype instead.

» The international country code for the Maldives is ☑960. All Maldives numbers have seven digits and there are no area codes.

» To make an international call, dial ☑00, then the country code, area code and number.

Time

The Maldives is five hours ahead of GMT, in the same time zone as Pakistan. When it's noon in the Maldives, it's 7am in London, 8am in Berlin and Rome, 12.30pm in India and Sri Lanka, 3pm in Singapore and 4pm in Tokyo.

The majority of resorts operate one hour ahead of Male time to give their guests the illusion of extra daylight in the evening and a longer sleep in the morning. This can make it tricky when arranging pick-up times and transfers, so always check whether you're being quoted a time in Male time or resort time.

Toilets

Male public toilets charge Rf2. On local islands, you may have to ask where the *fahana* is, although many people still use the town beach as a vast public latrine and rubbish dump. In general you're better off using toilets in cafes and restaurants in Male – they're usually cleaner and free.

Tourist Information

The official tourist office is the very helpful **Maldives Tourism Promotion Board** (www.visitmaldives. com), which has a fantastic website and a desk at the airport in Male. However, most tourism promotion is done by private travel agents, tour operators and resorts.

THOSE UNPRONOUNCEABLE ATOLLS

Confusingly enough, the 26 atolls of the Maldives are divided for official purposes into 21 administrative districts, which are named by the letters of the Thaana alphabet and as such are a lot easier to pronounce. Would you rather talk about South Miladhunmadulu Atoll or Noonu? Thought so. However, it's not that simple, as the traditional atoll names are still universally used for North and South Male Atolls, North and South Ari Atoll and Addu Atoll in the far south, so we also use these instead of the more obscure names Kaafu, Alif and Seenu. The following table gives both traditional and administrative names for most parts of the country; those marked with an asterisk are the ones used in this book.

ADMINISTRATIVE NAME	ATOLL NAME
Alifu	Ari Atoll*
Baa*	South Maalhosmadulu Atoll
Dhaalu*	South Nilandhe Atoll
Faafu*	North Nilandhe Atoll
Gaafu Alifu*	North Huvadhoo Atoll
Gaafu Dhaalu*	South Huvadhoo Atoll
Gnaviyani*	Fuvahmulah Atoll
Haa Alifu*	North Thiladhunmathee Atoll
Haa Dhaal*	South Thiladhunmathee Atoll & Maamakunudhoo Atoll
Kaafu	Male Atoll*
Laamu*	Hadhdunmathee Atoll
Lhaviyani*	Faadhippolhu Atoll
Meemu*	Mulaku Atoll
Noonu*	South Miladhunmadulu Atoll
Raa*	North Maalhosmadulu Atoll
Seenu	Addu Atoll*
Shaviyani*	North Miladhunmadulu Atoll
Thaa*	Kolhumadulu Atoll
Vaavu*	Felidhe Atoll

Travellers with Disabilities

At Male International Airport, passengers must use steps to get on and off planes, but it should be no problem to get assistance for mobility-challenged passengers.

Transfers to nearby resorts are by dhoni or speedboat and a person in a wheelchair or with limited mobility will need assistance, which the crews will always be happy to provide. Transfer to more distant resorts is often by seaplanes, which can be more difficult to access, but staff are quite experienced in assisting passengers in wheelchairs or with limited mobility.

Most resorts have ground-level rooms, few steps, and reasonably smooth paths to beaches, boat jetties and all public areas, but some of the more rustic and 'ecofriendly' resorts have a lot of sand floors. Staff – something there's never a shortage of in the Maldives – will be on hand to assist disabled guests. When you decide on a resort, call them directly and ask about the layout. It's usually a good idea for guests to advise their tour agency of any special needs, but if you want to find out about specific facilities, it's best to contact the resort itself.

Many resort activities are potentially suitable for disabled guests. Fishing trips and excursions to inhabited islands should be easy, but uninhabited islands may be more difficult to disembark on. Catamaran sailing and canoeing are possibilities, especially if you've had experience in these activities. Anyone who can swim will be able to enjoy snorkelling. The **International Association for Handicapped Divers** (www.iahd.org) provides advice and assistance for anyone with a physical disability who wishes to scuba dive. Resort dive schools should be able to arrange a special course or program for any group of four or more people with a similar disability.

No dogs are permitted in the Maldives, so it's not a destination for anyone dependent on a guide dog.

Visas

The Maldives issues a 30-day stamp on arrival to holders of all passports. Citizens of India, Pakistan, Bangladesh or Nepal are given a 90-day stamp. If you want to stay longer you'll either need to apply for an extension to the 30-day stamp or leave the country when your 30 days is up, then return.

While officially you're supposed to show immigration officials US$30 for every day's stay, this is not usually enforced, and showing a credit card will placate concerns. However, you should know the name of your resort or hotel and be able to show a return air ticket out of the country if asked by immigration officials.

Visa Extensions

To apply for an extension, go to the **Department of Immigration & Emigration** (☑332 3910; Ameer Ahmed Magu, near corner with Jumhooree Maidan; ☺9am-3pm Sun-Thu), near Jumhooree Maidan in Male. Fill in the Application for Permit Extension form, which will need to be co-signed by a local sponsor. The main requirement is evidence that you have accommodation, so it's best to have your resort, travel agent or guesthouse manager act as a sponsor and apply on your behalf. Have your sponsor sign the form, and bring it back to the office, along with your passport, a passport photo and your air ticket out of the country. You have to have a confirmed booking for the new departure date before you can get the extension – fortunately, the airlines don't ask to see a visa extension before they'll change the date of your flight. Proof of sufficient funds (US$30 per day) or a credit card may also be required. You'll be asked to leave the documents at the office and return in a couple of days to pick up the passport with its extended visa (get a receipt for your passport).

Extensions are for a maximum of 30 days. Overstaying your visa (or extension), even by an hour, can be a major hassle, as you may not be allowed to board your flight. If this happens, you will have to go back to Male, book another flight, get a visa extension and pay a fine before you can leave.

Volunteering

There are few volunteering opportunities in the Maldives, but those that do exist tend to be worthwhile projects involving sustainable development, wildlife protection and teaching. Bear in mind that for the most part, volunteers will be living on small, remote islands without many creature comforts (including alcohol!), so it's important to be prepared for that.

However, the experience can be extremely rewarding. The **Maldivian High Commission** (www.maldiveshighcommission.org/?id_w=22) can help with some placements and its webpage is useful for those considering volunteer work. Some excellent organisations include the following:

» www.maldiveswhale sharkresearch.org
» www.tinyislandvolunteers. com
» www.volunteermaldives. com

Women Travellers

Culturally, resorts are European enclaves and visiting women will not have to make too many adjustments. Topless bathing and nudity are strictly forbidden, but bikinis are perfectly acceptable on resort beaches.

Reasonably modest dress is appropriate when in Male – shorts should cover the thighs and shirts should cover the shoulders and not be very low cut. Women may be stared at on the street in Male, especially if their dress or demeanour is seen as provocative, but nothing more serious will happen. Local women don't go into teashops in Male, but a foreign woman with a male companion would not cause any excitement.

In more out-of-the-way parts of the country, quite conservative dress is in order. It is very unlikely that a foreign woman would be harassed or feel threatened on a local island, as Maldivian men are conservative and extremely respectful. They are very closed, small communities, and the fact that a foreign woman would be associated with a local sponsor should give a high level of security.

Work

There is an enormous work market for foreigners in the Maldives, as almost 50% of resort staff generally comes from abroad (a Maldivian law stipulates that 50% of all resort staff must be Maldivian). Resorts are keen to hire people with a background in the hospitality industry, including managers, administrators, divemasters, masseurs, biologists, chefs, sommeliers and yoga instructors, and the positions tend to be well compensated and provide for plenty of 'off-island' time.

Some useful websites:

» www.job-maldives.com
» www.jobinmaldives.com

Transport

GETTING THERE & AWAY

Entering the Country

Entering the Maldives is simple and hassle-free. However, you must know the name of your resort or hotel, so even if you haven't got one arranged, don't let immigration control know this, as you'll be marched to the nearest travel agency's airport desk and made to book something.

Passport

There are no restrictions on foreign nationals entering the country. Visas are not needed for visits of 30 days or less. Theoretically, travellers must have US$30 per day for the duration of their stay, though this is not usually enforced and producing a credit card is a perfectly good substitute if you're asked.

Air

Airports & Airlines

Almost every visitor to the Maldives arrives at **Male Ibrahim Nasir International Airport** (MLE; ☎332 5511; www.maldivesairport.aero), on the island of Hulhule, 2km across the water from the capital. It's a decent airport that is in the process of upgrading to a superb new world-class terminal. The only other international terminal in the country is **Gan International Airport** (GAN; ☎689 8010; www.gan airport.com), in the far south of the country. It mainly gets flights from Male, but also has direct flights from Hong Kong with Mega Maldives and the odd charter flight.

The national carrier is Maldivian, connecting the Maldives to India and flying to all domestic terminals from the capital. The international carriers serving Male are a mixture of scheduled and charter airlines. Some airlines only fly in certain seasons and change services frequently.

Aeroflot (www.aeroflot.com)
Aerosvit (www.aerosvit.com)
Air Berlin (www.airberlin.com)
Air India (www.airindia.com)
Austrian (www.aua.com)
Bangkok Airways (www.bangkokair.com)
British Airways (www.ba.com)
Condor (www.catchafly-t.com)
Emirates (www.emirates.com)
Etihad (www.etihadairways.com)
First Choice (www.firstchoice.co.uk)
Malaysia Airlines (www.malaysiaairlines.com)
Mega Maldives Airlines (www.megamaldivesair.com)
Monarch (www.flymonarch.com)
Oman Air (www.omanair.com)
Qatar Airways (www.qatarairways.com)
Singapore Airlines (www.singaporeairlines.com)
SriLankan Airlines (www.srilankan.aero)

CLIMATE CHANGE & TRAVEL

Every form of transport that relies on carbon-based fuel generates CO_2, the main cause of human-induced climate change. Modern travel is dependent on aeroplanes, which might use less fuel per kilometre per person than most cars but travel much greater distances. The altitude at which aircraft emit gases (including CO_2) and particles also contributes to their climate change impact. Many websites offer 'carbon calculators' that allow people to estimate the carbon emissions generated by their journey and, for those who wish to do so, to offset the impact of the greenhouse gases emitted with contributions to portfolios of climate-friendly initiatives throughout the world. Lonely Planet offsets the carbon footprint of all staff and author travel.

Thomson Airways (www.thomson.co.uk)
Transaero (www.transaero.ru)

Tickets

If you're on a package, you'll usually have little or no choice about the airline you fly, as it will be part of the package. However, packages without flights are available, so it pays to shop around for both scheduled and charter deals. More and more chartered airlines are selling flight-only seats and these can be good deals, so check their websites as well as those of scheduled carriers. The other advantage of charter flights is that you can fly direct from Western Europe to Male, without the change in the Middle East or Sri Lanka common for scheduled airlines.

Flights can be booked online at lonelyplanet.com/bookings.

Sea

International Connections

While it may look like an obvious transport route, there are currently no scheduled boat connections between either India or Sri Lanka and the Maldives, nor do cargo ships generally take paying passengers. You might be lucky if you ask around in Colombo or Trivandrum, but it's unlikely.

Yacht

Yachts and super-yachts cruise Maldivian waters throughout the year – this is, after all, a playground for the rich and famous. However, with the Maldives being somewhat out of the way, this is not a standard port of call. But more yachts are coming through and official policy is becoming more welcoming. The negatives include the maze of reefs that can make it a hazardous place to cruise, the high fees for cruising permits, the officialdom, the restrictions on

---

> ## THINGS CHANGE...
>
> The information in this chapter is particularly vulnerable to change. Check directly with the airline or a travel agent to make sure you understand how a fare (and ticket you may buy) works and be aware of the security requirements for international travel. Shop carefully. The details given in this chapter should be regarded as pointers and are not a substitute for your own careful, up-to-date research.

---

where yachts can go and the absence of lively little ports with great eating options and waterfront bars.

A large marina has been built at Island Hideaway (see p95) in the far north of the country, and this is the only place currently set up for servicing yachts in a professional way. Addu, in the far south, has a sheltered anchorage, a tourist resort and refuelling and resupply facilities.

The three points where a yacht can get an initial 'clear in' are Uligamu (Haa Alifu) in the north, Hithadhoo/Gan (Addu Atoll) in the south, and Male. Call in on VHF channel 16 to the National Security Service (NSS) Coastguard and follow instructions. If you're just passing through and want to stop only briefly, a 72-hour permit is usually easy to arrange. If you want to stay longer in Maldivian waters, or stop for provisions, you'll have to do immigration, customs, port authority and quarantine checks, and get a cruising permit. This can be done at any of the three clear-in facilities.

If you want to stop at Male, ensure you arrive well before dark, go to the east side of Viligili island, between Viligili and Male, and call the coastguard on channel 16. Officially, all boats require a pilot, but this isn't usually insisted upon for boats under 30m. Carefully follow the coastguard's instructions on where to anchor, or you may find yourself in water that's very deep or too shallow. Then contact one of the

port agents, such as **Island Sailors** (☑ 333 2536; www.islandsailors.com) or **Century Star** (☑ 332 5353).

Port agents can arrange for port authority, immigration, customs and quarantine checks, and advise on repairs, refuelling etc. After the initial checks you'll be able to cross to the lagoon beside Hulhumale, the reclaimed land north of the airport. This is a good anchorage. The bigger stores, like STO Trade Centre and Fantasy, have quite a good range of provisions at reasonable prices. The port agents can advise on other necessities such as radio repairs, water and fuelling.

Cruising permits cost US$400 for the first month, the second month US$500. Customs, port and inspection charges increase with the size of the boat. You're nearly always able to stop at resorts to eat, drink, swim, dive and spend your money, but you should always call the resort first. Usually you have to be off the island by sunset.

Before you leave Maldivian waters, don't forget to 'clear out' at Uligamu, Hithadhoo or Male.

GETTING AROUND

Air

Airlines in the Maldives

Air is the main way to cover long distances in the Maldives. There are six airports in the country, all of which are linked to the capital by regular flights. The domestic carrier is the national carrier **Maldivian** (☑333 5544; www.maldivian.aero; Boduthaku-rufaanu Magu), which offers several daily flights to the following five regional airports. Flights fill up fast, so reserve in advance (booking online is possible) to ensure you get the flight you want.

Fuvahmulah (Gnaviyani, one daily flight, US$340 return, 70 minutes)

Gan (Addu, four to five flights daily, US$350 return, 70 minutes)

Hanimaadhoo (Haa Dhaalu, five flights daily, US$275 return, one hour)

Kaadedhdhoo (Gaafu Dhaalu, two to three flights daily, US$305 return, 70 minutes)

Kadhoo (Laamu, five flights daily, US$268 return, 50 minutes)

Seaplane

The use of seaplanes means that almost every corner of the country can be reached by air. Many travellers use the services of the two charter seaplane companies, **Trans Maldivian Airways** (☑334 8400; www.transmaldivian.com) and **Maldivian Air Taxi** (☑331 5201; www.maldivian airtaxi.com). Both fly tourists from the seaplane port next to Male International Airport out to resorts. They fly 18-seater DeHavilland Twin Otter seaplanes under contract to resorts throughout the Maldives, so you won't have any choice about who you fly with – normally each resort has a contract with just one of the carriers.

All seaplane transfers are made during daylight hours, and offer staggering views of the atolls, islands, reefs and lagoons. The cost is between US$200 and US$600 return, depending on the distance and the deal between the resorts, and it's generally included in the package price. If you book independently, the seaplane will be charged as an extra.

Charter flights for sight-seeing, photography and emergency evacuation can also be arranged. Call both companies for rates and availability. Note that cargo capacity on the seaplanes is limited to 20kg in most cases, with extra weight charged at a premium and some heavy items may have to wait for a later flight.

Boat

Boat safety is excellent in the Maldives.

Dhoni Charters

In Male, go along the waterfront to the eastern end of Boduthakurufaanu Magu by the airport ferry jetty and you'll find many dhonis waiting in the harbour. Some of these are available for charter to nearby islands. The price depends on where you want to go, for how long, and on your negotiating skills – somewhere between Rf1000 and Rf2000 for a day is a typical rate, but if you want to start at 6am and go nonstop for 12 hours, it could be quite a bit more. You can also charter a dhoni at most resorts, but it will cost more (anything from US$300 to US$600 per day) and you'll only get one if they're not all being used for excursions or diving trips.

Ferry

The Nasheed government introduced a public ferry network in 2010, and while it's not without its faults, all the inhabited islands in the country are now connected by ferry to at least somewhere else, even if it is just a couple of times a week. This means that if you have plenty of time, independent travel around the Maldives is now possible. These ferries will not, however, help you travel between resorts – you'll need to do this by far pricier speedboat or seaplane transfers.

We have included basic information about ferry routes, but for specific timings

you'll need to check with the guesthouse you're heading to (and unless you know someone on the island in question, you'll need to be heading to an island with a guesthouse on it, unless it's just a day trip).

Ferries are cheap and relatively slow compared to speedboats. They are time-tabled, but are also prone to delays due to bad weather or technical problems, so ferries are for those with plenty of time and patience.

Speedboat

Resorts in North and South Male Atoll, as well as some in Ari Atoll, offer transfer by speedboat, which costs anything from US$50 to US$300 return depending on the distance. This is generally included in the package price, but for independent travellers it's charged as an extra on leaving the resort.

The boats range from a small runabout with an outboard motor to a full multideck launch with an aircraft-type cabin.

Most big travel agencies can organise the charter of launches from Male, which, if you can afford it, is absolutely the best way to get around. **Inner Maldives** (www.innermaldives.com.mv) has good-value launches for charter at around $500 per day, excluding the (substantial) fuel prices. For the price you'll get the services of the captain and a couple of crew members for a 10-hour day. If chartering a boat for the day, standard practice is for the client to pay for the tank to be refuelled on arrival back at Male. Another well-priced and reliable company to hire launches from in Male is **Nazaki Marine** (www.nazaki.com).

Car & Motorcycle

The only places where visitors will need to travel by road are Male and the southernmost atoll, Addu. Taxis are available in both places and driving is on the left.

Health

The Maldives is not a dangerous destination, with few poisonous animals and – by regional standards – excellent health care and hygiene awareness. Staying healthy here is mainly about being sensible and careful.

BEFORE YOU GO

Insurance

Make sure that you have adequate health insurance and that it covers you for expensive evacuations by seaplane or speedboat, and for any diving risks. See p182 for details on diving insurance.

Recommended Vaccinations

The only vaccination officially required by the Maldives is one for yellow fever if you're coming from an area where yellow fever is endemic. Malaria prophylaxis is not necessary.

Medical Checklist

Be aware that in resorts all medical care will be available only through the resort doctor or, when the resort doesn't have a doctor in residence, from a nurse or a member of staff with access to basic medical supplies. Bringing a few basic supplies such as plasters for small cuts is a good idea, as is mosquito repellent for the evenings in some islands.

IN THE MALDIVES

Availability & Cost of Health Care

Most resorts have a resident doctor, or share one with another nearby resort. However, if you are seriously unwell it may be necessary to go to Male or the nearest atoll capital with a hospital if you're in a far-flung resort.

The Maldivian health service relies heavily on doctors, nurses and dentists from overseas, and facilities outside the capital are limited. The country's main hospital is the **Indira Gandhi Memorial Hospital** (☏3316647; www.mhsc.com.mv; Buruzu Magu) in Male. Male also has the **ADK Private Hospital** (☏3313553; www.adkhospital.mv; Sosun Magu), which offers high-quality care at high prices, but as it's important to travel with medical insurance to the Maldives, the cost shouldn't be too much of a worry. The capital island of each atoll has a government hospital or at least a health centre – these are being improved, but for any serious problem you'll have to go to Male. Patients requiring specialist operations may have to be evacuated to Colombo or Singapore, or taken home.

Dengue Fever

Mosquitoes aren't generally troublesome in Maldivian resorts because there are few areas of open fresh water where they can breed. However, they can be a problem at certain times of the year (usually after heavy rainfall), so if they do tend to annoy you, use repellent or burn mosquito coils, available from resort shops at vast expense (bring your own just in case). Dengue fever, a viral disease transmitted by mosquitoes, occurs in Maldivian villages but is not a significant risk on resort islands or in the capital.

Diving Health & Safety

Health Requirements

Officially, a doctor should check you over before you do a course, and fill out a form full of diving health questions. In practice, most dive schools will let you dive or do a course if you're under 50 years old and complete a medical questionnaire, but the check-up is still a good idea. This is especially so if you have any problem at all with your breathing, ears or sinuses. If you are an asthmatic, have any other chronic breathing difficulties or any inner-ear problems, you shouldn't do any scuba diving.

Diving Safely

The following laws apply to recreational diving in the Maldives, and divemasters should enforce them:

» Maximum depth is 30m – this is the law in the Maldives.

» Maximum time is 60 minutes.

» No decompression dives.

» Each diver must carry a dive computer.

» Obligatory three-minute safety stop at 5m.

» Last dive no later than 24 hours before a flight.

Decompression Sickness

This is a very serious condition – usually, though not always, associated with diver error. The most common symptoms are unusual fatigue or weakness; skin itch; pain in the arms, legs (joints or mid-limb) or torso; dizziness and vertigo; local numbness, tingling or paralysis; and shortness of breath. Signs may also include a blotchy skin rash, a tendency to favour an arm or a leg, staggering, coughing spasms, collapse or unconsciousness. These symptoms and signs can occur individually, or a number of them can appear at one time.

The most common causes of decompression sickness (or 'the bends' as it is commonly known) are diving too deep, staying at depth for too long or ascending too quickly. This results in nitrogen coming out of solution in the blood and forming bubbles, most commonly in the bones and particularly in the joints or in weak spots such as healed fracture sites.

Avoid flying after diving, as it causes nitrogen to come out of the blood even faster than it would at sea level. Low-altitude flights, like a seaplane transfer to the airport, may be just as dangerous because the aircraft are not pressurised.

The only treatment for decompression sickness is to put the patient into a recompression chamber. That puts a person back under pressure similar to that of the depth at which they were diving so nitrogen bubbles can be reabsorbed. The time required in the chamber is usually three to eight hours. There are decompression chambers at both Baros and Kuramathi resorts.

Insurance

All divers must purchase compulsory Maldivian diving insurance before their first dive in the Maldives. This will automatically be done at the dive school where you do your first dive, and is not expensive. This remains valid for 30 days, no matter where in the country you dive.

In addition to normal travel insurance, it's a very good idea to take out specific diving cover, which will pay for evacuation to a recompression facility and the cost of hyperbaric treatment in a chamber. Evacuation would normally be by chartered speedboat or seaplane (both very expensive). **Divers Alert Network** (DAN; www. diversalertnetwork.org) is a nonprofit diving-safety organisation. It can be contacted through most dive shops and clubs, and it offers a DAN TravelAssist policy that provides evacuation and recompression coverage.

Environmental Hazards

Most of the potential danger (you have to be extremely unlucky or foolhardy to actually get hurt) lies under the sea.

Anemones

These colourful creatures are poisonous, and putting your hand into one can give you a painful sting. If stung, consult a doctor as quickly as possible; the usual procedure is to soak the sting in vinegar.

Coral Cuts & Stings

Coral is sharp stuff and brushing up against it is likely to cause a cut or abrasion. Most corals contain poisons and you're likely to get some in any wound, along with tiny grains of broken coral. The result is that a small cut can take a long time to heal. Wash any coral cuts very thoroughly with fresh water and then treat them liberally with antiseptic. Brushing against fire coral or the feathery hydroid can give you a painful sting and a persistent itchy rash.

Heat Exhaustion

Dehydration and salt deficiency can cause heat exhaustion. Take the time to acclimatise to high temperatures, drink sufficient liquids and don't do anything too physically demanding.

Salt deficiency is characterised by fatigue, lethargy, headaches, giddiness and muscle cramps; salt tablets may help, but adding extra salt to your food is better.

Heatstroke

This serious condition can occur if the body's heat-regulating mechanism breaks down and the body temperature rises to dangerous levels. Long, continuous periods of exposure to high temperatures and insufficient fluids can leave you vulnerable to heatstroke.

The symptoms are feeling unwell, not sweating very much (or at all) and a high body temperature (39°C to 41°C, or 102°F to 106°F). Where sweating has ceased, the skin becomes flushed and red. Severe, throbbing headaches and lack of coordination will also occur, and the sufferer may be confused or aggressive. Hospitalisation is essential, but in the interim get victims out of the sun, remove their clothing, cover them with a wet sheet or towel and then fan continuously. Give them fluids if they are conscious.

Sea Urchins

Sea urchins generally grow on reefs, and most resorts remove them if they're a danger to casual waders in the shallows, though the waters are generally so clear that it's easy to spot them. Watch out though, as the spines are long and sharp, break off easily and once embedded in your flesh are very difficult to remove.

Stingrays

These rays lie on sandy sea beds, and if you step on one, its barbed tail can whip up into your leg and cause a nasty, poisoned wound. Sand can drift over stingrays, so they can become all but invisible while basking on the bottom. Fortunately, stingrays will usually glide away as you approach. If you're wading in the sandy shallows, try to shuffle along and make some noise. If stung, bathing the affected area in hot water is the best treatment; medical attention should be sought to ensure the wound is properly cleaned.

Stonefish

These fish lie on reefs and the sea bed, and are well

DRINKING WATER

Tap water in the Maldives is all treated rain water and it's not advisable to drink it, not least as it has generally got an unpleasant taste. Nearly all resorts supply drinking water to their guests for free – some poorer resorts make you pay for it. Either way, it's a far better option.

camouflaged. When stepped on, their sharp dorsal spines pop up and inject a venom that causes intense pain and sometimes death. Stonefish are usually found in shallow, muddy water, but also on rock and coral sea beds. They are another good reason not to walk on coral reefs.

Bathing the wound in very hot water reduces the pain and effects of the venom. An antivenene is available, and medical attention should be sought, as the after-effects can be long lasting.

Travelling with Children

The Maldives is an exceptionally safe destination for children, with almost no medical dangers from the environment. The biggest worry, as

with all travellers, will be the strength of the sun. Ensure than kids are well covered with waterproof sunscreen (it's best to bring this with you as the mark up in the resorts can be huge) and that they take it easy during the first few days.

Traveller's Diarrhoea

A change of water, food or climate can all cause a mild bout of diarrhoea, but a few rushed toilet trips with no other symptoms is not indicative of a serious problem. Dehydration is the main danger with any diarrhoea. Fluid replacement and re-hydration salts remain the mainstay in managing this condition.

Language

The language of the Maldives is Dhivehi (also commonly written as 'Divehi'). It is related to an ancient form of Sinhala, a Sri Lankan language, but also contains some Arabic, Hindi and English words. There are several dialects throughout the country.

English is widely spoken in Male, in the resorts, and by educated people throughout the country. English is also spoken on Addu, the southernmost atoll. On other islands, especially outside of the tourism zone, generally only Dhivehi is spoken.

The Romanisation of Dhivehi is not standardised, and words can be spelt in a variety of ways. This is most obvious in Maldivian place names, eg Majeedi is also spelt Majidi, Majeedhee and Majeedee; Hithadhoo also becomes Hithadhu and Hitadhu; and Fuamulak can be Fua Mulaku, Foahmmulah or Phoowa Moloku.

BASICS

Hello.	a-salam alekum
Hi.	kihine
Goodbye.	vale kumu salam
See you later.	fahung badaluvang
Peace.	salam
How are you?	haalu kihine?
Very well. (reply)	vara gada
Fine./Good./Great.	barabah
OK.	enge
Yes.	aa
No.	noo
Thank you.	shukuria

I/me	aharen/ma
you	kale
she/he	mina/ena
What did you say?	kike tha buni?
What is that?	mi korche?
How much is this?	mi kihavaraka?
I'm leaving.	aharen dani
Where are you going?	kong taka dani?
How much is the fare?	fi kihavare?

DHIVEHI SCRIPT

Dhivehi has its own script, Thaana. It was introduced by the Maldivian hero Thakurufaanu during the Islamic revival of the late 16th century. Dhivehi shares Arabic's right-to-left appearance for words (and left-to-right for numbers). The list below shows the letters of the Thaana alphabet and their closest English equivalents, and a few words to show the way the letters combine.

ޙ (h) ސ (sh) ނ (n) ރ (r) ބ (b)
ޅ (lh) ކ (k) އ (a) ވ (v) މ (m)
ފ (f) ތ (t) ދ (dh) ތ (th) ލ (l)
ގ (g) ޏ (gn) ސ (s) ޑ (d) ޒ (z)
ޓ (t) ޔ (y) ޕ (p) ޖ (j) ޗ (ch)

palm tree	ruh	
cat	bulhaa	
egg	bis	

bathroom	gifili
cheap	agu heyo
dance	nashani
eat	kani
enough	heo
(very) expensive	(vara) agu bodu
go	dani
inside	etere
little (people/places)	kuda
mosquito (net)	madiri (ge)
name	nang/nama
now	mihaaru
outside	berufarai
sail	duvani
sleep	nidani
stay	hunani
swim	fatani
toilet	fahana
walk	hingani
wash	donani
water (rain/well)	vaare/valu feng

EATING & DRINKING

I'm a vegetarian.	aharen ehves baavatheh ge maheh nukan
What is the local speciality?	dhivehi aanmu keumakee kobaa?
What is this?	mee ko-on cheh?
The meal was delicious.	keun varah meeru
Thank you for your hospitality.	be-heh-ti gaai kamah shukuriyya

PEOPLE & PLACES

atoll chief	atolu verin
evil spirit	jinni
father	bapa
fisherman	mas veri
foreigner (tourist/expat)	don miha
friend	ratehi
island chief	kateeb
mother	mama
prayer caller	mudeem
religious leader	gazi
toddy man	ra veri
VIP, upper-class person	befalu
atoll	atolu
house	ge
island	fushi/rah

lane, small street	golhi/higun
mosque	miskiiy
reef/lagoon	faru
sandbank	finolhu
street	magu

TIME, DAYS & NUMBERS

day	duvas
night	reggadu
today	miadu
tomorrow	madamma
tonight	mire
yesterday	iye
Monday	horma
Tuesday	angaara
Wednesday	buda
Thursday	brassfati
Friday	hukuru
Saturday	honihira
Sunday	aadita

1	eke
2	de
3	tine
4	hatare
5	fahe
6	haie
7	hate
8	ashe
9	nue
10	diha
11	egaara
12	baara
13	tera
14	saada
15	fanara
16	sorla
17	satara
18	ashara
19	onavihi
20	vihi
30	tiris
40	saalis
50	fansaas
60	fasdolaas
70	hai-diha
80	a-diha
90	nua-diha
100	sateka

GLOSSARY

atoll – ring of coral reefs or coral islands, or both, surrounding a lagoon; the English word 'atoll' is derived from the Dhivehi *atolu*

bai bala – traditional game where one team tries to tag another inside a circle

bashi – traditional women's team game played with a tennis ball, racket and net

BCD – buoyancy control device; a vest that holds air tanks on the back and can be inflated or deflated to control a diver's buoyancy and act as a life preserver; also called a buoyancy control vest (BCV)

bodu – big or great

bodu beru – literally 'big drum'; made from a hollow coconut log and covered with stingray skin; *bodu beru* is also Maldivian drum music, often used to accompany dancers

chew – wad of areca nut wrapped in an areca leaf, often with lime, cloves and other spices; commonly chewed after a meal

Dhiraagu – the Maldives telecommunications provider, it is jointly owned by the government and the British company Cable & Wireless

Dhivehi – language and people of the Maldives, also spelt 'Divehi'

Dhivehi Raajje – 'Island Kingdom'; what Maldivians call the Maldives

dhoni – Maldivian boat, probably derived from an Arabian dhow; formerly sail-powered, many dhonis are now equipped with a diesel engine

divemaster – male or female diver qualified to supervise and lead dives, but not necessarily a qualified instructor

faru – also called *faro*; ring-shaped reef within an atoll, often with an island in the middle

feyli – traditional sarong, usually dark with light-coloured horizontal bands near the hem

finolhu – sparsely vegetated sand bank

fushi – island

garudia – a soup made from dried and smoked fish, often eaten with rice, lime and chilli.

giri – coral formation that rises steeply from the atoll floor and almost reaches the surface; see also *thila*

hawitta – ancient mound found in the southern atolls; archaeologists believe these mounds were the foundations of Buddhist temples

hedhikaa – finger food; also called 'short eats'

hingun – wide lane

house reef – coral reef adjacent to a resort island, used by guests for snorkelling and diving

inner-reef slope – where a reef slopes down inside an atoll; see also *outer-reef slope*

joli – also called *jorli*; net seat suspended from a rectangular frame; typically there are four or five seats together outside a house

kandu – sea channel; connecting the waters of an atoll to the open sea; feeding grounds for pelagics, such as sharks, stingrays, manta rays and turtles; good dive sites, but subject to strong currents

kateeb – chief of an island

long eats – a substantial meal with rice and *roshi*

magu – wide street

mas – fish

miskiiy – mosque

mudhim – muezzin; the person who calls Muslims to prayer

munnaaru – minaret, a mosque's tower

NSS – National Security Service; the Maldivian army, navy, coastguard and police force

outer-reef slope – outer edge of an atoll facing open sea, where reefs slope down towards the ocean floor; see also *inner-reef slope*

PADI – Professional Association of Diving Instructors; commercial organisation that sets diving standards and training requirements and accredits instructors

pelagic – open-sea species such as sharks, manta rays, tuna, barracuda and whales

Quran – also spelt Koran; Islam's holy book

raa veri – toddy seller

Ramazan – Maldivian spelling of Ramadan, the Muslim month of fasting

Redin – legendary race of people believed by modern Maldivians to have been the first settlers in the archipelago and the builders of the pre-Islamic *hawittas*

reef – ridge or plateau close to the sea surface; Maldivian atolls and islands are surrounded by coral reefs

reef flat – shallow area of reef top that stretches out from a lagoon to where the reef slopes down into the deeper surrounding water

roshi – unleavened bread

short eats – finger food; also called *hedhikaa*

STO – State Trading Organisation

Thaana – Dhivehi script; the written language unique to the Maldives

thila – coral formation that rises steeply from the atoll floor to within 5m to 15m of the surface; see also *giri*

thundu kunaa – finely woven reed mats, particularly those from Gaafu Dhaalu

undholi – wooden seat, typically suspended under a shady tree so the swinging motion provides a cooling breeze

Wataniya – Kuwaiti mobile phone provider operating one of the Maldives' two networks

LANGUAGE GLOSSARY

behind the scenes

SEND US YOUR FEEDBACK

We love to hear from travellers – your comments keep us on our toes and help make our books better. Our well-travelled team reads every word on what you loved or loathed about this book. Although we cannot reply individually to postal submissions, we always guarantee that your feedback goes straight to the appropriate authors, in time for the next edition. Each person who sends us information is thanked in the next edition – the most useful submissions are rewarded with a selection of digital PDF chapters.

Visit **lonelyplanet.com/contact** to submit your updates and suggestions or to ask for help. Our award-winning website also features inspirational travel stories, news and discussions.

Note: We may edit, reproduce and incorporate your comments in Lonely Planet products such as guidebooks, websites and digital products, so let us know if you don't want your comments reproduced or your name acknowledged. For a copy of our privacy policy visit lonelyplanet.com/privacy.

OUR READERS

Many thanks to the travellers who used the last edition and wrote to us with helpful hints, useful advice and interesting anecdotes: Kevin Dillow, Murray Laing, Nancy and Chris Mayberry, Yuriko Momoki, Kevin Judah White.

AUTHOR THANKS

Tom Masters

Many thanks to the scores of resort managers and other staff who helped me arrange visits to remote islands, often going out of their way to make things happen. More specifically, in the Maldives thanks to Ali Rilwan, Eagan Mohamed Badeeu, Raki Bench, Ashley Hood, Kate Hollamby, Jason Kruse, Allo Saeed, Ahmed Zahir, Richard Rees, Maseem Nizaki, Paul Roberts, Zuhair Mohammed and Ahmed Naseer. Thanks also to the folks at Lonely Planet for their hard work on this book.

ACKNOWLEDGMENTS

Climate map data adapted from Peel MC, Finlayson BL & McMahon TA (2007) 'Updated World Map of the Köppen-Geiger Climate Classification', *Hydrology and Earth System Sciences*, 11, 163344.

Cover photograph: A dhoni on a tropical beach at Velassaru, South Male Atoll, Kaafu, Maldives. Felix Hug/Lonely Planet Images ©

Many of the images in this guide are available for licensing from Lonely Planet Images: www.lonelyplanetimages.com.

This Book

This 8th edition of Lonely Planet's Maldives guidebook was researched and written by Tom Masters. The previous two editions were also written by Tom Masters. This guidebook was commissioned in Lonely Planet's Melbourne office, and produced by the following:

Commissioning Editors
Kate Morgan, Glenn van der Knijff

Coordinating Editors
Simon Williamson, Ross Taylor
Coordinating Cartographer Julie Dodkins
Coordinating Layout Designer Virginia Moreno
Managing Editor Brigitte Ellemor
Senior Editor Andi Jones
Managing Cartographers
Shahara Ahmed, Adrian Persoglia

Managing Layout Designer Jane Hart
Assisting Editor Kristin Odijk
Cover Research Naomi Parker
Internal Image Research Aude Vauconsant
Language Content Annelies Mertens
Thanks to Ryan Evans, Larissa Frost, Trent Paton, Gerard Walker

NOTES

NOTES

index

how to use this book

These symbols will help you find the listings you want:

⊙ Sights	⌂ Tours	☻ Drinking
🐾 Beaches	✦ Festivals & Events	☆ Entertainment
🏃 Activities	🛏 Sleeping	🛍 Shopping
🍴 Courses	✕ Eating	❶ Information/Transport

These symbols give you the vital information for each listing:

🕿 Telephone Numbers	🛜 Wi-Fi Access	🚌 Bus
⊙ Opening Hours	🏊 Swimming Pool	🚢 Ferry
Ⓟ Parking	🥗 Vegetarian Selection	
⊖ Nonsmoking	📖 English-Language Menu	
✳ Air-Conditioning	👪 Family-Friendly	
@ Internet Access	🐾 Pet-Friendly	

Reviews are organised by author preference.

Look out for these icons:

TOP CHOICE Our author's recommendation

FREE No payment required

A green or sustainable option

Our authors have nominated these places as demonstrating a strong commitment to sustainability – for example by supporting local communities and producers, operating in an environmentally friendly way, or supporting conservation projects.

Map Legend

Sights
- ⊙ Beach
- Buddhist
- Castle
- Christian
- Hindu
- Islamic
- Jewish
- Monument
- Museum/Gallery
- Ruin
- Winery/Vineyard
- Zoo
- Other Sight

Activities, Courses & Tours
- Diving/Snorkelling
- Canoeing/Kayaking
- Skiing
- Surfing
- Swimming/Pool
- Walking
- Windsurfing
- Other Activity/Course/Tour

Sleeping
- Sleeping
- Camping

Eating
- Eating

Drinking
- Drinking
- Cafe

Entertainment
- Entertainment

Shopping
- Shopping

Information
- Post Office
- Tourist Information

Transport
- Airport
- Border Crossing
- Bus
- Cable Car/Funicular
- Cycling
- Ferry
- Metro
- Monorail
- Parking
- S-Bahn
- Taxi
- Train/Railway
- Tram
- Tube Station
- U-Bahn
- Other Transport

Routes
- Tollway
- Freeway
- Primary
- Secondary
- Tertiary
- Lane
- Unsealed Road
- Plaza/Mall
- Steps
- Tunnel
- Pedestrian Overpass
- Walking Tour
- Walking Tour Detour
- Path

Boundaries
- International
- State/Province
- Disputed
- Regional/Suburb
- Marine Park
- Cliff
- Wall

Population
- Capital (National)
- Capital (State/Province)
- City/Large Town
- Town/Village

Geographic
- Hut/Shelter
- Lighthouse
- Lookout
- Mountain/Volcano
- Oasis
- Park
- Pass
- Picnic Area
- Waterfall

Hydrography
- River/Creek
- Intermittent River
- Swamp/Mangrove
- Reef
- Canal
- Water
- Dry/Salt/Intermittent Lake
- Glacier

Areas
- Beach/Desert
- Cemetery (Christian)
- Cemetery (Other)
- Park/Forest
- Sportsground
- Sight (Building)
- Top Sight (Building)

OUR STORY

A beat-up old car, a few dollars in the pocket and a sense of adventure. In 1972 that's all Tony and Maureen Wheeler needed for the trip of a lifetime – across Europe and Asia overland to Australia. It took several months, and at the end – broke but inspired – they sat at their kitchen table writing and stapling together their first travel guide, *Across Asia on the Cheap*. Within a week they'd sold 1500 copies. Lonely Planet was born.

Today, Lonely Planet has offices in Melbourne, London and Oakland, with more than 600 staff and writers. We share Tony's belief that 'a great guidebook should do three things: inform, educate and amuse'.

OUR WRITER

Tom Masters

Tom is a Berlin-based travel writer who has written widely about the Maldives since first covering the country for Lonely Planet in 2006. During his first research trip to the Maldives he found it under the heavy hand of a 30-year dictatorship, by his second visit it had its first democratically elected president, and during his most recent time there Tom was caught up in the coup against President Nasheed, proving that things are never dull in this quickly changing country. You can see more of Tom's work at www.tommasters.net.

Published by Lonely Planet Publications Pty Ltd
ABN 36 005 607 983
8th edition – October 2012
ISBN 978 1 74179 803 6
© Lonely Planet 2012   Photographs © as indicated 2012
10 9 8 7 6 5 4 3 2 1
Printed in China